Scarlet and Black

Scarlet and Black

Volume 1

Slavery and Dispossession
in Rutgers History

EDITED BY MARISA J. FUENTES AND
DEBORAH GRAY WHITE

RUTGERS UNIVERSITY PRESS

NEW BRUNSWICK, CAMDEN, AND NEWARK, NEW JERSEY, AND LONDON

1766-2016

RUTGERS
250

PCN 2016955389

ISBN 978-0-8135-9152-0 (pbk.)

ISBN 978-0-8135-9210-7 (ePub)

ISBN 978-0-8135-9211-4 (Mobi)

ISBN 978-0-8135-9212-1 (Web PDF)

The paper used in this publication meets the requirements of the American National Standard for Information Sciences—Permanence of Paper for Printed Library Materials, ANSI Z39.48-1992.

www.rutgersuniversitypress.org

Manufactured in the United States of America

CONTENTS

FOREWORD

The first stitch of this incredible project, *Scarlet and Black*, was sewn on May 11, 2015. On that day, in my office in Rutgers University's iconic Old Queen's Building, I met with a small group of students to discuss the current state of race relations at Rutgers. In the course of our conversation, the students made themselves clear: improving the current racial and cultural climate at Rutgers was impossible without answering questions about the university's early history. After a decade at Rutgers as a dean, and then administrator, I felt that I was quite familiar with the oft-told narrative of our beginning days: the Dutch Reformed Church, the royal charter (1766), the first name (Queen's College), the benefactor (Colonel Henry Rutgers), the second name (Rutgers College), and the land grant designation from the Morrill Act (1862), which launched the institution's research ambitions.

That accepted record was incomplete, the students said. They pointed to Craig Steven Wilder's 2013 book, *Ebony and Ivy: Race, Slavery, and the Troubled History of America's Universities* as having clues to a deeper, more painful narrative that had yet to be told. Wilder, a professor of American history at the Massachusetts Institute of Technology, made reference in his book to many of our prominent founding families and their involvement in enslavement— Livingston, Hardenbergh, and Rutgers himself.

The subsequent exploration of the missing narrative of slavery and dispossession, requested by the students and undertaken by the university, must be put in context. Mere months after that meeting in May, many campuses throughout the country were heaved into turmoil as encounters between students and administrators gave rise to renewed activism and questions around what a university's responsibilities are in providing to its students an inclusive and supportive academic environment. Intersecting with these conversations was the university's planned year-long celebration of its 250th anniversary. Running from November 10, 2015 to November 10, 2016, the commemoration sought to pay tribute to an institution whose impact on our country over a quarter of a millennium could be rivaled only by a venerable few. A true telling of our early history was never more due—and never more necessary.

From these converging factors, we have *Scarlet and Black: Slavery and Dispossession in Rutgers History.* The book is the result of the work of the Committee on Enslaved and Disenfranchised Populations in Rutgers History, which I formed in the fall of 2015. I asked the committee, chaired by Board of Governors Distinguished Professor of History Deborah Gray White, to seek out the untold history that we have ignored for too long, such as that our campus is built on land taken from the Lenni Lenape and that a number of our founders and early benefactors were slaveholders. Given our history as a colonial college, these facts are not unique to Rutgers, but I believed it was time that we began to recognize the role that disadvantaged populations such as African Americans and Native tribes played in the university's development.

Rutgers is not the first institution to wrestle with such issues. Brown University, for instance, founded just two years before Rutgers, formed a committee charged by its then-president, Ruth Simmons, to "examine the University's historical entanglement with slavery and the slave trade and report our findings openly and truthfully." The Brown committee's report was extensive and honest, and I asked our committee, which was to be composed of students, faculty, and staff, for the same vigorous pursuit of the truth.

Many of the truths reported within these pages by a dedicated team of researchers are complicated and uncomfortable. Take the example of Theodore Frelinghuysen, scion of one of the most influential and revered families of his day and ours. Frelinghuysen, whose forbears were early supporters of Rutgers's founding, was a notable national figure in public life during the early and middle part of the nineteenth century and served for twelve years (1850–1862) as Rutgers's seventh president. Before his time at Rutgers, he rose to prominence first as New Jersey attorney general, then as a United States senator (1829–1835). It was as a senator that he gained notoriety as a fierce opponent of the removal of Native Americans from their lands. His six-hour speech against the Indian Removal Act of 1830 was not enough to halt its passing, but the "Christian Statesman," as he was known, told his colleagues that "the Indians are men, endowed with kindred faculties and powers with ourselves"; he demanded to know "in what code of the law of nations, or by what process of abstract deduction, their rights have been extinguished?" Frelinghuysen was also an ardent opponent of slavery, calling the abhorrent institution a "moral evil." Though his opposition to slavery is well documented, Frelinghuysen supported a gradual end to its practice and was a proponent and leader of the American Colonization Society, which sought to remove blacks from America and "repatriate" them to Africa.

This example and many others in this book raise complex questions for the university to consider as we begin our introspection and reconciliation with the past. During this celebratory year, I have repeatedly said that to truly praise Rutgers, we must honestly know it; and to do that, we must gain a fuller understanding of it. With this book, the first volume of *Scarlet and Black*, we have begun to do that. It covers the early decades of Rutgers history; in the works are other volumes that will carry the story up to the present.

While reviewing the manuscript for this book, I couldn't help but recall that conversation with our students in May 2015. I kept thinking about them and about our committee's discovery that an enslaved man named Will helped lay the foundation of Old Queen's, our original and distinctive building—the building that houses my office and where we held that very first discussion. After reading the chapter in this book entitled "His Name Was Will," I thought again of the students and of our conversation and I remarked to myself: "if only they knew." Now they do.

Richard L. Edwards
Chancellor, Rutgers University—New Brunswick

Scarlet and Black

Introduction

Scarlet and Black–A Reconciliation

Deborah Gray White

Chair of the Committee on the Enslaved and Disfranchised in Rutgers History

In September 1749 the slave ship *Wolf* left New York City for Africa where it would troll the west coast, eventually buying and imprisoning 147 Africans, most of whom were children. Before it returned to New York in May 1751, with its human cargo packed like sardines in its hold, it had littered the Atlantic Ocean with eighty-one dead black bodies—again, most of them children. They had succumbed to the vessel's diseased environment, particularly the conditions that allowed twelve- to thirteen-inch worms to incubate the stomachs and intestines of its youthful captives. On May 21 the surviving sixty-six were auctioned off for sale by Philip Livingston, the *Wolf*'s principal investor/slave trader merchant. Seventeen years later, Livingston became a founder of Queen's College, the school that would eventually be named for another son of a slave-owning family, Henry Rutgers.[1] The first president of the college, Jacob Hardenbergh, and its first tutor, Frederick Frelinghuysen, were also slave owners.[2]

The Rutgers connection to slavery was neither casual nor accidental—nor unusual. Like most early American colleges Rutgers depended on slaves to build its campuses and serve its students and faculty; it depended on the sale of black people to fund its very existence. The faculty and curriculum at Rutgers and other early American colleges reinforced the theological and scientific racism that provided the ideological and spiritual justification for the free labor of Africans, the absolute power of slave owners, and the separation of the races.

1

Through their leadership of the state and regional boards of the American Colonization Society (ACS), men like John Henry Livingston (Rutgers president, 1810–1824), the Reverend Philip Milledoler (Rutgers president, 1824–1840), Henry Rutgers (trustee after whom the college is named), and Theodore Frelinghuysen, Rutgers's seventh president, were among the most ardent anti-abolitionists in the Mid-Atlantic. Defending the ACS position that free blacks were better off colonizing and Christianizing Africa than becoming full-fledged citizens of the United States, Frelinghuysen, a passionate defender of Native American rights to their southeastern lands, proclaimed African Americans to be "a depressed and separate race" who were "licentious, ignorant, and irritated."[3]

The history of the long relationship between the American academy and American slavery and racism has only recently gained our attention. Confrontations over the Confederate flag and other Confederate memorials, demands for racial equality that migrated to American campuses from protests against the killing of unarmed blacks by heavily armed police and civilian whites, and the perceived rollback of the academy's commitment to diversity and inclusion have all sparked renewed interest in the historic connection between the nation's oldest colleges and the institutional racism that was forged in the holds of slave ships.

The book *Ebony and Ivy*, by MIT historian Craig Steven Wilder, has also drawn our attention to the marriage of American colleges to the slave economy and the cultural subjugation of Native Americans. In his book, subtitled *Race, Slavery, and the Troubled History of America's Universities*, Wilder documents how merchants leveraged the slave economy by investing in early American colleges. He shows how the benefactors, administrators, professors, tutors, and graduates of Harvard, Yale, Princeton, and Rutgers, among many others, became slave merchants and owners, Southern planters, evangelizing missionaries, scientific racist ideologues, and slavery apologists. Like historian Edmund Morgan, who demonstrated the dependence of American freedom on American slavery, Wilder proves that African slavery "subsidized" American colonies and colleges and was the "precondition for the rise of higher education in the Americas."[4] The American academy, writes Wilder, "never stood apart from American slavery—in fact it stood beside church and state as the third pillar of a civilization built on bondage."[5]

The 250th anniversary of the founding of Rutgers University is an appropriate time for the Rutgers community to do what other schools have done and are doing—reconcile with its connection to the enslavement and debasement of African Americans and the disfranchisement and elimination of Native American people and culture. For example, the revelations involving Georgetown University's sale of 272 slaves in 1838 to save the Jesuit school from bankruptcy has recently garnered headlines.[6] But Georgetown is but one of many institutions studying their relationship to the heinous institution. There is the 2001 Yale study *Yale, Slavery, and Abolition,* published in tandem with the school's 300th anniversary celebration, which looks at the way slave-trading money sustained Yale and its students and how Yale officials led the opposition that stopped construction in New Haven of what would have been the nation's first black college.[7] In 2003 Brown University issued its *Slavery and Justice Report* and in turn inspired Harvard students to dig into their institution's history with slavery, resulting in the 2011 study *Harvard and Slavery: Seeking a Forgotten History.* The book looks at Harvard's history with slavery from the colonial through the antebellum periods and the way that slavery is remembered at Harvard.[8] And this year, 2016, has seen the exponential growth of the consortium Universities Studying Slavery (USS). Begun in 2015 when thirteen schools in Virginia established Virginia's Colleges and Universities Studying Slavery (VCUSS), the USS now has expanded to include the Universities of Mississippi, North Carolina, and South Carolina, as well as Hollins University in Roanoke, Virginia.[9]

These research projects have uncovered history that has led to a reckoning at colleges and universities. Georgetown, for example, has sought out the descendants of the slaves who were sold to pay the debts that kept it from closing. It has pledged to actively recruit these descendants and give them preferential status in the admissions process. It has also pledged to offer a formal apology, create an institute for the study of slavery, and erect a public memorial to the slaves whose labor benefited the institution.[10] After heated debates over whether to change the name of Calhoun College (a residential college named after South Carolina's arch proslaveryite and secessionist), Yale officials decided to keep the name as a way to encourage the campus community to confront and teach the history of slavery. It also, however, decided to name one of its new residential colleges after black rights activist Pauli Murray and to substitute "head of college" for the title "master" in all of the residential colleges.[11] In ridding the school of the moniker "master" for heads of residential colleges, both Yale and Harvard followed Princeton's lead. Princeton replaced "master" with "head of college," while Harvard now calls residential college heads "faculty deans."[12]

Things changed at Virginia's Washington and Lee University as well. In April 2015, President Richard Ruscio laid a historical marker on his campus to commemorate the lives of black men, women, and children who were bequeathed to the school in the estate of one of its benefactors.[13] In his remarks on that occasion Ruscio noted that the marker was not the politically correct thing to do but that it was *historically* correct and "a step towards justice." President Ruscio recognized that stories about slavery made people uncomfortable, but, he said, "Acknowledging those times when we failed in the past can serve to strengthen our resolve for the future."

Scarlet and Black: Slavery and Dispossession in Rutgers History is presented in the spirit of Ruscio's directive. Researched and written by Rutgers graduate and undergraduate students and history faculty member Camilla Townsend, it represents a first step in Rutgers's journey of reconciliation with its history as a school built on the dispossession and dehumanization of Native Americans, Africans, and African Americans. It is by no means a complete history but a work in progress. It initiates the study of a long overdue history of a school that spans three separate New Jersey campuses (Camden, New Brunswick, and Newark) and five learning communities in New Brunswick alone. The 250th anniversary should be, and is, a time of celebration, but the writers of this first volume on African and Native Americans in Rutgers's history also want it to be a time of reflection—reflection on Rutgers's past as a way to improve its future.

Scarlet and Black has seven chapters of varying lengths and an epilogue. The chapters begin with the story of the way Native Americans were dispossessed of the land on which Rutgers was built years before ground was broken on the college. It looks at how and why Rutgers failed to enroll Native American converts to Christianity and at the ideological position taken by Rutgers's leaders on the question of Indian Removal. The last chapter explains how Rutgers benefited from the land-grant Morrill Act of 1862, which allowed New Jersey to sell land taken from western Native Americans for the benefit of Rutgers.

The chapters in between our investigations of Native Americans address slavery in Rutgers's history and slavery's impact on African Americans in New Brunswick. First, we look at the way slavery figured in the political economy of New Jersey and the critical connection between the state and the Dutch Reformed Church. We show the wealth that was generated by slavery and the slave trade, and how and to what affect that wealth was transferred to Rutgers by its early benefactors. We then take a close look at a few of the wills researchers have uncovered. These wills reveal the premeditated inhumanity of slavery as leaders associated with Rutgers passed down people like property, separated children from parents, disposed of the aged and infirm, and exposed the illicit interracial sex that took place in the privacy of households. Here we trace the treatment of the parents of Sojourner Truth, the nineteenth-century freedom fighter whose parents were owned and bequeathed by Colonel Johannes Hardenbergh, whose son Jacob Rutsen Hardenbergh was the first president of Rutgers. From here our focus shifts more centrally to African Americans and how they survived, resisted, and negotiated their enslaved existence. We examine New Brunswick runaway ads for what they tell us about the resistance of local blacks and at the narrative of Ukasaw Gronniosaw, who was enslaved to the Frelinghuysen family, for clues about the physical and psychological trials of slavery. We identify Will, a slave who was hired out to help build Old Queen's, the first building established at Rutgers. Our look at blacks in New Brunswick also surveys the landscape of the town as we demonstrate how black life was circumscribed by physical structures of unfreedom, particularly the gaol.[14] We review the history that posits New Brunswick as an important stop on the Underground Railroad and complicate that history with information about the precarity of free and enslaved black life in New Brunswick. As Chapter 5 demonstrates, black precarity had a lot to do with the gradual emancipation laws in New Jersey, which did not free slaves born before 1804 and set terms of service for those born after 1804 at twenty-one years for females and twenty-five years for males. As ministers, faculty, and presidents of Rutgers justified the separation of blacks and whites and the removal of African Americans back to Africa, New Brunswick African Americans joined the national resistance movement and argued strenuously for their rights as American citizens.

As much of the history that *Scarlet and Black: Slavery and Dispossession in Rutgers History* unveils, it only scratches the surface. There are still more records to scour, more wills to analyze, more early maps to scrutinize, more speeches to interpret, and more real lives to excavate. There is Rutgers's relationship with blacks and Native Americans in the late nineteenth and twentieth centuries and its treatment of these populations as it expanded to Douglass, Busch, Cook, and Livingston Colleges in New Brunswick and Piscataway, and also to Newark and Camden. And, of course, yet to be included in Rutgers's reconciliation is the important history of Rutgers and the black freedom movement. Still, though just a beginning, we believe that this history of Rutgers and slavery has many uses and we suggest ways to begin utilizing it in the epilogue, which represents the thinking of the Committee on the Enslaved and Disfranchised in Rutgers History, the committee established by Chancellor Richard Edwards and chaired by myself, to begin this reconciliation.

Scarlet and black are the colors Rutgers uses to represent itself to the nation and world. They are the colors our athletes compete in, the colors our graduates and administrators wear on celebratory occasions, and the colors that distinguish Rutgers from every other university in the United States. Here we use these colors to signify something else: the blood that was spilled on the banks of the Raritan River by those dispossessed of their land and the bodies that labored unrecompensed so that Rutgers could be built and sustained. We offer this history as a usable one—not to tear down or weaken this very renowned, robust, and growing institution but rather to strengthen it and help direct its course for the future.

1

"I Am Old and Weak . . . and You Are Young and Strong . . ."

The Intersecting Histories of Rutgers University and the Lenni Lenape

Camilla Townsend

With Ugonna Amaechi, Jacob Arnay, Shelby Berner, Lynn Biernacki, Vanessa Bodossian, Megan Brink, Joseph Cuzzolino, Melissa Deutsch, Emily Edelman, Esther Esquenazi, Brian Hagerty, Blaise Hode, Dana Jordan, Andrew Kim, Eric Knittel, Brianna Leider, Jessica MacDonald, Kathleen Margeotes, Anjelica Matcho, William Nisley, Elisheva Rosen, Ethan Smith, Amanda Stein, Chad Stewart, Ryan Von Sauers

When the indigenous people along the banks of the Raritan were first becoming acquainted with the Dutch settlers who had come to live among them, they responded with humor whenever possible. They loved to tease the newcomers, testing to see how much they could get them to believe, and then laughing over the results in private. A missionary who lived among the Lenape years later—and came to speak their language fluently—explained: "They are fond of the marvelous, and when they find a white man inclined to listen to their tales of wonder, or credulous enough to believe their superstitious notions, there are always some among them ready to entertain him with tales of that description, as it gives them an opportunity of diverting themselves in their leisure hours, by relating such fabulous stories, while they laugh at the same time at their being able to deceive a people who think themselves so superior to them in wisdom and knowledge."[1]

The people's cultural proclivity to try to see what was funny in any situation was to stand them in good stead over the next two centuries. For while the newcomers planted a colony and watched it grow and become New Jersey and while its people multiplied and founded schools and universities to guarantee their children's future, the Lenape, meaning "the people" in the Algonkian tongue they spoke,[2] watched their world dwindle and their children grow hungry. They survived four stages—first, the period of living with the Dutch until the latter were suddenly replaced by the English, under whom they lost their land; second, the eighteenth-century wars which ultimately solidified the colonists' political position and permanently ended the Lenape's freedom to move about and live wherever they could in Central Jersey; third, the founding of Rutgers University in the 1760s and the decision of its trustees to fund the education of any remaining Lenape youths outside of New Jersey, rather than at Rutgers, leading to devastating isolation and grief for the community's potential leaders; and fourth, the early nineteenth-century debate over Removal in which Rutgers people played a major role, during which time the last of the Lenape were pressured to move westward.

This essay describes a gradual but deadly process in which one community paid with their very lives for the successes of another group. Yet the Native Americans who lived through it, and the handful of descendants in Jersey and greater numbers of descendants in Wisconsin and Oklahoma, despite all their losses, never lost their humanity. The archival record was created by those who vanquished them in a political and economic sense, but the writers of this essay have nevertheless sought in that very archival record evidence of the Lenape's rich intellectual life, their humor, and their astute observations of what was happening to them and their children.

The Lenape before Rutgers

Although it was Dutch traders who founded the initial European settlements in today's New Jersey, it was Dutch missionaries who were the first to embark on an intellectual exchange with the people who already inhabited the area. In the 1620s, Jonas Michaelius, the first minister to arrive in New Amsterdam, held several meetings with local Algonkian-speaking groups.[3] They invited him to sit with them in a circle so that they might converse and deliberate. There had been Dutch traders in the area since 1609, and someone—it is not clear who—had become bilingual enough to function as an interpreter. Michaelius thought he learned that their word for God was *Manitou*, or "Menetto" as he said. He assumed that Menetto was the devil himself, but the word really referred to the element of the divine that might inhabit many different spirits or elements of nature; the root is common to a number of Algonkian languages. Michaelius was unwilling to say that God was the European name for Manitou ("for that would be blasphemy"), so he asked for their word for chief—*sachem*, he was told—and then explained that God was like a king, the highest of sachems ruling over other sachems. Some, "in order to express regard and friendship," as he put it, nodded politely and responded with the word *orith*, meaning "good."[4] But most were visibly unconvinced. The idea that the Dutchman's god was a high king "appeared to them like a dream." Some even began to "mutter and shake their heads as if it were a silly fable." He could not understand the conversation they held among themselves, which made him feel confused, vulnerable, and dependent, like a child. He did not like it, and when he wrote home to his superior, he turned his feelings outward and said their tongue was "a made-up childish language."[5]

In fact, Michaelius's failure to obtain any baptisms at all among the Lenape left him with feelings of impotence and rage. "I find them entirely savage and wild, strangers to all decency, yea, uncivil and stupid as garden poles, proficient in all wickedness and godlessness; devilish men, who serve nobody but the devil, that is, the spirit, which in their language, they call Menetto." The task of converting them, he concluded, was utterly hopeless. Yet he was an ordained minister and an educator, and he was under explicit instructions to teach the heathens what they most needed to know. He had a suggestion. "It would be well then to leave the parents as they are, and begin with the children who are still young. . . . They ought in youth to be separated from their parents; yea, from their whole nation. For, without this, they would forthwith be as much accustomed as their parents to the heathenish tricks and deviltries which are kneaded naturally into their hearts by themselves through a just judgment of God."[6] (The Dutch settlers did not have the time, funds, or even the inclination to begin to bring indigenous children into boarding schools, but the idea would continue to circulate among missionaries until it bore fruit in later years.)

Unbeknownst to Michaelius, the Lenape priests and leading men could not accept the simple story of God and of Genesis that he seemed to offer them, for in the universe they knew, humanity's origination had been a highly complex affair. Each tribe in the region—indeed, even each individual within each tribe—could and did tell the story slightly differently, for they knew it was the essence that mattered, not the details (except in an artistic sense, they would have added, for a good storyteller was worth his or her salt). The story as it was told almost always began in the sky, where divine man-beings and woman-beings dwelt together in harmony, knowing nothing of death or sorrow. But at last a woman-being gave birth to a child, and as the child (a daughter) came into the universe, her father went out of it, and the gods knew sorrow for the first time. At first the child's weeping knew no bounds when she realized her father was dead, but she became reconciled to losing him when she found she could always climb a ladder, sit by his remains, and communicate with him, sometimes even laughing at the stories he told her. Eventually he told her it was time to marry. The husband chosen was cruel to her, but he provided venison for the household, and so she endured with fortitude for her people's sake. One day her partner uprooted a tree whose roots extended down into the world below, leaving a great gaping hole. He told her to sit next to the hole—and then he placed his fingers on the nape of her neck and pushed her through. "She kept falling in darkness. After a while she passed through it. She looked about her in all directions and saw on all sides of her that everything was blue in color. . . . She knew nothing of the thing she saw, but in truth she now was looking on a great expanse of water, though she did not know it. This is what she saw: on the surface of the water, floating about hither and thither, like veritable canoes, were all the types of ducks."[7] The first one to notice her called out and said a female being was coming up from the depths, but another bird corrected him and said a better way to describe it was that a woman was falling from the sky. The birds held a great council and decided to save her. They flew close together and caught her and set her gently down on a giant turtle's back. Then the water mammals—the beaver, otter, and muskrat—each in turn volunteered to dive down deep and bring up some mud, gradually turning her new home into the earth.

The woman-being delivered a child there on earth, a daughter. And that daughter conceived a child by a visiting warrior (a manitou) who laid an arrow— or was it two arrows?—down beside her and then left, never to return. She gave birth to twins, the first human beings. In the womb, the brothers argued. One was concerned for his mother and dived down the passage the proper way into the world of light. But the other did not care about her sufferings and emerged some other way, cutting his way into the world like a flint-knife and killing his mother. His grandmother, the Woman Who Fell from the Sky, did not know that he had done this and she cradled him and cared for him. "It was amazing how much she loved him," crooned the storytellers, as they went on to describe the psychological and material complexities that ensued among human beings.

The creation story contained many elements in common with other Native Americans' origin myths—that humans emerged from past beings who showed both cruelty and generosity and are thus themselves destined to be similar, that death makes room for new life, that people endure much for one another's sake, that people are utterly dependent upon animals, that the first human was not alone but came as a pair of twins, that there are worlds within worlds and parallel worlds, and that even a bit of algae growing on a turtle's shell may be a microcosm of the earth. Some of their traditional tales even shared highly specific plot elements with the narratives of other North American Indians—for example, an account of a feast that was put on as a deception, where the supposedly joyous dancers brought weapons they secretly planned to use.[8] That the stories across the continent shared so many elements is not surprising when we think of the way they were told—around firesides, with neighbors from across the river visiting, or a wife from another tribe present, or perhaps a prisoner of war who had been adopted into the community as a child recalling another possibility.

In fact, despite Michaelius's sense of failure, we know that the Lenape were listening to what the missionaries had to say, weighing it, and finding some of it appealing or at least interesting. In the 1650s, the Swede Peter Lindeström traveled in South Jersey, writing a report for the government of New Sweden (based in today's Delaware). He mentioned that he met several individuals who were already well versed in the life of Christ, "which they consider[ed] a fable."[9] And there is ample evidence that the Lenape were quite taken with the story of Dido in the *Aeneid.* Most European missionaries in the seventeenth century traveled with a copy of Vergil's great work in their trunks.[10] All of them had had classical educations and read Latin. And many of them, as early colonizers, were drawn to the story of the heroic Trojan who traveled far to found a great civilization on a distant shore (Rome, in the land of Italy). The story of Dido was especially beloved. A princess who fled political troubles in her home city-state of Tyre, she landed on the shores of North Africa and asked the people to give her only as much land as a cowhide could cover. Then she tricked the natives by making a spiral cut to turn the hide into a very long rope. The rope encircled enough land to establish a small city, and she founded Carthage.[11]

The Lenape took this tale as recounted to them by enthusiastic missionaries, passed it on, and in future generations incorporated it into a humorous tall-tale of their own. "A great many years ago," one storyteller began, in the mid-eighteenth century, "when men with a white skin had never yet been seen in the land, some Indians who were out fishing, at a place where the sea widens, espied at a great distance something remarkably large floating on the water, such as they had never seen before." He went on:

> They hurried out together, and saw with astonishment the phenomenon which now appeared to their sight, but could not agree upon what it was; some believed it to be an uncommonly large fish or animal, while others were of opinion it must be a very big house floating on the sea. . . . They sent off a number of runners and watermen to carry the news to their scattered chiefs, that they might send off in every direction for the warriors, with a message that they should come on immediately.[12]

As the ship approached nearer, they at length concluded that it must be a great Manitou coming to visit them, and assembling on what was later called York Island, they asked the women to prepare a great feast as a fitting reception for him.

In the story, when the white men approach and disembark, there is general confusion, as the two sets of people do not understand each other at all. One of the newcomers pours an "unknown substance" into a small cup or glass. "He

drinks, has the glass filled again, and hands it to the chief standing next to him."
Each chief receives the cup, smells it, wrinkles his nose in distaste, and passes it
on. At length one of the young men, a brave warrior, declares to the crowd that
they are being dangerously rude and takes a great swig. "Every eye was fixed on
the resolute chief, to see what the effect the unknown liquor would produce. He
soon began to stagger, and at last fell prostrate on the ground." His companions
were distraught and angry, thinking him dead. At this point in the narration,
the storyteller began to act, switching back to the present tense once again as
he mimed the scene surrounding the purportedly expired young warrior: "He
wakes again! He jumps up and declares—that he has enjoyed the most delicious
sensations, and that he never before felt himself so happy as after he had drunk
the cup! He asks for more."[13]

In the midst of the laughter, to underscore the point as to how naïve their
grandparents had been, the storyteller now added that the Dutch brought axes
and hoes to trade and that when the Indians received them, they knew not what
to do with them. "They had them hanging to their waists as ornaments," he said.
They walked around bearing that great weight for a long time, he remarked, and
he imitated a man almost toppled by the burden of an axe-necklace. It seems
unlikely that people who had been making tomahawks for many generations
would be unable to determine the use of an axe head or that the narrator's
listeners took this assertion at all seriously. Rather, he was trying to make his
audience laugh again. At last he wove in his own version of the story of Dido:

> As the whites became daily more familiar to the Indians, they at last pro-
> posed to stay with them, and asked only for so much ground for a garden
> lot, as, they said, the hide of a bullock would cover or encompass, which
> hide was spread before them. The Indians readily granted this apparently
> reasonable request; but the whites then took a knife, and beginning at
> one end of the hide, cut it up to a long rope, not thicker than a child's
> finger, so that by the time the whole was cut up, it made a great heap;
> they then took the rope at one end, and drew it gently along, carefully
> avoiding its breaking. It was drawn out into a circular form, and being
> closed at its ends encompassed a large piece of ground. The Indians were
> surprised at the superior wit of the whites, but did not wish to contend
> with them about a little land, as they still had enough for themselves.[14]

The listeners would have thought ruefully of all they wished their forebears
had known a hundred years earlier—about rum, trade goods, and European
trickery. But in the 1620s and 1630s, there was no way they could have foreseen
what was to come. The Dutch remained largely in New Amsterdam and points
north (a small settlement in Bergen, today's Jersey City, did not draw many people), and the Swedes when they came in 1638 mostly stayed at the mouth of the

Delaware.[15] A handful of Swedish men came inland to trade and stayed to marry local women, and a small number of enslaved Africans fled the Dutch and established communities in the northern hills, but there were not enough of either group to change the politics of the region. In fact, the people living near the Raritan River rarely ever saw a Swede or a Dutchman at that time. If anything, the presence of the newcomers at the fringes of their world seemed to be an advantage. The Europeans sold metal tools and woven cloth that made the Indians' lives as hunters and part-time farmers infinitely easier. They enthusiastically adopted the knives, axes, hoes, spades, shovels, awls, needles, scissors, and kettles, as well as the linen, cotton, and wool fabrics. To obtain these goods, they brought the newcomers baskets full of corn, beautiful blankets woven of dyed feathers,[16] and—mostly—stacks of animal pelts. The Europeans preferred beaver furs, but they traded for all kinds. In this new market, a medium of exchange was needed, and all sides settled for wampum, white and mother-of-pearl shell beads that the Lenape had long used for decorative purposes. As the supply of animals began to dwindle, proximity to the coast helped the Lenape to focus on making beads and trading for them in quantities never known before. They braided them into their hair, draped glistening strings from their ceremonial clothing, and buried their dead with large quantities. To their horror, white traders began to rob their graveyards, and they learned to be more careful and remove the boxes of wampum themselves after a period of mourning.[17]

The Dutch were quick to take offense and used violence with wild abandon. On what the Dutch called Staten Island a brutal war unfolded in the 1640s, and word of it certainly spread along the Raritan. Some of the warriors may well have gone to help their allies fight the newcomers.[18] The Lenape were no strangers to warfare, but when they killed, they killed one or two or in the worst of battles maybe as many as ten or twelve. When these newcomers fought, they killed by the dozens, without any apparent thought of the retribution and ongoing violence that must follow. The Dutch said they thought there were teaching the "savages" (*vilden*) a lesson, but the lesson they intended was not the one that those they attacked chose to learn. The violence around New Amsterdam escalated, and it also extended north into Iroquoian lands, where there were still enough beaver left to be worth fighting over. Nevertheless, by virtue of their location, the people of the Raritan remained relatively unscathed by violence during these decades.

A specter that did haunt the people, however, was disease. Waves of influenza and smallpox brought the population of ten to twelve thousand people who once had lived in what we call Jersey down to much smaller numbers. We have no way of counting the losses today, but everyone who left any account agrees that they occurred. Even so, Lenape lands in this period were still filled with sovereign villages; they continued to plant their corn and hunt and fish and trade, despite their reduced numbers. As of 1660, their numbers could have begun to climb again, if given the chance.

Then in 1664 four English warships sailed into New Amsterdam's harbor. Peter Stuyvesant, the Dutch governor, capitulated peacefully. A few years later, New Holland was officially turned over to the British Crown.[19] The English renamed the city New York, and across the river they founded the colony of New Jersey. Now settlers streamed in. In the New Amsterdam area, the Dutch had largely maintained it as just another trading outpost in their seaborne empire (which included colonies in the Caribbean and Asia as well); only a few had established farms, and those remained close to the city. England, on the other hand, swelled with surplus population who regularly arrived in the New World by the hundreds with the intent to farm. In addition, displaced New Netherlanders and their children, who felt they could not compete with the more powerful English settlers in New York City and the lower Hudson, now poured into the lands they perceived as open between the city and the Raritan River, establishing what would soon be called "the Dutch belt." In the meantime, after some additional skirmishing and negotiating, the former New Sweden, which had passed into Dutch hands in the 1650s, also became the property of England, and in 1682, the king gifted the region to the wealthy Quaker William Penn in settlement of a debt. Large numbers of Quakers and other English settlers soon established Philadelphia and several other towns along the Delaware, rapidly pushing deeper into the territory of New Jersey. In 1670, an English mapmaker would write about the territory of New Jersey that it was "at present inhabited only or most by Indians,"[20] but by 1700, there were an estimated 10,000 European settlers in the colony,[21] significantly outnumbering the remaining Lenape.

The British government was from the first well aware that the lands they were taking over were inhabited by Indians, and they wanted no wars with them. The Crown government gave Philip Cartaret, the proprietor to whom they awarded the colony, strict instructions to be kind to them. If he "should find any natives in our said Province of New Jersey," his people were to "treat them with all Humanity and Kindness, and not in anywise grieve or oppress them, but endeavor by a Christian carriage to manifest Piety, Justice and Charity, and in your conversation with them, the manifestation whereof will prove Beneficial to the Planters and likewise Advantageous to the Propagation of the Gospel."[22] Despite his desire that the colonists should eschew the use of violence, the king nevertheless intended that they fully settle the region. The idea was that any remaining Indians were to be compensated for their land and induced to sign legal agreements that would prevent them from returning to hunt or fish or gather again. As settlers cut back forests, planted crops, and fenced them in, the game upon which the Indians relied receded westward. As settlers sold each other pigs to launch new farms, they began to release increasing numbers of them to forage in the woods, and these destroyed the small fields of corn, beans, and pumpkins that the indigenous people were accustomed to planting and leaving unprotected.[23] When the Indians went hungry, they could buy food, but even this was easier said than done. A generation earlier, the Indians had exchanged furs for whatever they wanted, but now there were almost no beaver to be found. Wampum was no longer accepted as currency. They still had one item that the colonists would pay well for, however, and this was the land itself.

And so the Lenape began to bargain away their lands. Sometimes they made informal deals; sometimes the settlers insisted on appearing before one of the court justices and having everything recorded according to English law. In August of 1690, for instance, an English woman named Lydia Bowne, probably a widow, living near Middletown, down the coast from Perth Amboy, paid seven English pounds to a collective of Lenape sachems, named Iroseheote, Taphalaway, and Talinguanecan.[24] The three placed their marks (a distinct S, N, and T, respectively) on a document in the presence of three English witnesses, among them a relative of Lydia's named Captain John Bowne. Since this was a relatively early deed in the area, it is possible that the indigenous chiefs did not understand that they were being asked to alienate the land itself, as opposed to agreeing to share the rights to use it. It is also possible that they were not really chiefs at all or that, if they even were, their people did not believe they had the right to alienate the community's land. In any case, difficulties followed, for the Indians did not all leave immediately, as Lydia Bowne had apparently expected. Six years later, Captain John Bowne and one of the other witnesses came into court to swear that he had seen the said Indians sell their land to Lydia Bowne and that they had no further right to it. After that, the remaining Lenape must have departed, for no further complaints were lodged.

In November of 1714, two Indian sachems calling themselves Nowenibe and "Johnny" agreed to sell to two merchants named Elisha Parker and Adam Hude a large tract described as encompassing two of the hills or ridges near Woodbridge, in Middlesex County.[25] That the court reported they were paid "a competent sum of money" and were "therewith fully satisfied" leads one to suspect that they were paid a dismal price that the white men involved were embarrassed to place in the record. Perhaps they were even paid in alcohol. The Indians placed their marks, but again, there was trouble afterward. Most likely the Indians (or perhaps others unrelated to them) continued to take wood or birds from the trees or fish or shells from the stream that crossed the land. For the next year, the two white men who had witnessed the sale (neither of whom could write their names) were asked to return to court and say that they remembered the chiefs saying that they were "in the Actuall Possession" of the said land, "in our right from our fore fathers many many moons, moons further [back] than we know to reckon" and that they sold it "with all and Every thing and things thereon and thereunder, and Above and high as the clouds and as deep as the Center of the earth, forever to be and remain in the quiet possession of said Elisha Parker and Adam Hude." No doubt Elisha Parker and Adam Hude believed that quoting poetic language would make it seem more likely that the Indians really had promised not to take anything in or on the land at the time they sold it; they may not have actually spoken of the beautiful elements "thereon and thereunder," for none of that language appeared in the fulsome, detailed text of the original deed which the Indians actually signed.[26]

By the 1740s, the few remaining Indians in the area all had Christian names that they were known by to their white neighbors. In October of 1741, two sachems calling themselves Andrew Wolle (sometimes spelled "Woolley") and Peter Tule sold a Dutch American named John Peairs a fifty-acre tract near Perth Amboy for six pounds.[27] Land had grown more expensive: a similar amount of money had bought 500 acres for Lydia Bowne a generation before. Sadly, the place was specifically said to be the remnant of "the old settlement of the Indians in the Corporation of the City of Perth Amboy." These two sachems' people were the last ones living there, and they were selling. They specifically swore that they did so "with the Consent and approbation of the other Indian Confederates." They said good-bye to a place they knew well: the said land "joins to the said River thence west to the old Cart path that comes from South River to the old Indian Plantation, thence along ye Right hand old Cart path to a Chesnut tree wch stands a Little to the Left hand of the said path and adjoins to an old Stump thence on a straight Line to the old ford over Manelapon [Creek] at the place wch is Commonly Called the hott house." A few years later, Andrew Woolley was living near Cranbury, sometimes visiting other traditional lands of his people, such as some on the "Devil's Brook" that drained into the Millstone River in Middlesex County.[28]

A few Indians in the area were not free to sell up and leave. They were enslaved, subject to the same brutal punishment as enslaved Africans if they were to try to depart. Most of these were not Lenape, however. Rather, they were from the Carolinas, captured in Indian wars that were draining that region of its population and sold through slave-trading merchant houses in Charleston. Most such slaves were sold in the Caribbean, but a few were disposed of in Northern ports, such as Philadelphia and New York (and conceivably Perth Amboy). In New York City in the year 1708, for instance, there were about two hundred African and Indian slaves meeting regularly in the home of a minister, "always after candlelight" so that they could not be accused of shirking work; a number of Indians were baptized in the Dutch Reformed Church.[29] The sight made some of the white city folk tense, and so that fall the council passed a measure that "every Negro, Indian or Other slave that shall be found to . . . talk Impudently to any Christian shall suffer so many stripes [of the lash] at some publick place as the Justice of the Peace shall think fit." A month later, when a white family in Queens was found to have been murdered by their abused slaves, another measure was passed against any potentially bellicose "Negro, Indian or other Slave."[30] Lenape from the Raritan River area came to New York to trade, so they would have seen for themselves these Indian peoples who had known utter devastation and had no hope whatsoever in their eyes. We know with certainty that at least some local Lenape peoples were aware of the presence of the Indian slaves and distressed by it, for in January of 1706, the Pennsylvania legislature passed a law outlawing the importation of enslaved natives "from Carolina or other places" because it "hath been observed to give the Indians of this province some umbrage for suspicion and dissatisfaction."[31]

Because of the lack of such records as diaries or letters, it is very difficult to catch glimpses of individual Lenape assessing their options and making decisions in these decades of motion and turmoil, but occasionally an individual briefly emerges. One child, called Hannah in English, was born across the river in the province of Delaware in the early eighteenth century. When her father was forbidden by the local English landowner to continue to plant corn, he went away to Shamokin to see about moving his family. Shamokin was a new Lenape settlement to the west, on the Susquehanna River. "He never returned," she remembered later; she did not know why.[32] When her grandmother and mother grew afraid of potential violence, they moved the family across the river to New Jersey for a while, but eventually they returned to the lands they considered home. They sewed in exchange for their keep at different white households. After her grandmother and mother had died, Hannah went to live with an aunt in New Jersey, but she had "almost forgot [how] to talk Indian" and so again came back to the area. Some young Native women in her situation married white men or black men: to this day, there are small communities of people in the northern and southern reaches of New Jersey who recognize that they are descended from both Native American and African American people. (These are the state-recognized tribes, who since the 1970s have carried the names Nanticoke Lenni Lenape, Powhatan Renape, and Ramapough Lenape.)[33] Hannah, however, did not marry into such a group. She lived as a wanderer, making and selling baskets until she was old and the local populace forced her into the almshouse.

Another child, called Teedyuscung, was born in the early eighteenth century in the Trenton area.[34] His family, too, faced pressure to stop farming on the lands they were told they no longer owned and began to practice basket-making and broom-making. When he was a young man, he and his father and half-brothers made the decision to travel north to the Forks of the Delaware. Traveling with a group of men, Teedyuscung felt more confident than Hannah's father apparently did of his ability to wrest a future from the land somewhere, and so he brought along his wife and young baby. Later, after the infamous Walking Purchase robbed the Indians of the land to the west of the Forks, Teedyuscung and his group moved onward to the Susquehanna River Valley. Little by little, most of the surviving Lenape gathered there. By then, they were no longer called the Lenape, but rather the Delaware, named by the English for the river which had run along the lands where they once had lived—and where a few hundred of their relatives still eked out a living.

The Seven Years' War and the End of an Era

On a beautiful red-and-gold October day in 1758, about five hundred Indians met in Easton, Pennsylvania, with representatives of the colonies of Pennsylvania and New Jersey to talk about recent hostilities that were unfolding as part of the Seven Years' War.[35] About half were Haudenosaunee, or Six Nations of Iroquois, as they were by far the most powerful Native Americans in the Northeast, and the other half were various groups of Delaware and their close allies. Teedyuscung was there with about sixty members of the tribe he now led as sachem. He spoke English, but for form's sake, and for the sake of those Delaware who did not, they had an official translator. This was Stephen Calvin, one of the few Lenape left in New Jersey, who worked as a schoolteacher at a mission community run by Presbyterians. He was dressed formally in English clothing when he stepped forward to translate. First, he interpreted the flowery speeches of welcome made by Francis Bernard, governor of New Jersey, who was eager to minimize the violence on the northwest frontier. Then he waited for Teedyuscung, who had been demanding the floor from the start of the proceedings, to speak. After conveying a polite formulaic opening ("I desire all of you who are present will give ear to me," etc.), Calvin had no choice but to pass on Teedyuscung's anger, his unapologetic reference to the fact that his people had recently made war up and down the Pennsylvania frontier, and his refusal to promise to participate actively in the day's proceedings. "Brethren, I sit by, only to hear and see what you say to one another; for I have said what I have to say, to the governor of Pennsylvania, who sits here; he knows what has passed between us. I have made known to him the reasons why I struck him."[36] Whether Calvin felt a surge of pride in a fellow Delaware, or only pain as thought of the likely consequences of such words, we cannot know.

Certainly Calvin was not a simple interpreter, or a mere bystander. He and his people in Central Jersey had been through a great deal by the time he stood there at the Easton conference—where he was given the title "Mr."[37]—and he harbored substantial hope that the conference would yield tangible results for those whom he represented. That the Central Jersey "Delawares" were present as an organized body with an agenda was due in part—perhaps counterintuitively—to two white men, the brothers David and John Brainerd, originally from Connecticut.

The elder, David Brainerd,[38] had been expelled from Yale University in 1741 for what was perceived by the institution's administrators as his overzealous response to the spiritual enthusiasm of the Great Awakening. (He admitted to having said that one of his teachers "had no more grace than a chair.") The expulsion meant that he could not legally become a man of the cloth in Connecticut unless he traveled to Europe or to the even more conservative Harvard for his education. However, the Scottish Presbyterians suggested that they could name him a minister to the Indians, and he accepted gladly. He visited several Delaware sites in Pennsylvania but did not find a great welcome among these Indians who were desperately trying to reconstitute their indigenous way of life in the west. (Indeed, they later told his younger brother that "the white people were contriving a method to deprive them of their country in those parts, as they had done by the seaside, and to make slaves of them and their children as they did of the Negroes" and even that "the minister must not come [among them] because he was a white man, that if one white man came, another would desire it, etc. and so by-and-by they should lose their country.")[39] Undaunted, Brainerd traveled to South Jersey, where he had heard that the indigenous people might be more amenable. He had been told there were a large number at Crossweeksung (today's Crosswicks), but he was somewhat disappointed. He found the people scattered but made it his business to try to bring them together. In his diary entry for June 27, 1744, he wrote, "In the afternoon rode several miles to see if I could procure any lands for the poor Indians, that they might live together, and be under better advantages for instruction."[40] Brainerd would announce that he would preach on a certain day, and sometimes, apparently due to the efforts of the translator he had hired,[41] groups of people did appear. On December 17, 1744, he wrote:

> Went to the Indians, and discoursed to them near an hour, without any power to come close to their hearts. But at last I felt some fervency, and God helped me to speak with warmth. My Interpreter, also, was amazingly assisted, and I doubt not but 'the Spirit of God was upon him' . . . and presently upon this, most of the grown persons were much affected, and the tears ran down their cheeks; and one old man (I suppose, a hundred years old) was so affected, that he wept, and seemed convinced of the importance of what I taught them.[42]

Brainerd had a remarkable willingness to admit honestly that he sometimes preached without real caring and that it was only when genuine emotion—a genuine desire to help—came upon him, *and* when his interpreter felt a figurative kinship with him, that his hearers would feel a new hope and respond.

Within about a year, over sixty Indians were gathering frequently at Crossweeksung from the various places where they had been living, while Brainerd spoke to them about his efforts to collect funds to buy enough land so that they could live together permanently. Many, he said, were former "drunken wretches" who were putting alcohol behind them. Brainerd believed they had taken Christ to their hearts, and perhaps they had; it was also possible that they welcomed an opportunity to become a nation again, with enough land to live upon in something resembling the old ways.

In March of 1746, the local Indian man who had been helping Brainerd shepherd the group, and whom he called "the schoolmaster," became very ill. Brainerd does not name him, but it was almost certainly Stephen Calvin, who was always referred to by that title by the colonists. For several weeks, Brainerd nursed him. He voiced genuine feelings in his diary, complaining of how taxing it was to care for an invalid. But whether he planned it so or not, his effort paid off. The man recovered, and new bonds of caring had been formed. On April 5 he wrote: "A number of my dear Christian Indians came to my house, with whom I felt a sweet union of soul. My heart was knit to them, and I cannot say, I have felt such a sweet and fervent love to the brethren, for some time past: and I saw in them appearances of the same love."[43]

In May of 1746, Brainerd was able to establish a small community of about eighty acres which he named Bethel.[44] (It was just outside today's Jamesburg.) Andrew Woolley, who had sold his people's land near Perth Amboy a few years before, owned some land at the site,[45] which formed the nucleus of the acreage that was added to through purchase, and other chiefly families soon brought their people there. In the 1720s, the settlers had hanged a chief named Weequehela for killing a white man. He had been a wealthy and powerful sachem from the area that the English called Middlesex County. His surviving relatives used the surname Store or Stores, and some of them came. His only surviving daughter and her husband joined the community; the husband was the one who had been baptized as Stephen Calvin, he who worked as the community's schoolteacher.[46] Brainerd would eventually have about fifty students. Sadly, at this time he became increasingly subject to bouts of tubercular illness, which was gradually claiming his life. By November of that same year, he left to stay with white friends so that they could nurse him; in 1747 he died.

Eventually, David Brainerd's younger brother, John Brainerd, would take his place, but in the meantime, white neighbors began to organize to push the Indians out. Several wrote to the governor, Lewis Morris, saying that they feared so large a number of Indians would steal their livestock; they did not claim it had actually happened.[47] In August of 1749, the governor's son, Robert Hunter Morris, who had been named chief justice of New Jersey, sued four sachems for "trespassing" on property he claimed belonged to the Crown: Andrew Woolley,

Thomas Store, Philip Douty, and Stephen Calvin.[48] The proprietor of the province claimed they "cut down, too, and carried away . . . fifty oaks of the value of twenty pounds and fifty chestnut trees of the value of ten pounds" and then demanded payment of one hundred pounds for unspecified "damages." The sheriff couldn't find Andrew Woolley, but the other three appeared in court together on September 29, 1749. "How do you plead?" they were asked, and each one stepped forward and said clearly, "I plead not guilty." Thomas Store was unfamiliar with the pen, or perhaps very old; he placed a shaky X where he was told to sign. "Indian Philip" drew an elegant cross, and "Indian Stephen" (as they called the principal teacher of a school of fifty students) signed his name. An attorney named Richard Williams promised to defend them in the matter. And there the case seems to have been dropped. The chief justice was having difficulties on all sides, as white settlers were responding belligerently to rules imposed by the present proprietor, and he soon traveled to England to try to sort the matter out.[49] Still, the constant harassment was successful to some extent: within a few years, a number of the Bethel Indians had moved back to Crosswicks or gone elsewhere.

In 1756, war broke out between France and England on American soil, and the Indians were swept into the fray. The Delaware living in Pennsylvania found the English unreceptive to their needs whereas the French were very receptive. Most of them gradually withdrew deeper into Pennsylvania and eventually to the Ohio River Valley, fighting on the side of the French, though some fought with the English.[50] Northeastern Pennsylvania was engulfed. In 1757 and 1758, some of the warriors began to cross into northwestern New Jersey and attack isolated farms there. It was believed that Delawares who had migrated out of North Jersey (some called Munsee and some Minisink) over the preceding generation were responsible. The government of the province of New Jersey panicked and began to plan how to assuage the feelings of the Lenape who had once lived among them as well as placate those who had been left behind.

In February of 1758 there was a meeting at Crosswicks with representatives of as many of Jersey's Indians as could attend. The purpose was to create a listing of all the lands in New Jersey that the remaining sachems still felt that they owned, in order that they be recompensed accordingly. Two Delaware chiefs living on the Susquehanna attended, one of them being Teedyuscung, who claimed some of the Jersey lands of his childhood. But the majority of the Indians who came still resided in New Jersey.[51] Tom Evans had come from a small group of people who still lived in the Raritan Valley, and there were seven other leaders from three other isolated communities. Andrew Woolley and eight others represented the people of the Crossweeksung area. There were a large number from near the Bethel settlement: Thomas and Josiah Store; an elderly woman named Sarah Store, who was the widow of the well-known chief named Weequehela whom the English had hanged for murder in 1727; Stephen, James, and Peter Calvin; relatives of Andrew Woolley named Ebenezar and Joseph Woolley; Isaac Stille, named for a Swedish father or grandfather, who had moved most of his people inland from their lands near Great Egg Harbor to be part of Bethel;[52] and John Pompshire, an early convert of the Brainerds who now acted as chief translator.

Pompshire worked hard ascertaining what lands should be put on the list and how they should be described, but his heart must have been breaking. A few years earlier, in the fall of 1754, his eleven-year-old nephew, also named John, and one of the Woolley boys, a child named Jacob, had been sent by John Brainerd away from Bethel to go study with the minister Eleazar Wheelock in Connecticut. They were to be the first students in a new school for Indian children, the "Indian Charity School." (Later, it would move to New Hampshire, evolving into Dartmouth College.) They were not happy there. Within two years, it was evident that young John Pompshire was dying of the same tuberculosis that had killed David Brainerd. He was sent home, arriving in Central New Jersey around Christmas of 1756. "Poor little John tarried with us [at our house] for a while, but Seemed rather enclined to be among his Relations: And accordingly went to the Indian Town [at Bethel], where he had a comfortable, warm Lodging provided in his Uncle's House, and all the Comforts we could help him to. But he did not live long to need 'em: He departed this Life the 26th day of January [1757]."[53] Brainerd did not comment on his family's grief but rather on the likelihood that the child was on his way to heaven. "His whole behavior was Christian-like, and he has left us, I think, some Grounds for a comfortable Hope concerning him."

Despite their grief at the loss of young John, the people of Bethel clearly believed that their alliance with the Brainerd family was key to their future. That same spring of 1757, they agreed to send another Woolley child, Joseph, a cousin to the Jacob who was already at Wheelock's school, as well as Stephen Calvin's son, Hezekiah. Brainerd wrote to Wheelock, "Joseph Wolley [is] a child that has behaved himself Soberly, of a middleing good Capacity, naturally modest, and Something bashful." Hezekiah had probably been named for John Brainerd's own father, and Brainerd clearly had real affection for him. "He is a Smart little Fellow, but will want taking Care of. He loves to play, and will have his Hat in one Place & his Mittens in another." Brainerd added a comment that shows how short of money even the sachems were: "Josey you will See [comes] cloathed with poor little John's Apparrel." He closed his letter with a postscript to be passed on to the other Woolley child, the one who was living in Connecticut and who was evidently missed: "My kind love to little Jacob."[54]

So in the early months of 1758, it had only been a year before that John Pompshire had buried his nephew and only months before that Stephen Calvin had waved good-bye to his winsome son, Hezekiah. But they were nonetheless determined to address this business of gaining compensation for their lands, for it was their agenda to gain permanent title to a large tract of land within New Jersey where they could stay forever. And because of the war, and the fears created by the war, this was the moment to insist. The provincial government seemed amenable, but they wanted something in return: they wanted these men to help them indemnify the Delawares believed to be the ones making the violent incursions into New Jersey. They were willing to pay for peace, and they needed Pompshire and Calvin to help them. So in August, these two and a number of others met in Burlington with representatives from the colonial government and with emissaries from Calvin's and Pompshire's relatives living in Pennsylvania. They made it known that two months later, in October, there would be a massive gathering at Easton, where real payments would be made. Speaking through his interpreters, the governor of New Jersey commented, "Of late a great darkness hath overshadowed the land, but we hope that the sun is up that will disperse the clouds that have hindered us from seeing one another, and will make all our future days bright and pleasant."[55]

John Pompshire apparently grew tired, ill, or disgusted in the intervening weeks, for he did not travel to Easton. Instead Stephen Calvin went as the lead translator, with Isaac Stille to help him.[56] The English colonists asked for peace and the return of prisoners who had been taken; they also asked the reason that the hitherto nonviolent Delawares had behaved as they did. Thomas King, the chief of the Oneida (the easternmost branch of the Iroquoian peoples), explained:

> Our cousins the Minisinks tell us they were wronged out of a great deal of land [in New Jersey], and the English settling so fast, they were pushed back, and could not tell what lands belonged to them. They say, if we [made deals when we] have been drunk, tell us so: we may have forgot what we sold; but we trust to you the governor of Jersey, to take our cause in hand, and see that we have justice done us. We say, that we have here and there tracts of land, that have never been sold. You deal hardly with us; you claim all the wild creatures, and will not let us come on your land to hunt after them. You will not so much as let us peel a single tree; This is hard, and has given us great offence. The cattle you raise are your own, but those which are wild, are still ours, or should be common to both; for when we sold the land, we did not propose to deprive ourselves of hunting the wild deer, or using a stick of wood when we should have occasion.[57]

In the minutes, Stephen Calvin was now suddenly called the interpreter of the Delaware "and Minisink" languages when it was discovered that he could explain to the Minisink representative what Thomas King had just said in English. (It was in fact only a dialectical variation of his own language, but the colonials did not know that.) The provincial government offered the Minisinks "eight hundred Spanish dollars for their claim in New Jersey, an extraordinary price." Their Minisink chief turned to ask his Iroquoian mentor what to do. The experienced Thomas King answered smoothly:

> It was a fair and honourable offer, and that, if it was their own case, they would cheerfully accept of it; But as there were a great many persons to share in the purchase money, they recommended it to his excellency to add two hundred dollars more; and, if that was complied with, the report of it would be carried to all the nations [of Delaware in Pennsylvania], and would be a great proof of the affection and generosity of their brethren the English on this occasion, and would be very agreeable to them.[58]

Thus, the Indians got a thousand dollars, as well as wagons to carry them and the goods they intended to purchase with the money, all the way back to Pennsylvania. Teedyuscung asked in addition for a horse for his people's chief, who was old and infirm, "which was readily granted." In exchange, the Delaware leaders signed a paper agreeing that all of North Jersey to the mouth of the Raritan and inland officially belonged to the English. They promised there would be no more incursions by warriors. Nevertheless, the chief insisted that they might want to visit. "We desire, that if we should come into your province to see our old friends, and should have occasion for the bark of a tree to cover a cabin, or a little refreshment, that we should not be denied, but be treated as brethren."[59]

The commissioners kept their word to Stephen Calvin and his cohort. Following the conference, "in consequence of the expectations given the Indian inhabitants . . . in this colony south of Raritan," the province purchased a tract of 3,000 acres in Burlington County containing a sawmill and having access to the largely empty Pine Barrens. It was called the Brotherton Reservation and was understood to be in exchange for the remaining land claims of the Indians. About sixty Lenape moved there immediately, and more followed.[60] It was a hopeful moment.

Lost Opportunities

Despite this gain, the 1760s turned out to be a terribly painful decade for the province's Indian people. There were practical problems on the reservation: the land was not good for farming; the sawmill burned down in 1762 and there were no resources to replace it; neighboring settlers poached on their lands, taking their firewood and livestock, and the Indians did not have the means to fight them in court.[61] Worst of all, the most energetic and intelligent of their young people, on whom the community placed all their hopes for the future, were regularly pulled away from their families and sent to Wheelock's school in Connecticut, where loneliness and isolation regularly destroyed them.

There is deep irony here, for it was in this very decade that Rutgers University and its associated grammar school were founded on the nearby banks of the Raritan River; both went seeking students,[62] yet neither considered the indigenous people. At the time, although other colonial colleges considered it their mandate to educate "heathen" Indians, Rutgers did not. On the contrary, the founders distanced themselves from such a plan. In the 1740s, in the period when David Brainerd was expelled from Yale, numerous men of the cloth had begun to feel strongly that Harvard and Yale had too tight a stranglehold over the American ministry and that neither was receptive enough to the New Light, the energies of the Great Awakening. Presbyterians (among them the same men who supported David Brainerd's mission to the Indians) soon founded Princeton University (then the College of New Jersey). In the 1750s, when the Dutch Church underwent a great crisis, King's College offered to have one of the school's professors of divinity be regularly appointed from among the members of the Dutch Church, so as to amalgamate the local Dutch population's interests with those of the school. In the furor that followed, Rutgers University (then Queen's College) was founded as a separate institution, obtaining its charter in 1766. In Scotland, the Presbyterian Society for Propagating Christian Knowledge among the Indians of North America raised funds to educate the "heathens," and some of those monies were funneled to Princeton. Queen's College, on the other hand, had been self-consciously created for the sons of the Dutch alone; its administrators harbored no fantasies of converting Indians and collected no charitable funds to pay for their tuition. Instead, perhaps to salve their consciences, the Dutch Reformed Church gave generously to Wheelock's school in New England at this time.[63]

By the mid-1760s, both the Woolley cousins who had been sent away to school came to grief. Jacob had arrived in Connecticut first, in 1754. He said good-bye to young John Pompshire in 1757 when the latter became ill and was sent home; Jacob soldiered on alone, soon welcoming several New England Indian boys. In about 1760, he was sent back to New Jersey, but not to Brotherton, where his family was. Rather, with the help of John Brainerd, he was enrolled in Princeton, where the Society for Propagating Christian Knowledge had promised to pay his expenses (though the school found them delinquent in doing so). He was miserable. At first, he made a half-hearted effort. "I like College as well as ever, only I think it is too much Confinement; because I want to travel some where or other & get acquainted with Mankind. For I don't see as I am likely ever to learn anything else [here], but the Languages & Sciences."[64] By the fall of 1762, his sense of the place had entirely soured, and the deans decided to send him back to Wheelock. "He seems to have lost in a great degree all Sense of Honour as to his Behaviour here, as he is fully sensible that he is now looked upon by the greatest part of the Students in a disreputable Light."[65] Back in Connecticut, he signed a "confession" (written by Wheelock) of having been guilty of drinking, doubling and swinging his fists, daring God Almighty to damn him, going away without leave, uttering ungrateful expressions toward Mr. Wheelock, and so on. "And all this has been greatly aggravated by the peculiar Obligations I am under to God & Man, by whose Goodness & their Charity I have been so distinguished from all my Nation."[66] Younger Indian students, including his cousin Joseph, had to bear witness to his contrition and sign as witnesses to his confession. He wandered in neighboring towns in deep depression. Other Indian students at the school, among them the son of the famous Iroquois chief Joseph Brant, lent him money.[67] A former friend ran into him. "I tryd every method that Occurred to my mind, to induce him to be free and open hearted; but to little purpose. He rather seemed to decline making me any Answer though his Silence appeared not to be the effect of Obstinacy & Contempt, but rather of Confusion or not knowing what to Say."[68] Jacob's cousin, Joseph, later heard that he joined the army[69] (as many Indians did during the Seven Years' War), but beyond that he never heard of him again. During the same period when Jacob had been at Princeton, the younger Joseph was thrilling his teachers in Connecticut. Wheelock apparently tried hard to encourage him: he bought a bear's hide to have made into a coat for him and paid for plenty of candles and paper.[70] In 1764, in the wake of the recent disaster at Princeton, Joseph moved on, not to college, but to a position as a schoolteacher in Onondaga (Haudenosaunee or Iroquois country). He was profoundly lonely, and the next year, in 1765, he died.[71]

Joseph had traveled to the Connecticut school in April 1757 when he was a young teenager, together with the much younger Hezekiah Calvin, the nine-year-old son of Stephen Calvin. With his quick intelligence, Hezekiah became Wheelock's favorite. By the time he was eleven, he could read Vergil in the original and write Latin in a beautiful hand. His tutor used a pencil to create lines on the smooth paper, and he copied out some of his favorite maxims, such as *Nemo mortalium omnibus Horis Sapit* ("No mortal man is wise at all times") and *Donec eris foelix multos numerabis Amicos* ("When you are happy, you will have many friends").[72] When he was fourteen, Wheelock was buying him his own Latin books.[73]

By 1765 it was understood that Hezekiah was to follow Joseph up to Iroquois country, and Joseph awaited his arrival eagerly[74] (though he would not live to see him, as it turned out). Hezekiah, however, had his doubts about the project. He wrote a note to Wheelock begging to be allowed to return to New Jersey just once to see his people before he traveled north. As always, he wrote with great rapidity, skipping little words in his eagerness to express his next thoughts: "I seem as if I wanted to go up among the Indians & try to do them some good as far as it lays in [my] Power. And I want to go home too to see my Friends & relatives once more this Side [of] Eternity (ie) if they are in the land of the Living. I think I shall never try to see that Country no more if I could but only See my Parents this [one] time."[75] It is clear from the note that Hezekiah was not in active touch with his people by mail, for he was not even sure who was alive and who was dead. It is not clear if he was allowed to go to Brotherton for a visit, but it seems unlikely, given the cost of travel and comments he later made.

By early August of 1766, he found himself in upstate New York. He was forced to tell Wheelock that the local Indians "were very loth to send their Children [to school], for what reason I know not." He described the situation: "They would make excuses that they had work for them to do, so that they could not send them yet, but they would send them Tomorrow & So on till I told them I would leave 'em, that I could not stay with them Doing Nothing, and on the Morrow they sent Five Children." He continued to struggle with establishing the school, at the end of his first letter saying, "It is true I should be glad to keep School here all my Days but all these things make me faint hearted, together [with] my wanting to see my father, Mother & relations."[76]

Within about a month—at some point in September—Hezekiah gave up all thought of staying forever among the Mohawks (where he could not speak the language and felt like a "dumb stump that has no tongue").[77] He did not wait for permission to leave but instead made his own way back to Connecticut, presumably hitching rides and working for his keep here and there, arriving at his old school by the end of winter. Wheelock, surprisingly, received him kindly.[78] He seemed to understand that part of the problem was that Hezekiah was in love with Mary Secuter, a Narragansett girl who had studied at the school and now worked in the Wheelock household. Hezekiah wrote to Mary's father: "It may be no small thing that I have to acquaint you with, the design that lay between your Daughter Moley, and me. Pardon me if I blush to Name it, that is *Matrimony* but I shall not attempt it without your Consent & approbation."[79] Mary, or Molly, enclosed a note of her own as well, but unfortunately, her father refused his permission, apparently because Hezekiah had no source of income.

Over the course of the summer of 1767, Wheelock wrote to John Brainerd in New Jersey and proposed to send Hezekiah home to teach in the school at Brotherton.[80] One problem was that what he would earn doing such work would not support a wife. The implication was that neither of the young pair was equipped, after the education they had had, to live as part-time farmers and part-time foragers, like the other Indians at Brotherton; certainly the evangelizing ministers wanted them to live in such a way as to model Christian values. John Brainerd wrote back many months later, apparently making a veiled reference to Stephen Calvin's budding alcoholism. "It won't due for Hezekiah to be anywhere near his father."[81] Wheelock spoke to Hezekiah and asked him to think about it all. When Hezekiah wrote to Wheelock, he revealed some surprising reactions. He didn't want to leave Molly, but he would, if Wheelock told him "as a father" that it would be best. His real concern seemed to be that he needed to "learn somewhat of my own Native Language that I might be the better fitted for the design you have in view."[82] It had been too many years; he no longer trusted himself to be able to speak the Lenape language that his father moved in and out of so fluently. He was delighted, but also somewhat overwhelmed, to be looking toward New Jersey and home at last. "My Mind is full. I cant express myself."

The result of the exchange was that Hezekiah was bound out as some form of apprentice to learn a mechanical trade, apparently so that he might be able to support a family back in Jersey. However, his impatience to set off soon made him miserable. "I shall turn out as Jacob Wolley did if I tarry much longer."[83] He began to drink a great deal. He thought of running away to sea. "There is something that makes me want to go home, what, I can't tell. Home is in my Mind all the time. I want to go Home soon & see my Relations."[84] Such comments became almost a refrain in letters he poured out to Wheelock.

In June of 1768 he went to Charlestown, on the coast of Rhode Island, where Molly was living with her family, having gone home because she had been caught drinking once too often.[85] (Wheelock had allowed him to make such visits in the past, in November even giving him the money for the trip.) Now Molly did not know what to say to Hezekiah. He pressed her to marry him and go with him to New Jersey, and her parents were by now convinced that she should. But she knew that he drank, that he flirted with other girls ("he has no regards for me more than he has for any giral"); she would have to give up everything she knew if she went with him and thus be vulnerable. At Wheelock's school, girls were boarded with local families to learn housewifery, attending class once a week; the kind of education she had received showed in her writing: "I have had more regards for Calvin that I ever had for anny Indian in my life I have minded him far enough I think (tho I have the same love as ever I had)." Once they had agreed "nothing [would] part us but death." Because of her doubts now, she feared he would always be bitter even if she married him. "He will always think I like hem not." She asked Wheelock what to do.[86]

Meanwhile, Hezekiah had already left for home. Before he went, he said things in his cups that he may or may not later have regretted. A mutual acquaintance wrote to Wheelock to report to him what the former student had been heard saying:

> That you have took from him his Silver Watch & Shoe Buckels with other things which his Father gave him,—that there is a large quantity's of Rice, Coffee, Flower [flour] & Sugars sent from ye corporation in Scotland to support ye Indians in your School, which you Sell, together with ye Cloths

which are sent . . . and Cloath them with that that's mean—That ye best Cloths he has his Father gave him. That Mary Secuter & Sarah Simon has been kept as close to work, as if they were your Slaves & have had no priviledge in ye School Since last Fall, nor one Copper allow'd em for their Labour. That Mary ask'd for a small piece of Cloth to make a pr of Slippers, which you would not allow her,—'twas too good for Indians &c. . . . That you won't give no more of ye Indians more learning than to Read & Write—'twill make them Impudent; for which they are all about to leave you.[87]

Hezekiah wrote a last note to Wheelock. "It seems to me as if I was willing to go to hell sooner or later. I believe it is best for me to be turned out of the School, for I shall never be good for anything, let me go home & Labour for my Living & not to stay & live upon Christ here to no purpose but to serve the Devil. I should be glad to be a helper in the Cause, but I am so hardened in Sin, I don't think that ever I shall be any better."[88] Then he went to Newport and boarded a boat to Philadelphia. From there, he hoped it would be easy to find his way to Brotherton and his father, Stephen Calvin.

In early 1769, Wheelock wrote, "I hear that poor Hezekiah Calvin has got into Prison . . . for forging a pass for a Negro & that it is probable he will fare badly. I hope God will humble him & do him Good by it."[89] Back in Jersey, John Brainerd told Stephen Calvin of his son's "bad" behavior and tried to induce him to make some sort of apology that he could pass on to Wheelock. However, Brainerd had to report that Calvin "did not desire me to write anything about it."[90] It could have gone hard with Hezekiah, but this was only 1769, not yet the harsh antebellum years of the Fugitive Slave Law, and somehow, Hezekiah managed to get himself released. On June 22, John Brainerd suddenly dropped everything to write to Wheelock, "Hezekiah Calvin is this minute come into my house." He had come to see Brainerd before returning to New England to see old friends there. Perhaps he had not given up on convincing Molly to marry him. "He has behaved pretty well, for anything I know, since he has been in these parts. I have given him the offer of the school if he could behave steady and well: he talks of accepting the offer after his return."[91] In 1772, Hezekiah was living in Jersey but hadn't settled down to teaching.[92]

A few months after Hezekiah left so dramatically in 1768, Wheelock suddenly made the decision to send home another Delaware student, a girl named Miriam Stores, almost certainly from the family of Thomas Stores. Wheelock may have been attempting to do "damage control" in New Jersey, sending home a student who would give the school a better report than would Hezekiah. She had arrived in Connecticut years earlier in 1761, when the school had first sent out a call for girls. (Whether the Stores family felt that it was their turn, since both the Woolley and Calvin families were already represented at the school, or whether they were told it was their duty to handle this request, as the other families had already incurred the loss of at least one child, we will never know.) Wheelock had seemed delighted with her. "She has sometimes seem'd almost to forget that she was a Tenant of the lower World, and at the Same Time appeared intirely free from ostentation or any degree of Enthusiastic Wildness."[93] Miriam grew from little girl to grown woman over the course of a few short years: she needed new shoes regularly and then in 1765 "a gown" and then a cap to cover her long hair.[94]

Wheelock certainly had every reason to assume that Miriam would say positive things about his endeavors—and she largely did. But it would have been better for his purposes had he been as watchful of her safety as he would have been in the case of any young white woman, for she had a harrowing time aboard the boat on which she sailed. She had gotten as far as New York City when she wrote to Wheelock to report on the progress of her journey. First she joked, "The Doctor will need [his knowledge of] the Greeke to read my writing," but then she reminded him that since she left his house she had heard "instead of prayers, filthy talk." Eventually she was more specific about what the voyage from Connecticut had been like. "I lay [awake] many a night, and for fear of one mans bad intention in his heart as I thought." She said she learned from the man's own lips after they finally disembarked that he had indeed been biding his time, waiting for an opportunity ("that was his end and aim") but that he had at least expressed something like remorse ("he was mistaken he owned").[95] Once she was in New York City, it was only a few days more before she was in the arms of her family. "Her poor old parents were overjoyed to see her."[96] Brainerd said he would try to help her find work in "a tailor's shop," for which she had been fitted, but that in the meantime she was working in Bridgetown (present-day Mount Holly) as a domestic servant. He could not say that he was pleased by her attitude. "I took the opportunity to talk with her and she appeared considerably affected, but on the whole, I did not discover so good a temper as I could desire." Brainerd continued to find Miriam to be different from the pious girl he had imagined; she remained unhappy. Eventually, she left Bridgetown and moved not to Brotherton but rather back to "where the Indians formerly lived"—meaning apparently either Bethel or perhaps Middlesex County.[97]

In Brotherton, times remained difficult. They still had limited means and no help came to the people from the education of their children at Wheelock's distant school, as they once had hoped it would. At the end of the Seven Years' War, a Brotherton resident named Joseph Peepy, who had conversed with Teedyscung and other Delawares living in Pennsylvania at the Crosswicks conference in 1758,[98] chose to move to the Ohio Valley, and in 1767 he came back to invite all the Jersey Indians to join their cousins in the West. Thomas Store, Stephen Calvin, Isaac Still, and the others were unconvinced. Working with John

Brainerd, they wrote a formal response: "We have here a good house for the worship of God, another for our children to go to school in, besides our dwelling houses and many comfortable accommodations, all of which we shall lose if we remove."[99] But they did not really have enough land to make a living without the sawmill that had burned down. They had been used to supplementing small-scale agriculture with hunting and foraging widely, and this they could no longer do, by the terms of the agreement they had signed during the war. Thus only a few years later, in 1771, after another visit from one of the Ohio Delaware, Stephen Calvin tried to convince his fellows to sell their lands and move west— at one point even forging some of their signatures to move a deal along—but the effort fizzled for lack of community agreement.[100] Calvin, tragically, took to drink in this period—or else suffered from some other form of dementia—but he made one key decision most astutely: a younger son born in 1755, who could easily have been sent to Connecticut in the 1760s, as his brother Hezekiah had been, was kept at home to be educated in his own father's schoolhouse. His Lenape name was Shawuskukhkung, or Flattened Grass;[101] his Christian name was Bartholomew. He grew up with his mind and spirit uncrushed, happy and healthy, and when he was an adolescent, in the early 1770s, John Brainerd arranged for the Presbyterian Society for Propagating Christian Knowledge to pay for his tuition at nearby Princeton. He studied there for two years, only leaving when the Revolution broke out and the Presbyterians ceased to pay the bills.[102] He lived to help his people when the era of Removal inevitably came.

Early in the Revolutionary War, the patriot forces approached the Delaware living in Ohio and in September of 1778 signed a treaty with them (often referred to as the first formal treaty between the United States and an Indian nation). White Eyes, the leading chief, asked for and received key concessions, among them the remarkable Article 6: "And it is further agreed on between the contracting parties . . . [in future] *to form a state whereof the Delaware nation shall be the head*, and have a representative in Congress."[103] As a sign of good faith, White Eyes left his son (then age eight) and two adolescent nephews to be educated at Princeton, as Jacob Woolley and Bartholomew Calvin had been, on the understanding that their expenses would be paid through the relinquishment of claims to particular lands that had once belonged to their people. But, of course, the members of Congress had no actual intention, in the event of their victory, of creating a fourteenth state to be inhabited and governed by Indians, or even of letting it become publicly known that they had ever considered doing so. White Eyes, the only leader likely to insist on the implementation of the treaty in the future, was murdered a few months later, although it was announced that he had died of smallpox. Colonel George Morgan, who had been instrumental in making all the arrangements, was horrified at what his countrymen had done: "White Eyes was treacherously put to death, at the moment of his greatest Exertions to serve the United States in whose service he held the Commission of a Colonel. . . . I have carefully concealed and shall continue to conceal from young [George] White Eyes [at Princeton] the manner of his Father's death."[104] Meanwhile, George and his cousins were entirely miserable at the school, so distant from their home in Ohio, and constantly begged leave to go. However, members of a committee commissioned by the Continental Congress were "upon the whole . . . of opinion that in the present situation of affairs with the Indians it would be impolitic to send these youths back to their country."[105]

The Revolution was proving to be devastating for the Jersey Lenape as well. There was military activity in the area, making it difficult for all farmers, but they in particular did not have the means to live as they once had done, in a world in which the sawmill was gone, their land was shrinking, and, most especially, where it was impossible for them to wander freely. A few local Quakers went to visit and found the Brothertons "in a very poor Sufering Condition." One of the men made a plow to give to Mary Calvin so she could attempt to farm on behalf of her family;[106] she was probably Stephen Calvin's wife, or perhaps sister, as she was now considered the head of the lineage, Stephen having died or at least ceasing to function in public. The Revolution, which was to bring such great change and such a sense of excitement and possibility to so many young people of that generation, brought an end to the Lenape of New Jersey. At the end of the century, they would decide to sell the Brotherton land and move out of the state. There were about eighty-five of them left; they hired twelve wagons to take them and their belongings to New Brunswick, from where they began their long journey.[107]

Rutgers and the Early National Indian Question

In the winter of 1832, Bartholomew Calvin (the younger son of Stephen Calvin and brother of Hezekiah), composed a letter.[108] He was writing to a number of graduates of Queen's College (Rutgers) and the College of New Jersey (Princeton), the men who now comprised the State Legislature of New Jersey. He himself had attended Princeton for a brief period in the 1770s, alongside the suffering young George White Eyes, and he longed to use his education to make legalistic and rhetorical points. But he also wanted his letter to be effective, to sway the white men whose attitudes he knew so well. So he began the way he knew his audience would want an Indian to begin: "My brethren, I am old, and weak and poor, and therefore a fit representative of my people. You are young, and strong, and rich, and therefore fit representatives of your people." Then, however, he veered into the erudite language he preferred to use. "But let me beg you for a moment to lay aside the recollections of your strength and our weakness, that your minds may be prepared to examine with candor the subject of our claims." In 1802, Calvin and his people had sold their Brotherton land and moved north to join another band of Christian Indians living in New York State; from there they had since removed to Wisconsin, where they yet lived. His people had been compensated for their land, but not for the usufruct rights they had enjoyed in the Pine Barrens. "Our tradition informs us, and I believe it corresponds with your records, that the right of fishing in all the rivers and bays south of the Raritan, and of hunting in all unenclosed lands, was never relinquished, but on the contrary was expressly reserved in our last treaty, held at Crosswicks in 1758." Bartholomew Calvin knew well what the treaty records showed, for his father, Stephen, was the one who had negotiated and translated at the time of the writing of the treaty. He was also clearly well acquainted with the law. For him, the only real difficulty in his task lay in composing a letter that would be acceptable to his audience.

As a highly literate man who was now in his seventies, Bartholomew knew that he was addressing a world of middle-aged men who had come of age imagining Indians as noble savages. The trend had begun almost as soon as the Revolutionary War had been won and the last of the East Coast Indians defeated. In 1795, the wide-ranging intellectual Samuel Mitchill—who was partially of Dutch descent and would go on to help found and become vice president of a short-lived Rutgers Medical College—gave a popular address to a social club in Manhattan, the "Tamany Society," founded in 1789 and named for Chief Tamanend, one of the Lenape chiefs with whom William Penn had once dealt.[109] Such clubs, named for Indian tribes and structured according to fictive native polities, were rapidly becoming more common, with New Jersey likewise soon boasting "Leni Lenape Lodges."[110] Mitchill delighted his audience when he said he had decided not to give a retrospective on the war but to change topic altogether. "For the bird, who used of old, to carry tidings to the ear of Tammany, and is now his messenger, between the world of spirits and those whom he loves on earth, just now, whispered in mine, something that I must communicate to his fans. I shall, therefore, talk to you concerning the life, character and exploits of YOUR GREAT FATHER TAMMANY."[111]

Tammany was beloved because he had been a "good Indian" who did not make war or evince any memorable hostility. "It was a maxim of conduct, with the sagacious savage, far more refined and excellent, than prevails among most of our civilized, enlightened and Christian legislators, that putting revenge and retaliation entirely out of the question, a fellow man ought not to be degraded to the condition of slave."[112] According to Mitchill, the chief's high notions of peace had helped create the country that was now a new nation, one destined to greatness when measured by principles of justice. But here Mitchill faced a problem: if he and his cohort were going to find the roots of their nation's greatness among the noble savages who once had lived there, they would find themselves quickly outstripped by Spanish America, whose people were the symbolic heirs of the far more extraordinary Aztec and Inca empires. Through a sleight of hand, Mitchill resolved the issue: he had the spirit of the original Inca, and that of Moctezuma's ancestor, to pass forward through time and come to beg Tamanend in the 1600s to visit their ancient lands and establish his high political ideals among them. He did so and "laid down the principles and chalked the great out-lines that formed afterwards the happy government of Peru; which would have continued to this day flourishing and excellent, had it not been overturned by the cursed enterprize of Pizarro."[113] Mitchill was almost overwhelmed when he thought of the greatness from which the young United States was descended, on a figurative level: "Let Asia extol her Zamolxis, Confucius, and Zoroaster; let Africa be proud of her Dido, Ptolemy, and Barbarossa; let Europe applaud her numberless worthies. . . . Where among them all, will you find coercion so tempered by gentleness, influence so co-operative with legal authority, and speculation so happily connected with practices as in the Institutions of Tammany?!"[114]

At the time, citizens of the still fragile young nation were eager to find mythological antecedents of whom they could be proud: stories of grateful Indians who signaled the supposed *rightness* of the colonists' taking of the continent served their purposes beautifully. In 1800, an English tourist named John Davis published a short novel titled *The Farmer of New-Jersey*. In it, he introduced to modern readers the story of Pocahontas. The farmer's son is asked to tell a story as the family sits around the fire. He offers one about "Pocahontas, an Indian Queen." He begins with the excellent Captain Smith of the first English settlement at Jamestown. He "bartered his goods with the Indians . . . and was often an umpire in quarrels between them and the whites." Eventually, he was captured by the Indians and condemned to being burned at the stake. Unable to watch an innocent man die, "Pocahontas . . . threw her arms around the prisoner, and declared, that unless he was pardoned she would be burned with him." (The real John Smith had included a single sentence about a beautiful Indian girl saving him from being clubbed in his 1624 book; he loved to describe beautiful girls saving his life everywhere he went. Either John Davis had read Smith's book, or more likely, he had been entertained in his travels in America by someone who had. That person clearly had read about the South Asian tradition of *sati* which Englishmen loved to abhor, for there was an overlay of that idea here which Smith himself had never introduced.) In any case, this particular segment of *The Farmer of New-Jersey* was well loved. In his 1802 book, *Travels of Four Years and a Half in the United States of America*, John Davis developed the theme into a fifty-page digression, and by 1806 he had decided simply to write a historical romance on the topic, calling his work *The First Settlers of Virginia:*

A Historical Novel. On the last page, the author mourned the disappearance of Pocahontas's people. "The race of Indians has been destroyed by the inroads of the whites! Surveyors with long chains have measured the wilderness and lawyers contended for the right of possession. Beneath those forests, once the favoured seat of freedom, the swarthy slave groans under the scourges of an imperious task master."[115]

What most American readers loved to dwell on, however, were not the losses of Pocahontas's people—or allusions to the ongoing sin of slavery—but rather the gains to the colonists which she, like the mythical Tammany, had purportedly helped make possible. Playwright James Barker was explicitly nationalist in his thinking when he chose Pocahontas as his subject in 1808. "We have yet to acquire and maintain a steady, temperate and consistent consciousness of our country's worth and value, without resorting to French naturalists to learn the size of our persons; or to British tourists to ascertain the state of our morals and manners."[116] He decided to write and direct *The Indian Princess; or, La Belle Sauvage.*[117] The show opened in Philadelphia to great acclaim; white citizens of the Delaware Valley eagerly went to see it. There, they came to know a Pocahontas who is such a very noble savage that she mourns having killed a flamingo. "I will use my bow no longer; I go out to the wood, and my heart is light; but while my arrow flies, I sorrow; and when the bird drops through the branches, tears come into mine eyes. I will no longer use my bow."[118] After she meets John Smith and he teaches her that the earth is round and there are many lands upon it, she asks sweetly, "My brother, will you teach the red men?"[119] The other Indians in the play are violent and villainous, but Pocahontas is a "good Indian" who loves white men and white culture better than Indian men or Indian culture, and through her efforts, a virtuous young country is born. The plot of the show lived on, moving far beyond the Delaware Valley, first as a chapter in Noah Webster's textbook and then in countless stories and paintings, becoming a permanent part of American lore.[120]

The early decades of American literature are known for having produced James Fenimore Cooper's *Last of the Mohicans* (1826) and other works concerning disappearing Indians. As a topic, the Lenape fared no differently from other tribes. In 1839, Samuel Janney published a lengthy story poem, "The Last of the Lenape," in which a good Indian saves a white settler family. "Then did his tribe all melt away." The author does not explain how the tribe "melts away"; it happens as if it were a natural phenomenon.[121] Over a decade earlier, Nicholas Marcellus Hentz had produced *Tadeuskund, the Last King of the Lenape* (1825), a book about Teedyuscung, the Delaware chief well known to Bartholomew Calvin's father, Stephen. The author was a radical Frenchman living in America, and he worked harder to defend the Indian than did Samuel Janney. When a heavily accented Dutch colonist condemns the Lenape on grounds that they "spoil our larders, blunder [plunder] our orchards and steal our gattle [cattle]," the narrator has a Quaker answer him:

> Are they created by a meaner power than the author of *our* lives? Has the hand that formed them impressed a baser stamp on their brow? And the blood that flows from their soiled wounds, is it blood, forsooth, or the vain effusion of useless flued? No. The inspiration of the Almighty hath given them understanding. They are shaped like us; they are our image; they are our brothers, and hold erect a countenance that speaks their noble thoughts and our shame.[122]

The Frenchman Hentz was in effect intervening in what had by the 1820s become (at least temporarily) *the* subject of national debate—that is, the question as to whether or not the last of the East Coast Indians should be removed and sent to live in territories in the West. No one could avoid the question: people of all stripes talked about it—men and women, old and young, rich and poor, black and white. The people of the "Dutch Belt," who founded and populated Rutgers University, certainly did. We can get a sense of their views in their regional newspaper, the *Christian Intelligencer*, published by the Dutch Reformed Church beginning in 1830 and read throughout the greater New York area. There they mentioned the start of classes at Rutgers University in the fall (where annual tuition, incidentals, and room and board totaled $123 per annum) and they regularly published advertisements for the associated grammar school (a classical education for $25 per annum; a basic English education for $20).[123] The editor, Charles Westbrook, was also a trustee of Rutgers University.[124] The paper covered a wide range of news, reprinting pieces from a variety of other papers, and included many articles on Native Americans. Generally, up and down the coast, serious Christians tended to be against Removal, focusing on the radical equality of souls. But the Dutch Reformed Church was different. There were in fact some ministers among them who ardently *espoused* Removal; indeed, the Reverend John Freeman Schermerhorn, who had been educated in New England at the staunchly conservative Andover, accepted the position of Indian commissioner under President Andrew Jackson in 1832 and became the mastermind of the actual Removal.[125] Other Dutch Reformed men of the cloth were opposed to many of Schermerhorn's ideas; he later, for example, became estranged from the Rutgers College trustees.[126] The staff of the paper—and presumably, most of their readers—seem to have held middle-of-the-road views, gradually becoming more accepting than not of the basic tenets of the pro-Removal faction (namely, that even educating the Indians would be useless and that for their own protection there was therefore nothing to be done but move them west).

For the editor, Westbrook, Indians simply were not a primary concern, even in discussions of evangelism. For him, the most important project was to raise the next generation of *white* citizens to be profoundly religious. He reprinted a lengthy article arguing that if ordinary white Americans were allowed to become secular, the results would be more disastrous than in the case of infidel people of color in other lands:

> The[ir] people are prepared for this [irreligion], having been transformed into beasts of burden by the long influence of superstition and the domination of privileged orders. But if the people of America speaking the English language should lose nearly all the religious restraint, which now exerts so salutary an influence in our land, they will be a very different sort of men from the Chinese, or the inhabitants of Turkey, or Spain. All determined to gratify themselves, and none willing to submit to others;—all having arms in their hands, and refusing to surrender them; wickedness and violence will reign with tremendous and indomitable energy.[127]

In keeping with this concern about future white lawlessness and truculence, the Dutch Reformed Church sent no missionaries to the Indians at this time, focusing rather on the settler population. However, the *Christian Intelligencer* did cover the efforts of other proselytizing Christians working with Native Americans. As of 1830, they were still reporting positive results from these efforts: the Mohegans in Connecticut were doing well under church influence, as were the Creeks, the Cherokees, and so on. A Methodist missionary in Ojibwe country in Minnesota—who was also a linguist known for developing an effective syllabary—quoted a dying Indian, first giving the words he purportedly uttered in halting English: "I got no more child leave on earth, Jesus take him my little boy, and I suppose Jesus take care of him, and my wife and girl, suppose I die. Oh my heart very happy. I think I see him Jesus by and by and all my good brothers there in heaven." Then the missionary quoted the man in Ojibwe: *O wa-wa-neh Keshamunetoo, kagate sah, nekichi wahwe shaindum oomae nintainkg* ("O thank you Good Spirit truly I am very glad in my heart").[128]

Over the next few years, as the national debate on the Indian question reached its crescendo, the paper's coverage became more conservative. The editors included pieces by Lewis Cass,[129] a famous apologist for Removal, who argued that it was in the Indians' best interests to be separated from white society by large distances, because Indians could not adapt themselves to education or work and only ended up drunk and dependent. In 1832 Westbrook himself explicitly commented: "As true friends of the Indians we have been decidedly in favor of the voluntary Indian colonization beyond the Mississippi. . . . We have, most unfortunately for the trial of our patience, humanity, and practical wisdom, the colored population in our bosom and the Indians upon our back. The colonization of the former in Africa, and of the latter beyond the Mississippi, affords the only feasible prospect of deliverance from these evils in a manner to maintain consciences void of offense toward God and Man."[130] The editor urged people to give money toward this cause, and the minutes of the General Synod reveal that the ministers were urged to appeal to their congregations, but there is no evidence that any money the Church raised in this guise was actually spent in Indian Country.[131]

However, like all churches, the Dutch Reformed Church did harbor some more radical disciples, and these found a sort of home at Queen's College, renamed Rutgers College in the 1820s.[132] The students' enthusiasm for defending the Indians' right to remain in their ancestral homelands seems to have been generated by the active involvement in university life of the free-thinking Frelinghuysen family, who had a long pedigree in the area. The minister Theodorus Jacobus Frelinghuysen (1691–1747) came from Holland in the 1720s and established the family line. He participated passionately in the Great Awakening, believing in the equality of all souls, which gave rise to accusations that he was "heretical, Quakerish, and Labadistic," that, indeed, there was "an unquiet spirit under the ministry . . . in the churches of the Reverend Frelinghuysen, which are along the Raritan."[133] Two of his sons, who were also ministers, worked long and hard with other Church members to establish Queen's College in the 1760s. One of his sons, Frederick Frelinghuysen (1743–1804), was the only instructor at Queen's for several years, during one of the periods when the school was struggling. He was elected as a delegate to the Continental Congress and later fought in the war. Afterward, he served in several public capacities. Frederick's son, Theodore Frelinghuysen, was in 1829 elected as a senator from New Jersey, at which time one of Theodore's young cousins was attending Rutgers while Theodore's own adopted son (an orphaned nephew) was about to enroll.[134]

Senator Theodore Frelinghuysen—who would later be Henry Clay's vice-presidential running mate in his bid for the presidency on the Whig ticket in 1844 and who would serve as the seventh president of Rutgers from 1850 to 1862—became famous across the nation in April of 1830 when he delivered a six-hour speech, spread over a three-day period, on the evils of passing the proposed Indian Removal Act. "Do the obligations of justice change with the color of the skin?" he demanded heatedly. "Is it one of the prerogatives of the white man, that he may disregard the dictates of moral principles, when an Indian shall be concerned? No, sir. In that severe and impartial scrutiny, which futurity will cast over the subject, the righteous award will be, that those very causes which are now pleaded for the relaxed enforcement of the rules of equity, urged upon us not only a ridged execution of the highest justice, to the very letter, but claimed at our hands a generous and magnanimous policy."[135] Parts of Frelinghuysen's speech were printed in newspapers across the country, but Andrew Jackson still got his Act of Removal. In May of 1830 it passed the Senate (28 to 19) and the House (102 to 97).

The highly organized Cherokee Nation of Georgia immediately responded by bringing a lawsuit all the way to the Supreme Court. Their case was dismissed on grounds that if it were true that they were a nation unto themselves, then the Supreme Court had no jurisdiction over them; however, Chief Justice John Marshall made it clear that he might welcome a different case. The Indians' cause and the legal suspense created by the decision fired the imaginations of many idealistic young people. Samuel Worcester from Vermont went down to Georgia as a missionary to the Cherokee. There he was informed—as he had known he would be—that he would need to take an oath of loyalty to the state of Georgia, as all white residents of the reservation now had to do. He refused. He was arrested and sentenced to four years hard labor. His lawyers appealed the case to the Supreme Court.[136]

Meanwhile, during that same year of 1831, Rutgers students worked to mobilize local opinion against the Indian Removal Act and in favor of striking it down. Nearly all students belonged to either the Philoclean or Peithessophian Society. These were recently founded literary clubs around which much of university life revolved. As members, the students pooled their resources in order to be able to buy books different from the ones in the school library—that is, books about nonreligious themes—and they met weekly to discuss concerns of the day. At the February 4 meeting of the Philoclean Society, the students excitedly decided to ask the Honorable Theodore Frelinghuysen to deliver the society's annual address at commencement on July 19.[137] *The Christian Intelligencer* reported a large turnout when he came. Some of the students later gave mini-disquisitions (among them Frelinghuysen's young cousin, who likewise took an interest in the indigenous people and spoke of the tragic fall of the Aztecs).[138] But it was Frelinghuysen's afternoon speech that most electrified. He had to be cautious in this context: he could not actually specifically mention the Indian Removal Act by name in a nonpartisan commencement speech, yet he found a way to speak of what he hoped young Americans would do in the upcoming years:

> No age of the world has surpassed the present in moral and political interest. . . . At some dark periods, the course of human freedom seems to have been crushed by the force of absolute power—and then for a season, the friends of man rise again to the assertion of her rights, and display in their struggles, an energy of unyielding resolution, which constrains even tyrants to bow before it. . . . But [then] again our hopes are dashed by the rising waves of oppression, and long years of ignoble acquiescence advance to pretensions and fortify the claims of power.[139]

Frelinghuysen reminded his listeners that their fathers and grandfathers had fought a great Revolution whose work was not yet finished. He said their generation had choices to make; they could not pretend otherwise. "My young friends, your future example will be most powerfully felt, for or against your country. It cannot be avoided. You cannot, if you desired it, become mere negative beings. . . . No, truth will either rejoice in your agency, or weep over the wrongs you have inflicted on her cause."[140] Frelinghuysen could not mention "Red men" but he could indeed speak of another race. He was speaking, he said very specifically, to white people, who had horrifying doings to answer for. "If moral ruin has passed upon our race, is the way of deliverance of no moment?"[141]

When school reopened in September, the Philocleans discussed copies of the speech that they had since had printed; they eventually decided that three copies should be given to each member and that each of them should distribute them judiciously, with the hope of heightening the awareness of as many people as possible. The original copy the senator had given them, they declared, should be placed in the archives of the society.[142] Meanwhile, in October, the competing Peithessophian Society held a debate on the question "Was the removal of the Indians beyond the Mississippi justifiable?"[143]

The entire country, Rutgers included, was by now awaiting the resolution of the case *Worcester v. Georgia*. In the late spring of 1832, the decision was handed down. Samuel Worcester had won his case that the state of Georgia had no jurisdiction over him when he was on Cherokee land—which in turn meant that the Cherokee and, by extension, other Indians had had their right to sovereignty upheld. In some circles, there were parties; almost certainly there was one at Old Queen's, with young Frederick Frelinghuysen (Theodore's adopted son) there as a student. (His scribblings and those of his friends give evidence of his joyous disposition as a youth.)[144] However, the merriment was short-lived. President Jackson soon made it clear that he would not enforce the court's ruling. Young Samuel Worcester was not released.[145] A few years later, the Georgia militia removed the Cherokee at bayonet point. By that time, Frelinghuysen had lost his bid for reelection to the Senate.

The Lenape who had left New Jersey three decades before were clearly following the national drama in the newspapers. They must have known about Frelinghuysen's speech to the Senate, about his popularity in New Jersey, about the animated conversations that were occurring throughout 1831 at Rutgers and elsewhere. It could not have been an accident that toward the end of 1831, they made the decision to present their own petition to this eager and sympathetic crowd. In early 1832 Bartholomew Calvin traveled from Wisconsin back to his homeland and had his letter presented to the assembly at Trenton. He brilliantly alternated between making threats of a lawsuit that could go as high as the Supreme Court ("The courts would consider our claims valid were we to exercise them. . . . It is not, however, our wish to excite litigation") and expressing belief in the kindness and wisdom of those he addressed ("We have ever looked up to the leading characters of the United States, and to the leading characters of this state in particular, as our fathers, protectors and friends").[146] New Jersey historians have liked to aver that the assemblymen cheered the letter and approved the state's purchase of the Indians' fishing and hunting rights wholeheartedly, but in truth the reaction was probably somewhat more muted: they passed a measure to pay the Lenape $2,000 in exchange for relinquishing all claims forever—not unanimously, but rather by a vote of twenty-seven to sixteen.[147]

Bartholomew Calvin did not forget to write a thank-you letter. "The final act of intercourse between the state of New Jersey and the Delaware Indians, who once owned nearly the whole of its territory, has now been consummated, and in a manner which must redound to the honor of this growing state, and in all probability to the prolongation of the existence of a wasted, yet grateful people." "There may be some who would despise an Indian benediction," he added. But the "ear of the great Sovereign of the Universe . . . is still open to our cry," he insisted, and whether these college-educated leaders of men felt they needed it or not, he would ask God to bless them.[148] He took the documents promising payment back to his remaining people in Wisconsin.

Two Epilogues

At Rutgers and in the rest of New Jersey, the after-tale is largely one of silence. Throughout the nineteenth century, Delaware people were repeatedly moved west, then west again, ultimately landing in Oklahoma, where they still live today. The people at Rutgers never wrote or commented on their painful odyssey; if they wrote about the Lenape at all, they wrote of them as long gone, as disappeared. The fervor of 1831 had entirely dissipated. The Rutgers community turned its face away. The only moment, in fact, when any Indians seemed at all relevant came in 1862 with the passage of the Morrill Act. Thanks to its terms, each state received the proceeds of the sale of a certain amount of Indian land in the west in exchange for committing to the pursuit of the study of science and engineering. Rutgers was selected as New Jersey's "land-grant" college and thus rose tremendously in stature.[149] No one thanked the Indians for the value of their land.

A few days after Christmas of 1890, the U.S. Seventh Cavalry opened fire on a band of Sioux near Wounded Knee Creek, South Dakota, and obliterated them. The act became a badge of shame to the nation and many people spoke of it and its significance. But other than the Quakers, few people in New Jersey commented, and there is no trace of anyone at Rutgers saying anything at all.[150] In the succeeding years, in fact, local people seem to have particularly enjoyed an amateur theater production of a play written by a local judge called *Tom Quick, Indian Fighter*,[151] in which a Pennsylvania settler whose family was killed by Indians in the Seven Years' War attempts to kill every single Indian he finds.

There were periods of interest in "Indian relics" in the twentieth century, but for many years, there was no sustained course work available to Rutgers students. In the 1930s, a Sioux woman, Neiome Whitecloud, who got a job teaching at the new Essie-Olive-Abeel School in Hackensack, had to take a course in Newark at the Normal School in order to learn something of her forebears.[152] She forbore to comment on the derogatory statements that were made in class. It was not until the 1970s that Rutgers students seem to have become energized on the issue of Native American rights. In the winter of 1973, the Pine Ridge Reservation Sioux working in tandem with AIM (American Indian Movement) members took over the site of the 1890 Wounded Knee massacre, and the televised spectacle became a media sensation. For a sustained period, Rutgers students filled the pages of the *Targum* with sympathetic coverage of the events, mostly taken from the Associated Press.[153] As a show of solidarity, they organized a march from the College Avenue quad to the U.S. Army Recruiting Center in New Brunswick that drew over five hundred students. As it did for much of the country, Wounded Knee seems to have marked a shift, the beginning of genuine interest in Native American affairs on the part of Rutgers students and faculty.

Meanwhile, during all those unfolding years, the Delaware Indians had been moving west and building homes and moving again and starting over once more. In the early twentieth century, professors from Columbia University who were inventing the new field of anthropology sought them out in Oklahoma and recorded some of their stories, which had both stayed the same and yet changed over the years. An elder named Julius Fouts told of the "Creation of the White Man."[154]

They say that the origin of the white man came in the early life of the Delaware Indians. When the white man was first created, there was no other natives then on earth except the Indians.

At this time they were visited by a man of an unknown nation, who began to teach the Indians a religion, telling them how they should live, et cetera. And this stranger resembled the Indians themselves in color and disposition.

Then the stranger departed from the Indians, going towards a nearby stream. When he reached the stream it was flowing nicely, and in it he saw great heaps of foam accumulated on the water—and took particular notice of this, giving the situation much study.

Now this man had been sent by God to the Indians to teach them the way to live. After meditating for a time, he decided he could create man himself out of the heaps of foam.

He then gathered some of the foam and made a man, making him like the Indians. But at the finish of his creation, this being looked fairer in color, and from that time there were men of this kind. They were strong in body and increased rapidly in population.

When they became many, he had no further influence over them. They would not heed the teachings of their creator. He could find no way to induce them to observe his commands. They became boisterous and mean, very unruly, and he could not control them. So he decided to go back to God.

And when he had journeyed until near to his destination, he met his brother, near a great gorge or canyon. He told his brother that his nation of people had become unruly and disobedient to him. "I taught the way to live, but they would not heed my commands, they killed me."

His brother asked him then, "Will you give our people over to me? If you give them to me I shall teach them the way of living, and every mechanical trade and benefit to mankind, and shall make them a wise nation and provide all things for their future use."

The man then consented to give these people over to his brother, for him to teach and command to the best of his ability and power. The brother then took charge of these people and taught them all mechanical trades and industries, and then the paleface people began to learn by practice the better means of progress. Success followed, and social life and happiness was soon established among them. But this man also taught them to scheme and how to mislead their brethren to their own satisfaction.

The creator of these people soon discovered that his brother was very much wiser than himself, and that his brother had been **condemned** by God because he was selfish, headstrong, and disobedient, and false to Him. It was for this reason he had offered his services to his brother to take command of the people he had created on earth, and to this day we find more *evil than goodness throughout the entire world and that evil is the stronger in every respect.*

Here Julius Fouts paused. He might have been finished. But he decided he was not. He and his people had long been told that they themselves were the creatures of the devil, but he had some thoughts about that. "The condemned man must have been Satan," he added, "who was so false to God that he could no longer arrange to stay with Him, so he was sent away to earth where he met his brother at the great gorge."

Did the Oklahoma Lenape man believe that white people had been taught how to behave by Satan himself? Was this how he explained the history his people had endured? Or was he teasing, trying to get the young anthropologist to smile at his irony? No one asked him, and now it is too late. We shall never know with certainty. Yet the Lenape descendants in Oklahoma doubtless have their theories.

2

Old Money

Rutgers University and the Political Economy of Slavery in New Jersey

Kendra Boyd, Miya Carey, and Christopher Blakley

Wealth accumulated from participation in slavery created a colonial aristocracy whose members would found Queen's College, serve as its trustees and officers, and patronize the institution as pupils. Prominent slaveholding families donated money and land to Queen's College (Rutgers), which helped the college reopen and remain in operation when it struggled financially. These families had relationships with Queen's College for generations. Prominent individuals who descended from the colonial aristocracy passed their wealth and privilege to subsequent generations, and the college continued to benefit from "old money" that was earned through the economic exploitation of enslaved people.

In *Ebony and Ivy: Race, Slavery, and the Troubled History of America's Universities*, Craig Steven Wilder traces the development of America's institutions of higher education from the early colonial period through the nineteenth century. His research demonstrates that the creation and development of American universities "were thoroughly intertwined" with the slave trade and decline of indigenous peoples in the Americas. Queen's College was among the early institutions to benefit from the profound "economic and social forces" of the slave trade.[1] This chapter builds on Wilder's work to provide an overview of the political and economic climate that existed at the time of the founding of Queen's College, and how the growth of the slave trade facilitated the development of these institutions.

The story of Rutgers University and slavery in New Jersey both originate in the Netherlands. The Dutch West India Company and the Dutch Reformed Church were two institutions that played a key role in the development of the economy in the Mid-Atlantic region and Queen's College. As historian James

Gigantino has noted, slavery's beginning in New Jersey cannot be divorced from its interaction with the Atlantic world and its relationship with neighboring New York. In 1626 the first African slaves arrived in New Netherland (New York) to work for the Dutch West India Company. This company of merchants traded in the West Indies (Caribbean) and dominated the Atlantic slave trade. It also enacted a "patroon" system, which granted vast tracts of land in the New Netherland colony to European settlers. Slave labor soon became extremely important to the region as few European immigrants chose to settle there and the colony suffered chronic labor shortages. By 1630, Dutch and Walloon settlers had spread to the west bank of the Hudson River in present-day Bergen County and brought the first slaves to New Jersey. The Dutch had settled New Brunswick by 1681.[2]

Queen's College would be founded within the slaving belt of East Jersey, where slave trading and slaveholding was common. Under British rule, East and West Jersey operated as separate proprietary colonies for twenty-eight years (1674–1702) before reuniting as a royal colony in 1702. Slavery in East Jersey was greatly influenced by the West Indies. Planters from Barbados, along with their slaves, came in droves to East Jersey and New York in the 1660s and 1670s. By 1700 Barbadian immigrants owned the largest concentration of slaves, whom they forced to labor on large estates granted by the colony proprietors. After East and West Jersey reunited, the colony passed, in 1704, a slave code that used previous East Jersey statutes as a model and included provisions influenced by the Barbadians. The 1704 law imposed severe restrictions on black people, including prohibiting slaves and free blacks from owning property.[3] By the time Queen's College was established, the institution of slavery was entrenched in the political, economic, and social facets of New Jersey, especially in East Jersey counties. This included Middlesex County, the future home of Queen's College.

The Dutch Reformed Church was also a key institution that shaped the culture of New Jersey. Prior to the founding of Queen's College there was no seminary in the Americas to train those who aspired to be ministers in the Dutch Reformed Church. Prospective ministers had to take the long, dangerous, and expensive journey to Amsterdam for their education and ordination. Some Dutch ministers in New York and New Jersey favored autonomy for colonial churches, rather than having to submit to the Church in Amsterdam. Through the efforts of colonial ministers such as the Reverend Theodore Frelinghuysen (1724–1761), a Dutch college was established in New Brunswick. Queen's College received its charter in 1766 and in 1771 commenced instruction "to cultivate Piety, Learning, and Liberty."[4]

Yet in the early colonial era, colleges functioned as tools of empire. Wilder calls them "imperial instruments akin to armories and forts, a part of the colonial garrison." They educated future colonial administrators, advanced civilizing missions, and sought to spread Christianity to indigenous peoples and "extend European rule over foreign nations."[5] Britain supported colleges in the colonies financially in the early portion of the seventeenth century, but as a growing merchant class began to gain power and wealth by mid-century, colonists were able to finance their projects "without metropolitan interference."[6] Merchants became the major financiers of higher education, and in the case of Queen's College, they along with Dutch ministers founded the institution.[7] The Dutch Reformed Church did not see the enslavement of Africans as a social evil or moral sin.[8] Thus, many of college's early trustees and officers, students, and donors came from wealthy families with financial ties to slavery.

By the mid-eighteenth century, trade with Africa and the West Indies reshaped cities in New England and the Mid-Atlantic. Shops sprouted in port cities, and grand homes were filled with luxury goods from Europe and the Caribbean. Members of New York's old guard branched out into the shipping and insurance industries: "These were the families that laid the foundations of the metropolis."[9] They sat on boards and founded major social institutions such as New York Hospital and the first public library in New York City. Prior to the American Revolution, sixteen merchants served as trustees of King's College (Columbia University). Merchants were integrated into the Atlantic economy, and as the slave trade grew, so did their wealth.

In addition to merchants, slave traders and planters gained power in colonial society, allowing them to take "guardianship over education." The development of campuses was intertwined with merchants' and planters' rise to power in the decades leading up to the American Revolution. According to Wilder, "Slaveholders became college presidents. The wealth of the traders determined the locations and decided the fates of colonial schools. Profits from the sale and purchase of human beings paid for campuses and swelled college trusts. And the politics of the campus conformed to the presence and demands of slaveholding students as colleges aggressively cultivated a social environment attractive to the sons of wealthy families."[10]

Take for example, Jasper Farmar, who was born into a middle-class family and began his career as a slave ship captain. In 1739, he forged a contract with John Walther of New York and Arnot Schuyler of New Jersey to captain the maiden voyage of their ship, *Catherine.* Farmar sailed to Angola and returned with 130 people to Perth Amboy, New Jersey, and New York City. Thirty Africans died aboard *Catherine* during the journey from Angola to the colonies.[11] Farmar continued as a slave ship captain and went on to command voyages between New York and London, which proved to be more lucrative. He eventually garnered enough capital to invest in his own ships and partnered with his brother Samuel to open a merchant house. By mid-century, Farmar was involved in slaving ventures with John Watts, a merchant and trustee of King's College. Farmar amassed enough money to send his son, also named Jasper, to Queen's College.[12] Farmar demonstrates that the emergence of merchants not only financed schools but also supplied the wealth to send students to college. The tie to slavery was not only at the administrative level but present within the student body.

The slave trade also lined the pockets of those who founded and became the trustees of Queen's College. The charter trustees came from some of the most prominent slave-trading and slaveholding families in the region. The founding president, Jacob Hardenbergh, was a slave owner. The first tutor, Frederick Frelinghuysen, Hardenbergh's stepson, also owned slaves. The earliest graduates came from Dutch slaveholding families, including the Schencks, Van Cortlandts, and Van Hornes.[13] The trustees, Philip Livingston, Robert Livingston, Theodorus Van Wyck, Peter Schenck, and Abraham Hasbrouck, were all from prominent slave-trading and slaveholding families in the region. In the Mid-Atlantic and New England regions, the greatest period of expansion in higher education occurred at the peak of the African slave trade. By the 1750s, the number of trustees involved in this trade increased.[14] Two of Queen's College's original 1766 trustees were brothers Philip Livingston (1716–1778) and Robert Livingston (1708–1790), who came from the prominent Livingston Manor in upstate New York.[15] Many of the early trustees were not residents of New Jersey but of New York City, because of the Dutch Reformed Church's strong presence in that city. The Livingstons belonged to the "colonial aristocracy" and its members were "distinguished culturally from their humbler neighbors," in wealth and manners.[16] This landed family traced its roots back to the first Robert Livingston (1654–1728), a Scotsman brought up in the Netherlands who arrived in the New York colony in 1675. By 1686 he had assembled the 160,000-acre tract called Livingston Manor.[17] The estate's great wealth was acquired in part by the labor of enslaved people. The first Robert Livingston purchased several slaves in New York City to provide for the manor's labor needs and for his children's need for servants.[18]

Robert's son Philip (1686–1749) was a leading importer of slaves from Jamaica and Antigua during the 1730s.[19] In August 1733, Philip's sloop *Katherine* brought in fifty blacks from Jamaica, an unusually large shipment from that source.[20] He was also part-owner of a number of vessels, some of which were owned in partnership with his sons Philip and Robert, the Queen's College trustees. The younger Philip Livingston, who was a signer of the Declaration of Independence, continued in his father's slave-trading business and became a merchant in New York City. He also received "slaves and commercial slaving interests" from his parents and his in-laws, the Van Brugh family.[21] Philip and Robert Livingston's involvement with the slave trade was not exceptional among major mercantile families.[22] Thus, we can assume that other early trustees and Queen's College affiliates who were listed as New York merchants likely had financial ties to slavery.[23]

Robert and Philip's younger brother was William Livingston, the first governor of New Jersey following the American Revolution, for whom Rutgers
University's Livingston campus is named. William Livingston attended the Constitutional Convention and helped to frame the document that emerged from
its deliberations.[24] William was also a lawyer, but he apparently did not choose
the profession with much enthusiasm. Since his older brothers were merchants
and landowners, the family wanted him to look after its legal interests. Thus,
William was compelled into the law profession.[25] Livingston's connections with
New York's most prominent and wealthy families aided his legal career considerably; he executed their wills, drew up their deeds, and sued their delinquent
debtors. The Livingstons and their relations constituted the source of William's
earliest legal practice, and his membership in the legal profession served his
slave-trading family's financial interests.[26]

William Livingston's family connections also took him far in politics. In
1772 Livingston moved from New York to New Jersey and was elected governor
of New Jersey in 1776.[27] As governor, Livingston was sympathetic to abolitionists.
In 1786 he wrote that "slavery was an indelible blot . . . upon the character of
those who have so strongly asserted the unalienable rights of man."[28] In refer-
encing the Declaration of Independence, William highlighted the fact that the
liberal promises of the American Revolution stood beyond the reach of enslaved
people. At the beginning of the Revolution, the founding fathers declared, "We
hold these truths to be self-evident, that all men are created equal, that they
are endowed by their Creator with certain unalienable Rights, that among these
are Life, Liberty and the pursuit of Happiness." Yet all men were not equal, and
they did not pay an equal price for the nation's freedom from Britain. During
the Revolutionary War, landed families were able to flee from the battles taking place in New York and New Jersey. For example, John Henry Livingston, the
future president of Queen's College, was able to evade the danger of living in
Flatbush by fleeing to the manors of family and friends in upstate New York and
Connecticut.[29] These large estates, which served as safe havens, were built and
maintained by unfree blacks.

Like William Livingston, members of slaveholding families who opposed
slavery often occupied a place of contradiction. They condemned the institution while they benefited from the wealth it created. Likewise, the people closest to them continued to benefit financially from slavery.[30] Livingston worked
with Quaker abolitionists to instigate an end to the Atlantic slave trade and the
abolition of slavery in New Jersey. However, Livingston eventually abandoned
the combined plan, believing that trying for both ran the "risk of obtaining
nothing." He claimed it was "then prudence not to insist upon it, but to get what
we can and which paves the way for procuring the rest."[31] As the privileged and
wealthy governor of New Jersey, William Livingston could afford to have a "be

FIGURE 2.1 Reverend John Henry Livingston, president of Queen's College and professor of Theology. Special Collections and University Archives, Rutgers University Libraries.

patient" attitude. But enslaved men and women in New Jersey agonized every day that freedom remained elusive.

The prominent Livingston family continued to have close ties with Queen's College in the next generation. The fourth president of the college was the Reverend John Henry Livingston, who served from 1810 until his death in 1825.[32] In addition to being president, John Henry Livingston was a theological professor for the college. John Henry was the son-in-law and distant cousin of trustee Philip Livingston (1716–1778). Livingston had grown up in Poughkeepsie, New York, in a family who owned slaves and he had almost certainly owned slaves himself as late as 1790 while he was still in New York City, although by 1800 he apparently no longer did so.[33] John Henry Livingston's branch of the family was the least prosperous; his grandfather was the first Robert Livingston's youngest son, Gilbert. However, Gilbert Livingston did benefit financially from the family's slaveholding and was relatively wealthy. In fact, Gilbert apparently did not mind suffering a financial loss to demonstrate his mastery over his slaves. John Henry Livingston's grandfather once subjected a slave to a severe beating for the offense of having run away. The unfortunate man "died out of doggedness" within ten days.[34] For wealthy slaveholders like Gilbert Livingston, enslaved people's lives were expendable.

John Henry Livingston, who married his second cousin Sarah Livingston, never expected to participate in the slave-trading business of his father-in-law Philip. He was always an astute scholar, and after briefly studying law, he decided his true calling was to devote his life to God and the religious profession.[35] An event in 1765 made an unforgettable impression on John Henry and cemented his religious conversion and decision to devote himself to the ministry. For many months he had been ill with a constant pain in his chest along with a fever. In the spring of 1765, John decided that a voyage to the West Indies would improve his health. However, after making all the necessary arrangements and preparations for the trip, for some unexplainable reason, he lost all desire to go and "suddenly gave up the voyage." John later learned that the vessel he had planned to take to the West Indies had been seized and all who were on board were murdered. Realizing that he would have died had he gone on the voyage, he interpreted the outcome as Divine Providence working in his favor.[36] This moment of divine intervention that shaped the course of Livingston's life—and Queen's College—was tainted by slavery. Livingston had probably planned to visit the West Indies because the family had been importing slaves from the West Indies and had many connections there.[37]

Though he was not actively involved in his father-in-law's slave-trading business, John Henry Livingston did inherit some of his wealth from his slave-trading father-in-law. When Philip Livingston died in 1778, his daughter Sarah and son-in-law John Henry Livingston were named as heirs.[38] Excluding Brooklyn real estate left to his wife, Philip Livingston bequeathed all of his estate to be divided equally among his six children, which included Sarah Livingston. Since Philip's son Abraham had died not long after his father, part of his inheritance was also passed on to Henry Alexander Livingston, the son of John Henry and Sarah Livingston.[39]

Besides inheriting wealth, John Henry Livingston served as one of the administrators of Philip Livingston's estate. For decades after his father-in-law died, John Henry conducted business on behalf of the estate.[40] In his May 18, 1778, last will and testament Philip stipulated that the executors of his estate should sell whatever was necessary to settle his debts, and then divide the rest of his property among his children. Philip's property included "goods and Chattels" and it is plausible that John Henry Livingston could have overseen the sale of this property as one of the administrators of the estate.[41]

As president of Queen's College from 1810 through 1825, John Henry Livingston certainly encountered many enslaved persons in New Brunswick and the surrounding area.[42]

Livingston's former student Benjamin Taylor recalled a time he and the Reverend Livingston walked through New Brunswick where they encountered several people, including a young black man:

> As we passed down the street, the first person we met was a young colored man, who very politely bowed to the Doctor, who quickly replied, "Good morning, boy!" Turning his face toward me, he said, "my son, learn a lesson: never be outdone in politeness by a negro." Presently we met a prominent lawyer of the city. Stopping for a moment, he with his hand lifted his hat, and saluted him gracefully. Then having passed on a few steps, he said: "my son, always be very respectful to gentlemen of intelligence

FIGURE 2.2   Watercolor of Rutgers College by Theodore Sandford Doolittle, 1857. Special Collections and University Archives, Rutgers University Libraries.

and influence." Advancing somewhat further, he saw a venerable lady, the widow of a distinguished judge of our supreme courts, coming toward us. "My son, Mrs. Paterson is coming—a most estimable lady. We must be very courteous." Then, with both hands, in a most dignified manner, he took off his hat, and bade her good-morning. Turning to me, he [said], "my son, always remember there are distinctions in society. Ever have respect to the characters you meet with and the positions they occupy."[43]

From this we can see that Livingston saw blacks as the lowest in society. The young black man had to bow to the Reverend Livingston, something he probably had to do to most whites he encountered. He also had to bear being called a "boy" even though Taylor admits that the person he and Livingston encountered was in fact a young man.

The Livingstons were not the only aristocratic family with ties to the college. Stephen Van Rensselaer (1764–1839) served as a trustee of Queen's College from 1829 to 1839 and donated $1,000 for a professorship in 1824.[44] Van Rensselaer was the son-in-law of Philip Livingston (he married Sarah's sister Catherine), a descendant of Kiliaen Van Rensselaer, and a director of the Dutch West India Company, which had enacted the "patroon" system. Kiliaen Van Rensselaer was the most successful patroon and had a large estate in upstate New York called Rensselaerswyck, which he passed down to his male descendants.[45] The Manor of Rensselaerswyck relied on slave labor, and the family owned many slaves. Stephen Van Rensselaer inherited Rensselaerswyck in 1785 and became one of the wealthiest Americans of his era.[46] His brother Philip S. Van Rensselaer also donated a piece of land in New York to the college.[47] Stephen Van Rensselaer Jr. was also a trustee and donor to the college.[48]

After the Revolutionary War, America emerged as a new nation and had to define for itself the role slavery would take in the young country's future. Much of the United States, including New Jersey, chose to embrace or accept the institution of slavery as a vital part of their political, social, and economic life. Deference to white men's property rights resulted in gradual rather than immediate emancipation in most of the North. Northern merchants who profited from carrying slave-produced agricultural commodities from Southern states to foreign markets remained invested in the institution.[49] At the beginning of the nineteenth century, the new nation experienced unprecedented prosperity and rapid technological advances that created a "Market Revolution." Yet, the early Republic's bustling economy opened up new possibilities for some Americans precisely because it closed down opportunities for others.[50]

The Revolutionary War battles fought in New Jersey had caused much destruction and pushed the state into a deep economic recession. White New Jerseyans decided that slavery could spur economic recovery and thus refused to advance abolition, even as it moved forward in other Northern states.[51] The need to rebuild the devastated East Jersey economy and the growing demand for New Jersey's grain crops led to the growth of slavery in New Jersey during the two decades after the Revolution. Slave labor enabled New Jersey farmers to profit from the increased value of wheat and flour that the nation witnessed between 1780 and 1790. Uncompensated slave labor was the key factor that allowed New Jersey to keep pace with the worldwide demand for the state's foodstuffs.[52]

At the opening of the nineteenth century the city of New Brunswick was noted as a shipping and commercial point. Ships owned by locals such as John Voorhees sailed from the Raritan on voyages to Bermuda, the Bahamas, Jamaica, and Hispaniola in the West Indies, as well as to South Carolina, Delaware, North Carolina, and Georgia. Cargo shipped from New Brunswick included grain, pork, leather, and iron ore. Carriages were shipped to the South, and the vessels brought back sweet potatoes and other products.[53]

There were merchants and dealers of all types located on Church and Albany Streets. For example, Thomas Brush conducted a land and intelligence office. He was also an auctioneer who sold "houses, lots, plantations, negro men, wenches and children."[54] On business trips to New York, the city's merchants generally proceeded by private conveyances to what is now Jersey City and Hoboken, where they crossed New York Harbor either in a sailboat or rowboat. This journey took three days. It was not uncommon for businessmen to encounter "stray negroes" or blacks who could not give an accounting of their presence on the road. These "strays" were sometimes put in jail. If no owners appeared, they were sold to pay the expense of arrest and jail fees.[55] One of New Brunswick's principal merchants in the early nineteenth century was Jacob R. Hardenbergh Jr., one of Queen's College's early trustees and son of its first president.

While businesses in New Brunswick thrived in the early years of the nineteenth century, the same could not be said of Queen's College's financial situation, though its investors remained involved in slavery. Due to financial difficulties Queen's College fell on hard times and closed from 1795 to 1807. After a few years of renewed operation the college closed again from 1816 to 1825. Only the monetary donations from wealthy slaveholding benefactors saved the institution. In 1807 Queen's College president Ira Condict along with Andrew Kirkpatrick generated renewed interest in the college and raised $6,000 from patrons in and around New Brunswick. With this money they were able to construct "Old Queen's," the college's first permanent building, in 1809.[56] The land that Old Queen's was built on was donated by prominent families, whose wealth stemmed from their engagement with slavery. The family of James Parker, a former delegate to the Provincial Congress and an East Jersey proprietor, donated five acres bounding Somerset and George Streets, where Old Queen's was built in 1809.[57] James Parker was a merchant in New York City and the son of the owner of extensive landed property.[58] The Parker family held slaves as late as the 1820s. Mrs. Ann Parker of North Brunswick appears twice in the Middlesex County records for manumission of slaves. On March 31, 1817, a thirty-five-year-old woman named Charlotte was manumitted and on August 20, 1821, a twenty-three-year-old man named Edward was manumitted.[59] The Parkers were close friends with another family who had ties to the university. Jacob Dunham, whose father and brother were Queen's College trustees, was the Parker family's physician. Mrs. Ann Parker had a running account with Dr. Dunham, who visited Ann and Gertrude Parker on several occasions in the early 1820s. Dunham also treated the Parkers' "blk girl."[60]

The college's land expanded from the Parkers' donation to include a contribution from the Neilson family. Colonel John Neilson, who was elected as a trustee of the college in 1782, profited from personal and familial slaveholding connections. The colonel's uncle, James Neilson, arrived in New Brunswick in 1730.[61] At the time of his death, James Neilson held two enslaved men, "Negro Jack" and "Negro Sampson."[62] John Neilson, born March 11, 1745, at Raritan Landing, joined his Uncle James's shipping business and continued with it after James's death in 1783.[63] The business traded "corn, wines, rum, gin, flour, and cloths" between Madeira, the Dutch West Indies, and New Jersey. In her 1935 master's thesis, Thelma Doyle noted that in one case the Neilson business sold "a negro and that was for the sum of one thousand dollars."[64] In 1778 John also inherited his uncle's estate, including possession of Jack and Sampson.

John Neilson purchased and sold enslaved Africans before and after the Revolutionary War. On February 20, 1777, Neilson wrote to a fellow officer during the war, informing him, "I herewith send you the negro woman taken from Smith of Spotswood, two sight horses arrived last night from South Amboy."[65] According to a report by David J. Fowler, Neilson purchased at public vendue in November 1777 "a negro Man taken from the Enemy."[66] According to Fowler, this man may have appeared again in Neilson's records when in October 1779, a tailor, John Henry, billed Neilson for making a jacket "for your Negro Will."[67] In January 1787, Neilson bought "a certain negro Woman named Flora together with her two female Children, one called Phillis, the other Ann" from Anthony L. Bleecker of New York.[68]

In 1795, John Neilson bought the farm of John Voorhees in New Brunswick, where Neilson's slaves, and possibly free blacks as well, worked for decades.[69] In addition to purchasing enslaved Africans as chattel property, Neilson also purchased an enslaved man, it appears, through a form of indenture. In July 1798, Neilson purchased a "Negro Man named Tony" for a five-year-term, which, according to Fowler, was formally arranged between Neilson and Tony.[70] In 1815, Neilson purchased another enslaved man, Prince, for a period of four years.[71] John Neilson continued to buy and sell enslaved people in New Jersey well into the nineteenth century. Two receipts from Hannah Clark in 1814 and 1815 indicate Neilson sold two enslaved women, Grace and Dine, making a profit of $150 and $75, respectively, from the sale.[72]

John Neilson's son, James, was also a slaveholder and a major benefactor to Rutgers College. In 1814, he purchased an enslaved man, Lewis, from Joseph Baldwin in Newark for the sum of $126.[73] The following year, Neilson paid $250 to purchase an enslaved woman, Elizabeth.[74] In 1816, Neilson purchased another man, Mark, from a man in New Brunswick, Benjamin Taylor. In the receipt, Neilson promised to manumit Mark in 1821. However, almost two decades later in 1838, Neilson sold Mark to Abraham Ranby. In 1825, Neilson paid $100 for another enslaved woman named Jerima. In his will, James Neilson bequeathed a fund to the college.[75]

James Neilson pledged $500 to Rutgers as early as 1845 and continued to pay the college 6 percent interest on this sum until his death. He also maintained a scholarship of $30 per year. The New Brunswick Theological Seminary, closely affiliated with Rutgers, was likewise the beneficiary of Neilson's generosity. The *New Brunswick Fredonian* gave the following details concerning his gift in 1855 to the Seminary: "Mrs. Anna Hertzog of Philadelphia, having recently made a donation of $30,000 for the purpose of building a Theological Hall . . . Colonel James Neilson, of this city, has made the thing complete by giving five acres of ground to build the Hall on, situated back of the college adjoining the property of Messrs Bishop. For building purposes this ground is among the handsomest in this City, and will ever call up grateful recollections of its donor from the students of old Rutgers, who pursue the study of Theology."[76] James Neilson's son, James Neilson Jr., also studied at Rutgers, graduating in 1866 and later being elected as a trustee in 1886.[77]

The most substantial donation the college received during its period of financial troubles was from the Dutch minister Elias Van Bunschooten. A Queen's College trustee from 1787 to 1815, Van Bunschooten gave a gift of $14,640 ($13,840 in bonds payable over the next ten years and $800 cash) near the end of his life in 1814. When he died in 1815, Van Bunschooten left the college additional property amounting to over $4,000 in his will. His generous donation was to be used for "the purposes of theological education." Besides his role as a loyal trustee of Queen's College, Van Bunschooten was also influenced to give to the college by a "most moving and beautiful letter from his old schoolmate and life-long friend," John Henry Livingston, who was president of Queen's College at the time.[78]

Elias Van Bunschooten did not gain his wealth or social position from his occupation as a minister. He was a frontier preacher with a modest salary. The rural churches of the Delaware Valley where Van Bunschooten was called to serve as pastor were located in "a backwoods region whose scanty settlements were marked by much of that semi-barbarism by which civilization usually is temporarily overcome at its first contact with the wilderness, and was still haunted by those uncomfortable neighbors, the savage red men," as narrated by Van Bunschooten's descendant. [79] Additionally, throughout Van Bunschooten's time in the Delaware Valley "there was much friction over salary." His stipend of somewhat more than a hundred pounds was raised by the three congregations in unequal proportions and they were "much of the time in arrears."[80]

However, Van Bunschooten came from a wealthy slaveholding family. Elias was the son of Teunis Van Bunschooten, the owner of a large property near what became New Hackensack, approximately 1,196 acres of land in Duchess County, New York. Teunis was in fact "one of the three largest tax-payers in the county during the Revolution."[81] Teunis died in 1788 and his will left three of his sons land "together with all my slaves to be equally divided among them."[82] As the oldest son Elias inherited four-hundred pounds to "be paid to him in silver or gold" as well as a share of other property that was divided among Teunis's other children. Teunis had previously expended "upwards of two hundred and sixty pounds" toward Elias's education (Elias was from the generation of ministers that had made the journey to Amsterdam for their training and ordination).[83] Thus, Teunis Van Bunschooten's large landholding and reliance on slave labor also secured for Elias his education and future position in the Church.

Elias Van Bunschooten took his inheritance and invested it in a huge farm, which was worked by slaves. In about 1800, Van Bunschooten purchased a 700-acre farm where he built a mill and a "commodious mansion."[84] Elias's vast wealth was often attributed to his savvy business practices and his frugality. He was described as "systematic as a business man" and a "model farmer" who had every item of his business recorded carefully in his account books.[85] A family biographer concluded that through "industry and frugality Mr. Van Bunschooten rapidly increased his worldly substance."[86] Yet the uncompensated labor of people enslaved to Van Bunschooten was the true source of the wealth that he would pass on to Queen's College.

The Van Bunschoten family Bible recorded a long history of slave ownership.

> Of those slaves whose names are recorded in the old Dutch family bible, we know twelve sprung from the loins of the Nanna family, five from Cetty, fourteen from the tribe of Cay, twelve from the Ginna, twelve from Susanna, four from Betty, and others from Tudd, Ezebel and Robe Hearman Judge. The dates of births recorded range from July 30, 1749, when Susanna Betty was born, onwards through a succession of primitive names such as Nanna, Ginna, Cay Betty, Betty Susanna, Pegga Susanna, Caty Suanna, Eve Ginna, Robe Susanna, Nanna Betty, Adam Susanna, Cay Robe and many others, until the even century is reached when more common names appear, such as Silver in 1801, Simon in 1802, Dorcas in 1804, Ruth 1806, Alfred 1807 and Henry 1810.[87]

The Van Bunschooten family stories mention that Elias Van Bunschooten owned slaves. For example, one story tells of Van Bunschooten's frugality. "Whether in paying or receiving money he insisted upon 'the utmost farthing,' usually remarking that otherwise the account could never be balanced. He carried this so far that, in settling with a customer at his mill one day and finding that he was owed three cents, [Van Bunschooten] . . . sent a negro in chase who followed the fugitive creditor several miles and at last succeeded in making payment in full."[88] Another story about Elias Van Bunschooten featured his gardener, an old enslaved man named Caesar. According to the story, Caesar once ripped up the vines of the cucumbers Van Bunschooten liked after Elias had entered the garden and ruthlessly tore up the melons Caesar was growing. [89] In short, the bulk of the wealth Elias Van Bunschooten accumulated and ultimately donated to Queen's College came from his inheritance, which his father used slave labor to amass, and from Elias's farm, where he also used slave labor.

While not as large as Elias Van Bunschooten's, a financial gift from Colonel Henry Rutgers also came at a vital time for the college from money rooted in slavery. The university's namesake, Henry Rutgers, was a slaveholder during the time he served as a trustee and made donations to the college.[90] The federal census recorded that Rutgers owned two slaves in 1790, five slaves in 1800, three slaves in 1810, and one slave in 1820.[91] Upon his death, Rutgers's will recorded an enslaved woman named Hannah, described as his "Negro wench slave," whom his will stipulated was to be "supported out of my Estate."[92] In 1826 Colonel Rutgers donated the interest on a $5,000 bond and a bell to the school that was named after him.[93] This donation in the early years of the school's reopening certainly aided the college's financial stability. When the college reopened in 1825, its president, the Reverend Phillip Milledoler, suggested that Queen's College be renamed in honor of trustee Colonel Henry Rutgers. A devoted member of the Dutch Church, Rutgers epitomized the Christian qualities held in high esteem by both the synod and the trustees.[94]

Henry Rutgers had long-standing connections to slavery. Rutgers's family had profited from slavery since the early decades of the eighteenth century; his father and grandfather owned slaves, and other family members were also slave-holders. Three enslaved men—Quash, Galloway, and Jacob—owned by Henry Rutgers's grandfather Harmanus were implicated in the 1741 slave conspiracy in New York. Hendrick Rutgers, Henry's father, owned slaves who labored at his brewery in New York.[95]

Like many of the other slaveholders linked to Queen's College, Henry Rutgers had a conflicted relationship to slavery. In 1786, Rutgers added his name to a petition for a bill before the New York legislature "for checking the progress of Slavery in our Country."[96] The petition, also signed by Alexander Hamilton and other prominent New Yorkers, requested a law to prevent "the practice of exporting [enslaved people] like cattle and other articles of commerce, to the West-Indies and the Southern States."[97] Rutgers joined the American Colonization Society, and from 1817 to 1830 was annually elected vice president of the society. The year he joined the organization he manumitted one man, Thomas Boston. While Rutgers did support colonization as well as gradual emancipation, he never supported abolition in the United States. Upon his death, Rutgers's will stipulated that his "superannuated [slave]" was to be "supported out of my Estate."[98]

In 1824 Theodore Frelinghuysen, a U.S. senator and future president of Rutgers College, directly acknowledged the state of New Jersey's connection to the institution of slavery. Frelinghuysen asked New Jerseyans to "survey your cultivated fields, your comfortable habitations, your children rising around you to bless you. Who, under Providence, caused those hills to rejoice and those valleys to smile? Who ploughed those fields and cleared these forests? Remember the toils and tears of black men, and pay your debt to Africa."[99] Frelinghuysen admitted that New Jersey had a debt to enslaved people for the state's economic prosperity. However, he prescribed colonization as the best way for whites to repay this debt, something that most free blacks in New Jersey opposed. Still, Theodore Frelinghuysen recognized the ways New Jerseyans continued to benefit from slavery and the financial rewards that passed to subsequent generations of whites. Frelinghuysen's words also apply to Rutgers University. Queen's College would never have existed without the institution of slavery. This is not unique to Rutgers but rather reflects the legacy of all nine institutions of higher education chartered in the American colonies. All colonial colleges have an institutional history that is deeply intertwined with slavery.

Another few years of financial struggle closed the college again from 1816 to 1825.[100] Only the monetary donations from wealthy slaveholding benefactors saved the institution. Part of the university's duty in dealing with this history is to acknowledge that the United States of America—which sought freedom from Great Britain—and Queen's College—which was established to provide colonists more freedom from the Dutch Reformed Church in Amsterdam—only prospered because the freedom of Africans and their descendants was stolen and their labor exploited. Acknowledging the university's deep ties to slavery requires stating and accepting that Rutgers has not been "revolutionary for 250 years" in the eyes of enslaved and disenfranchised people in Rutgers's history, or their descendants. Rutgers, The State University of New Jersey, has been in step with the nation's historical trajectory, and this means that the institution participated in and benefited from the economic exploitation of marginalized groups.

Acknowledgments

We would like to especially thank Thomas Frusciano, Erika Gorder, Albert C. King, and David J. Fowler for their assistance with our research.

3

His Name Was Will

Remembering Enslaved Individuals in Rutgers History

Jesse Bayker, Christopher Blakley, and Kendra Boyd

For over 250 years, the black individuals whose labor helped build Queen's College have remained nameless and invisible. No more. The aim of this essay is simple: to name them, to tell their stories. They were ever present in the slaveholding world of the Dutch Reformed ministers who established Queen's College (later Rutgers College). Here the reader will encounter familiar names: Frelinghuysen, Hardenbergh, Neilson, and many more whose histories and contributions to the college are well known and well remembered. We add new names here: Will, Phillis, Dinah, and others, too, who served—and resisted—the men whose names we know so well.

As Rutgers University continues to engage its troubled and entangled history with the institution of chattel slavery and the Atlantic slave trade in the eighteenth and nineteenth centuries, one man's life and his relationship to the college's past offers an especially unique perspective that has been hidden in plain view for some time. In 1730, a slaveholder in New York sold Ukasaw Gronniosaw, a West African man, to a "Mr. Freelandhouse, a very gracious, good Minister" at Raritan, in Somerset County, New Jersey.[1] Gronniosaw's new master was in fact the Reverend Theodorus Jacobus Frelinghuysen (1691–1747), the Dutch Reformed minister whose family played a crucial role in the origins of Queen's College.[2] Reverend Frelinghuysen settled his family in the Raritan Valley, New Jersey, in 1720 and was an active evangelical minister during the First Great Awakening. His sons carried on his legacy. By 1750, his son John Frelinghuysen (1727–1754) took over the church at Raritan where he soon set to work instructing new ministers, including Jacob Rutsen Hardenbergh, who would go on to become the first president of Queen's College. Beginning at a church meeting in New York City in 1755, John's brother Theodore Frelinghuysen (1724–1761), along with other Dutch Reformed clergy, began to petition the Church to install a college and seminary in British America.[3] In 1759, Theodore Frelinghuysen traveled to the Netherlands for two years to seek funds for the new school, but he largely failed to get support in Europe and died on his return voyage to America. When the college founders secured a royal charter in 1766 and finally opened the school in 1771, Frederick Frelinghuysen (1753–1804), the son of John and grandson of Theodorus Jacobus, became the college's first tutor. The family continued to play a role in the early history of what would become Rutgers College. Frederick Frelinghuysen's son, Theodore Frelinghuysen (1787–1862),

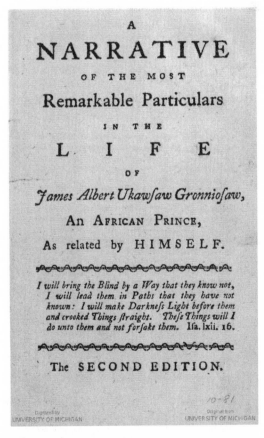

FIGURE 3.1 Title page of *A Narrative of the Most Remarkable Particulars in the Life of James Albert Ukawsaw Gronniosaw, an African Prince / written by himself* (Bath printed: Newport, Rhode Island: reprinted and sold by S. Southwick, in Queen-Street, 1774). Rutgers University Library.

became the seventh president of the college in 1850.[4] Today, the family name adorns a dormitory on the College Avenue campus in New Brunswick along the Raritan River.

While the Frelinghuysen family's connections to Queen's College and Rutgers College are well known, Gronniosaw does not appear in any major history of the university.[5] However, his remarkably itinerant life, which spanned the Atlantic world, his published *Narrative*, and his ongoing relationship to the Frelinghuysen family after being granted his freedom in 1747 make Gronniosaw a particularly interesting individual who deserves a place in the history of the college. His *Narrative*, for instance, underscores the diasporic and Atlantic dimensions of the enslaved African people who built Queen's College, or whose labor grounded the material wealth of the college's early officers, benefactors, and alumni. In one sense his life is extraordinary, given his ability to publicize his autobiography in print. However, his life might arguably be representative of the men, women, and children whom European traders bought, sold, and held as legal chattel throughout the Atlantic world. Examining Gronniosaw's life in detail, including his connection to the Frelinghuysen family, then, offers a starting point for understanding Queen's College, not only through the various circum-Atlantic networks that connected settlers in New Jersey and New York to their relatives and business contacts across the ocean in Europe but also as an institution founded with ties to West Africa and the Caribbean, and ultimately the Black Atlantic world.

Ukasaw Gronniosaw was most likely born around 1710 in Bournou (present-day northeastern Nigeria), the youngest of the six children of the eldest daughter of the king of Bournou.[6] As an adolescent, a merchant offered to take Gronniosaw south to the Gold Coast, where he promised Gronniosaw would see "houses with wings to them walk upon the water, and should also see the white folks."[7] The young man agreed and traveled a journey of over a thousand miles. On the coast he fell into trouble, as a local king believed him to be a spy and ordered Gronniosaw's execution. Moved by Gronniosaw's courage in the face of death, the king ultimately spared his life. Instead of beheading Gronniosaw, the king enslaved the young man, binding him to the merchant who had delivered him to the coast. Days after this ordeal, the merchant sold Gronniosaw to a Dutch slave ship bound for Barbados.[8]

Gronniosaw survived the Middle Passage.[9] After landing in Barbados, the captain of the Dutch slave ship sold Gronniosaw to a new master for $50. This new master was "Vanhorn, a young Gentleman" from New York City.[10] Vanhorn promptly took Gronniosaw north to New York and put him to work as a domestic servant performing duties like waiting at table, serving tea, and cleaning the silver. After some time, and troubles, a new master, the Reverend Frelinghuysen, persuaded Vanhorn to sell Gronniosaw again, this time for fifty pounds.

The New Jersey minister immediately set about instructing his new slave in the Christian faith, teaching him to kneel and pray to the Christian God—an alien figure to Gronniosaw who he learned was to be his "Father and BEST Friend."[11] However, Gronniosaw remained profoundly attached to his family in Bournou, whom he described in detail to Frelinghuysen. He pleaded to his master that above all he desired to return to his father in Bournou. "I wanted very much to see him," wrote Gronniosaw, "and likewise my dear mother, and sister, and I wish'd he would be so good as to send me home to them."[12] Frelinghuysen did not grant Gronniosaw his request and instead urged him to find solace in the Christian heavenly Father. Dislocation from his family in West Africa tortured Gronniosaw's mind and tested his spirit.

Gronniosaw found life at Raritan to be at times both hopeful and disturbing. Theodorus Frelinghuysen and his wife, Eva Terhune, who became fond of Gronniosaw, sent him to the schoolhouse of a Mr. Vanosdore. Gronniosaw came to enjoy school, where he learned to read. Yet at church on Sundays, Gronniosaw heard Frelinghuysen's sermons and felt "great agonies" because he feared his master's words were particularly aimed at him and "fancied, that [Frelinghuysen] observ'd [him] with unusual earnestness."[13] Gronniosaw felt Frelinghuysen hated him for not fully embracing or understanding his new faith and for not devoting himself to his new temporal and spiritual fathers. It appears Gronniosaw felt disturbed by the strangeness of his new religion and his new life as an enslaved man far from his homeland.[14]

After a maid of the Frelinghuysen household falsely accused Gronniosaw of buying tools with the minister's money, the young man fell further into despair and began to isolate himself from the family. Eva and Theodorus Frelinghuysen lent him books by John Bunyan and Richard Baxter, but he found both texts only worsened a sense of his profound wickedness and loneliness. After experiencing "agonies that cannot be described," Gronniosaw decided to take his own life by using a case-knife.[15] As he moved to strike himself, the knife folded, and he quit the attempt, fearing eternal damnation. "I could find no relief," he recalled of this time, "nor the least shadow of comfort; the extreme distress of my mind so affected my health that I continued very ill for three Days, and Nights."[16]

Gronniosaw continued to wish to die and slept outside of the house in the stable, miserably reflecting on his sinful nature. In the night, he recalled scripture from Frelinghuysen's sermons and sought out his schoolmaster, Mr. Vanosdore, for prayer and conversation. In the following days, Gronniosaw turned to the natural world for comfort, particularly "a large remarkably fine Oak-tree, in the midst of a wood" a quarter of a mile from his master's house.[17] Gronniosaw later recalled: "It was the highest pleasure I ever experienced to set under this Oak; for there I used to pour out all my complaints to the LORD: and when I had any particular grievance I used to go there, and talk to the tree, and tell my sorrows, as if it had been to a friend."[18] He sought out the tree, sometimes twice a day, and confessed to the tree what he believed to be his deeply wicked and sinful nature, and found "more comfort and consolation" there than anywhere else.[19]

Gronniosaw ultimately reconciled himself to the Christian faith and embraced his new religion as a wellspring of comfort. In his *Narrative*, he recalled one day being overwhelmed with love and peace upon reflecting on his new faith and cheerfully met with his schoolmaster to tell him of his true conversion. "I was now perfectly easy, and had hardly a wish to make beyond what I possess'd," he wrote, until "my temporal comforts were all blasted by the death of my dear and worthy Master Mr. Freelandhouse, who was taken from this world rather suddenly."[20] In 1747, Gronniosaw waited at Frelinghuysen's deathbed and "held his hand" when the minister departed.[21]

In his final moments, Theodorus Frelinghuysen granted Gronniosaw his freedom and ten pounds, but informed Gronniosaw that he intended for him to be kept in the household as a servant. Later, Gronniosaw learned that Frelinghuysen had also planned to take him to Holland and "had often mention'd [Gronniosaw] to some friends of his there that were desirous to see" the converted African man.[22] It appears the Reverend Frelinghuysen believed his successful evangelizing of his slave would impress his fellow ministers and possibly encourage future investments by the Dutch Reformed Church in British America.

Gronniosaw remained with the widow Eva Terhune at Raritan as a servant after his master's death in 1747. Frelinghuysen's death deeply affected Gronniosaw, whose depression returned as he began to believe he would ultimately become a "Cast-away" adrift in the world.[23] After Eva Terhune died in 1750, Gronniosaw continued with the family, serving the sons of his former master. Theodorus Frelinghuysen and Eva Terhune had five sons, all of whom became ministers, and all of whom died within a decade of their mother's passing. Gronniosaw later recalled moving from place to place as he served the Frelinghuysen brothers, but his exact travels and whereabouts in the 1750s are impossible to pin down from his *Narrative*.[24] Since John Frelinghuysen took over his late father's church in 1750, it seems likely that Gronniosaw would have stayed at Raritan until John Frelinghuysen's untimely death in 1754. John Frelinghuysen and his wife Dina Van Bergh set aside a room in their house for training Dutch Reformed ministers and frequently received guests in their home. As a domestic servant, Gronniosaw would be on hand to wait on the guests, and he may have poured tea for John Frelinghuysen's mentee Jacob Rutsen Hardenbergh on more than one occasion.

When John Frelinghuysen died suddenly in 1754, his widow, Dina Van Bergh, wrote to her brother-in-law Henricus Frelinghuysen about her grief. She also mentioned to Henricus: "As to the blacks, they are submissive to me, but I should like to be rid of them."[25] The black people working in Dina Van Bergh's household remained nameless in her letter, but Gronniosaw may have well been one of the people whom she was referring to when she said she wanted to "get rid" of her "blacks." Evidently, he was just one of several black people who served this family in the 1750s. Others may have provided services like cooking the family's meals or childcare for one-year-old son Frederick Frelinghuysen (future first tutor of Queen's College). Gronniosaw left Raritan, but it is possible that Dina Van Bergh continued to oversee black staff when she married Jacob Rutsen Hardenbergh two years later. After all, the up-and-coming minister and future Queen's College president came from a prominent slaveholding family.[26]

We cannot know with certainty where Gronniosaw was in 1755. He was likely serving Henricus or Theodore Frelinghuysen, the only two brothers still alive at this time. His recollection of service to the Frelinghuysen brothers, as well as his training as a butler, raise the possibility that he might have gone to New York City with Theodore Frelinghuysen in May of 1755. That month, a group of Dutch Reformed ministers convened a meeting where they first formulated a plan for a Dutch college in America.[27] At this key moment in the history of Queen's College, Gronniosaw may have been standing in the shadows ready to pour tea or fetch some wine for the prominent church leaders who assembled together. If he was there, Gronniosaw would have stood nearly unseen and certainly unheard at the back of the room as the white men discussed their hope of education for their sons.

After "it pleased God to take" another one of the Frelinghuysen brothers, Gronniosaw found himself "left quite destitute, without a friend in the world."[28] After leaving this family, Gronniosaw tried to find work in New York City but soon found himself indebted to a friend of one of the late Frelinghuysen brothers. This man threatened to sell Gronniosaw as a slave. Shocked at this turn of events, Gronniosaw knew that the threat of sale was illegal, but he also understood that he was extremely vulnerable in this situation. He recalled later: "Though I knew he had no right to do that, yet as I had no friend in the world to go to, it alarm'd me greatly."[29] To earn money to pay his debt, Gronniosaw ventured out of New York and traveled throughout the Caribbean for the next few years, first as a cook on a privateering ship and later as a soldier in the British Army.

Gronniosaw traveled to Saint-Domingue as a cook aboard the privateer, but he found the voyage difficult because his fellow sailors ridiculed and tormented him. Then Gronniosaw enlisted as a soldier in the 28th Regiment of Foot and fought in the Seven Years' War, traveling to Barbados, Martinique, and Cuba. After serving in the war, he became determined to travel to England and soon went to London, where he met with evangelical leaders including George Whitefield and Andrew Gifford. After staying in London for six weeks,

Gronniosaw was "recommended to the notice of some of [his] late Master Mr. Freelandhouse's acquaintance," who encouraged him to travel to the Netherlands. Gronniosaw left London for Holland, explaining his reasons thus: "My Master lived there before he bought me, and used to speak of me so respectfully among his friends there, that it raised in them a curiosity to see me; particularly the Gentlemen engaged in the Ministry, who expressed a desire to hear my experience and examine me."[30] In Amsterdam, Gronniosaw, who now took the name James Albert, sought out the friends, and possibly relatives, of Frelinghuysen. For seven weeks, Gronniosaw stood before a gathering of thirty-eight ministers every Thursday and recounted the details of his far-flung life. Gronniosaw supported himself for a year by working as a butler in a merchant's home. However, he never found support from the Frelinghuysen family in Holland and ultimately returned to England where he married and made contacts with several Quaker and Methodist clerics. In 1772 he published *A Narrative of the Most Remarkable Particulars in the Life of James Albert Ukawsaw Gronniosaw, an African Prince, As related by himself*, which he dedicated to Selina Hastings, countess of Huntingdon. In 1775, James Albert Ukasaw Gronniosaw died in Chester, England. In his obituary, he was remembered as one who lived a life of "many trials and embarrassments."[31]

From his enslavement as an adolescent to his freedom and itinerant life that spanned the Atlantic world, Gronniosaw remained profoundly influenced by his time spent in the Frelinghuysen household at Raritan. His period of enslavement and freedom among the Frelinghuysen family offers a window into the everyday life of enslaved Africans in New Jersey. Moreover, his remarkably frank and deeply personal descriptions of his mental state while enslaved are of great significance and value for understanding the inner lives of enslaved Africans in British America. Gronniosaw's commitment to finding the Frelinghuysen family in the Netherlands after he had been freed is particularly striking. In his last years, he worked to keep connected to his former master through his encounters with the Dutch Reformed ministers he met in Holland. It is not difficult to imagine him on the streets of Amsterdam, asking the clergy he encountered how he could find the Frelinghuysen family. It is also not difficult to imagine the disappointment and frustration he must have felt upon failing to find them. While the Frelinghuysen family undoubtedly deserves, and occupies, a hallowed place in the history of Queen's College, Gronniosaw, too, deserves a place in the recounting of the college's beginnings.

Gronniosaw is only one of many who connect Rutgers to West Africa and the Black Atlantic. Runaway notices in local and regional newspapers give us clues about the lives of the many enslaved individuals who served—and ran from—the founders, benefactors, and students of Queen's College. One of these enslaved people was Claus. This black man lived in New Brunswick around the same time when Ukasaw Gronniosaw came to serve the revivalist minister on the Raritan. We do not know whether Claus found comfort in talking to an oak tree or questioned the usefulness of his life as Gronniosaw had, but we do know that on August 23, 1741, he ran away from his master, Philip French. Claus was approximately forty-five years old at the time—about the same age as his master—and may have lived in New Brunswick for decades before running away. Whether he was born in Africa or in the Americas is unclear. He spoke at least two languages—Dutch and English. His master's advertisement described Claus as having a "yellowish Complexion" and being of "middle Stature." Claus was probably left-handed; he was accustomed to shoot a bow with his left hand. He enjoyed playing music, and he took his fiddle with him when he ran away, as well as some extra clothing. His attempt to get out of town may have involved crossing the river—this would have been a familiar route for Claus considering that his master owned ferry rights on the Raritan. Philip French offered a reward of three pounds for the runaway's capture, but we do not know whether he ever saw Claus again.[32]

In addition to owning ferry rights, Philip French owned large tracts of land in New Brunswick, and he continued to exploit slave labor for decades after 1741.[33] In 1766, French became one of the founding trustees of Queen's College.[34] Once the trustees chose New Brunswick as the location for the school in 1771, he sold to the college a tavern at the corner of French (Albany) and King (Neilson) streets. It was here, inside the former tavern, that the first college students received their instruction.[35]

Three years after Queen's College received its first charter, a young man named Jack ran away from his master, Ernestus Van Harlingen. Jack was twenty-one years old when he escaped from the farm at Millstone. He was described as "well built" and "yellowish" in color, standing five feet nine inches tall. Jack knew that running away from Millstone would not be easy. Like any free or enslaved person of color, anywhere he went, he faced the danger of being stopped and scrutinized by local whites who could demand to see his pass—paperwork showing that Jack was authorized to travel through the area. Over weeks or months leading up to his escape, Jack made plans to run away with his nineteen-year-old friend Ben, whose master was Leffert Waldron of Three Mile Run near New Brunswick. On Saturday, June 10, 1769, Jack and Ben met up and left the area together. Both of these young men were proficient speakers of Dutch and English, and may have learned how to read and write. Their masters believed that Jack and Ben forged or obtained a false pass that would help them travel away from the area.[36]

The Van Harlingen family maintained close ties to Queen's College from its inception, beginning with the Reverend Johannes Martinus Van Harlingen, who was one of the chief founders.[37] The founder's brother, Ernestus Van

Harlingen, was Jack's master. Ernestus Van Harlingen provided valuable support for Queen's College during the Revolutionary War. In 1780, after the students and faculty fled New Brunswick, Ernestus Van Harlingen opened his home in Millstone to the young scholars so that instruction could continue.[38] If Jack was ever captured and brought back to the farm at Millstone, he would be among the enslaved laborers who interacted with the students and faculty when the Van Harlingen homestead temporarily became the seat of Queen's College. Ernestus Van Harlingen was elected to the college's board of trustees in 1782.[39] He continued to hold black people in bondage at least until the early nineteenth century.[40] Unlike Jack and Ben, clever young men from the Van Harlingen family had the privilege of traveling between Millstone and New Brunswick without a pass. They also had the privilege of obtaining a college education, and in 1783, 1792, and 1809 three of them became proud graduates of Queen's College.[41]

A few months after Jack and Ben ran away from their masters, two men named Abraham and December came to New York City as cargo and were purchased by Abraham (Abram) Lott. Abraham Lott was a founding trustee of Queen's College.[42] He was a prosperous New York merchant and a slaveholder. On October 28, 1769, Lott made three transactions related to the purchase and sale of enslaved people in New York City. Lott sold two black men to Peter Remsen for ninety pounds.[43] He also purchased Abraham and December from Lucas Von Beverhoudt. Abraham and December had both been "imported" from the island of St. Croix.[44] It is probable that Von Beverhoudt was a slave trader and had brought the two men on a voyage from his home on the island of St. Thomas, not far from St. Croix.[45]

In the next decade, the Revolutionary War swept up the colonies and Abraham Lott's slaves. Abraham Lott had been the treasurer of New York Colony before the war and maintained loyalty to the British Crown during much of the conflict.[46] In the summer of 1781, Adam Hyler—a patriot privateer stationed in New Brunswick—made several raids on loyalists in New York Harbor. In one of these raids, Hyler robbed and captured Abraham Lott. Known to be a wealthy man, Lott was taken prisoner to New Brunswick along with two of his slaves. These two men may have been Abraham and December, or they could have been other enslaved individuals Lott purchased after 1769. While sailing up the Raritan River, Lott's captors divided their booty and realized that the bags of money they had taken from Lott contained halfpennies rather than guineas. Dissatisfied with their plunder and determined to make the best of the exploit, the patriots demanded more money. Abraham Lott then used his two slaves as ransom in order to secure his own release and be permitted to return home to New York.[47] We do not know what became of the two men after they fell into the possession of the patriots. Most likely they were sold in a state-sponsored auction. New Jersey patriots routinely sold off the enemy's confiscated property, including slaves, to finance the war.[48] One thing is clear: the war was not revolutionary for these black people. Whether enslaved to loyalists or patriots, they were still not free and the war would not bring about their liberty. In 1781, the same year that Abraham Lott used the lives of two black men to secure his freedom, Queen's College reopened in New Brunswick after intermittent wartime closures. When young white men came to study at the college, they may have brought enslaved servants with them to campus. It is difficult to pin down with certainty the names and identities of the enslaved individuals who served these young men in New Brunswick. One person who may have been on campus in the late 1780s was a boy named Sam. Sam was a black teenager who belonged to the Stevenson family of Hunterdon County.[49] Sam was a few years younger than Queen's College student James Stevenson. It was common for prosperous slaveholders to assign a black boy to serve their sons—a boy who would grow up and continue to serve his young master through college and beyond. Thus, it is possible that Sam came to New Brunswick when Stevenson enrolled in Queen's College. Stevenson graduated in 1789 and stayed on as a tutor the following year.[50] In 1790, Stevenson returned to Amwell, in Hunterdon County.

Two years later, on April 24, 1792, Sam ran away from Stevenson's household in Amwell. Sam was eighteen years old at this point. Whether Sam was ever captured, we do not know. If any white person in the area saw Sam, they might have recognized him from the notice published in the *Brunswick Gazette* where James Stevenson described the coarse gray clothes that Sam had on when he left. The outfit that Sam wore was rather unremarkable. Thus, any young black man wearing old shoes and a striped gray shirt might have been stopped on the road in the area and asked to take off his trousers so that suspicious whites could check whether the man had a "remarkable scar on one of his legs."[51] This scar was the main identifying feature that might give Sam away and earn his captor $8.

The Stevenson family continued their connection with the school in the early nineteenth century. When the college reopened, Stevenson's son James Stevenson Jr. enrolled as a student and also took charge of the attached grammar school from 1809 until 1811.[52] Shortly before his son graduated from Queen's College, James Stevenson lost his older brother, John Stevenson, and became the executor of the brother's estate. James Stevenson followed the instructions laid out in his brother's will: to sell all of the enslaved men and women belonging to John Stevenson's estate, excepting one girl named Isabel.[53] Among the people James Stevenson sold for his brother's estate would have been a woman named Rode and her two-year-old son, Daniel.[54] By 1813, James Stevenson assumed public office in Hunterdon County, serving for over a decade as the director of the Board of Freeholders, all the while holding in bondage several black people, including Mary, Pattie, and Jude and their young children.[55]

Another young black man whose scars made him vulnerable to detection was Dick. He was about seventeen or eighteen years old when he endeavored to escape from attorney Alpheus Freeman in the summer of 1807. His master's advertisement in a New Brunswick newspaper described Dick as a "mulatto boy." Dick was a short teenager with several conspicuous burns and scars on his body. Some of these marks could have resulted from violence that Dick might have experienced at the hands of his masters. Suspicious whites would have readily seen deep scars on Dick's feet and toes because the young man ran away barefoot and poorly clothed and did not take anything with him from his master's house (other escapees frequently took extra clothing on the road). Unlike Jack and Ben, who carefully planned their escape, Dick was probably moved to run suddenly by a traumatic event or some immediate threat of violence.[56] His master, Alpheus Freeman, was one of the earliest graduates of Queen's College. Freeman received his degree in 1788 and established a law practice in New Brunswick.[57] He owned several properties, including a large building on the corner of George Street and Prince (Bayard) Street, and it might have been from this location that Dick ran in 1807. In addition to Dick, a young black woman toiled in Freeman's household. She was two years younger than Dick, and when Alpheus Freeman died in 1815, the administrators of Freeman's estate touted that they had a "stout, active and healthy" twenty-four-year-old black woman for sale.[58]

Many enslaved people experienced not only the hardships of uncompensated labor but also the ultimate reminder of their status as chattel property— the slave sale—at the hands of Queen's College affiliates. Surviving records of slave sales tell us who profited from the institution of slavery but give us only fragmentary evidence of enslaved people's lives and identities. For example, county tax records report only numbers of slaves and not their identities, and auction advertisements in local newspapers never list the names of enslaved individuals whose bodies and labor were for sale. After all, prospective buyers did not care about the identities of the enslaved. Thus, sellers listed only the age, gender, and skill set of the enslaved worker, occasionally with a note about their purported obedience. Sales were traumatic for enslaved men, women, and children who were torn away from their families and communities.[59]

Among those who bought and sold enslaved laborers was Jacob Rutsen Hardenbergh Jr. (1767–1841). He was the son of the first president of Queen's College, Jacob Rutsen Hardenbergh Sr. (1736–1790), and Dina Van Bergh. The junior Hardenbergh attended the college and graduated in 1788 during his father's tenure as president.[60] After his father's death, young Hardenbergh was elected trustee. In 1793, he stepped up to the office of secretary of the board of trustees.[61] That same year, he acquired an enslaved worker for his household. In 1795, the year Queen's College closed its doors due to financial difficulties, Hardenbergh acquired a second slave.[62] By 1800, Hardenbergh decided to sell a thirty-five-year-old black woman who had been cooking meals for his family for several years. Jacob R. Hardenbergh's advertisement noted that the woman was "sober and honest, sold for no other reason than being dissatisfied with the place of her master's residence."[63] Evidently, this woman disliked living at Somerville where her master took her, and she made her feelings known. Like many others who had been arbitrarily separated from their families by slaveholders, she probably missed her loved ones and pressed her master to allow her the opportunity to get closer to them.

Another man whose fate hung in the hands of a prominent Queen's College trustee was Jef. In 1794, Colonel John Neilson (1745–1833) contemplated purchasing Jef from Mr. Mattison of Princeton. At this point, Neilson had been a trustee of the college for a dozen years, and he would continue in that role until his death in 1833.[64] Whether Jef ever became Neilson's property is unclear, but the letters that Neilson exchanged about the potential sale give a glimpse into Jef's life and provide insight into how Neilson selected slaves for particular qualities. After Neilson learned that Mr. Mattison wanted to sell Jef for the price of ninety pounds, Neilson hoped to evaluate the price by learning of the man's "general Character." Neilson wrote to his friend Robert Finley asking him to visit the Mattison household and ascertain the black man's age, if he was "free from the monstrous vice of frequent intoxication," if he had been "faithful to [his] masters service," if he possessed a "constitutional turn for Industry," if he evinced a "degree of ingenuity," and if he demonstrated a "desire of improving his mind." Neilson asked more specifically if the man had been acquainted with caring for horses or gardening, two skills he seems to have particularly prized.[65]

Two days later, Robert Finley replied from Princeton with his answers. Finley wrote that Jef was twenty-one years old, was known to be "habitually sober" and faithful, and that though he showed little ingenuity he seemed eager to improve himself if given the opportunity. Finley reported that Jef had some experience with horses and possessed considerable expertise at raising a kitchen garden. Jef's only flaw, Finley wrote, was that he was "too much given to stay from home at night, tho, he supposed it arises from his loneliness at home."[66]

Robert Finley's response to John Neilson raises the issue of what "home" meant to enslaved people like Jef. Finley considered Jef's frequent absence from his master's household to be a flaw. But for many enslaved people, their master's house did not feel like home. When Jef left his master's house, most likely he was not "stay[ing] from home at night" as Finley suggested. Instead, Jef was probably going to a place that felt more like home. In Princeton, as in New Brunswick, the institution of slavery kept families apart. Jef's loneliness at his master's house likely resulted from separation from his loved ones. Besides being separated from parents by way of a sale, young black men also frequently married black women who served another master and lived in another household. Thus, Jef may have walked for hours at night to see his wife or visit his parents, sacrificing his sleep for the chance to briefly feel a warm embrace.

Another Queen's College officer who benefited from slave sales was Abraham Blauvelt. Blauvelt was an early alumnus of Queen's College, following in the footsteps of his two brothers to graduate in 1789.[67] He was elected to the board of trustees in 1800 and immediately succeeded Jacob Rutsen Hardenbergh Jr. as the secretary of the board.[68] He worked with Ira Condict to reopen the college in 1807 and became the chairman of the Building Committee. In this key role, he oversaw the construction of the Queen's Building beginning in 1808 (this building is now known as "Old Queen's" and houses the offices of the president and the school's top administrators).[69] Abraham Blauvelt was a slaveholder, as evidenced by a certificate he sent to the Middlesex County clerk in 1813 to report that an enslaved woman in his household gave birth to a baby boy named Peter.[70] The boy would become a "slave for a term" under New Jersey's gradual abolition law and would be obliged to serve Blauvelt's family until 1838 unless he was sold to another master earlier.[71]

Besides his deep involvement in the college's affairs, Abraham Blauvelt spent much of his time publishing a local newspaper. He established the *Guardian; or, New Brunswick Advertiser* in 1792, three years after graduating from Queen's College.[72] For decades, he regularly published runaway slave notices and advertisements for slave sales in his newspaper. Blauvelt did more than just take money from advertisers who wanted to sell their enslaved chattel. He also acted as a middleman to arrange sales. Some sellers did not want to publish their own name and information in the newspaper, preferring to keep the transaction more private. In such cases, Blauvelt published advertisements like this item: "TO BE SOLD. A HEALTHY, likely Negro girl, about 14 years old. Enquire of the printer. Oct. 6, 1794."[73] Blauvelt's name does not appear in any of the advertisements for slave sales, but his readers knew very well what "enquire of the printer" meant.

A prospective slave buyer could stop by Blauvelt's home or meet him at Queen's College to ask for more information and set up a sale. For example, in the summer of 1809, while Blauvelt kept busy overseeing the building of Old Queen's, prospective buyers might meet him near the construction site and "enquire of the printer" about two individuals advertised in his newspaper. One was a twenty-five-year-old black woman who was an indentured servant with four years remaining on her indenture.[74] The second person whose sale Blauvelt hoped to arrange that summer was a nine-year-old boy who was a slave for life and who reportedly was "smart, active, and every way promising for a child of his years." Blauvelt assured the readers that they could buy the boy cheaply "on moderate and accommodating terms."[75] In all likelihood, Blauvelt did not provide his services for free and may have collected a fee (or a mutual favor) for the slave sales that he facilitated.[76]

At the construction site, Abraham Blauvelt may have also interacted with a black man named Will. Will was enslaved to Dr. Jacob Dunham, a physician who practiced medicine in New Brunswick for three decades.[77] It is unclear how Will came to Jacob Dunham's household; however, it is possible that Jacob Dunham inherited Will from his father's estate or purchased Will with the wealth he inherited. Jacob Dunham's father, Azariah Dunham, was an early trustee of Queen's College, a Revolutionary War colonel, the first mayor of New Brunswick after the war, an extensive landholder, and a slave owner.[78] Like countless other enslaved persons, Will's date and place of birth and his family history are absent from the archive. The fragmentary record of his life highlights his labor but obscures everything else about him.

In the fall of 1808, Will worked to lay the foundation for Old Queen's. The first evidence of Will's labor comes from an entry in an account book that contains the expenditures for erecting the building. On September 28, 1808, Abraham Blauvelt recorded a payment of $5.60 due Jacob Dunham "for labor of his negro."[79] Blauvelt noted that this payment was for work on the foundation. Almost a year after this initial payment for enslaved labor, Blauvelt paid out an additional $39.88 to Jacob Dunham on November 30, 1809. This time the charge was "for his negro's services" doing masonry work.[80] The enslaved man performing this labor remained nameless in Blauvelt's account book.

This man's identity would almost certainly be lost to history but for the fact that his white master kept a careful record of people who owed him money. Because he came from a prominent family in New Brunswick, Jacob Dunham's accounting ledger was preserved in the Rutgers Special Collections and University Archives. For many years, the physician meticulously recorded the money that white locals—and some free people of color—owed him for medical treatments that he provided. Alongside medical services, Dunham also recorded another income stream—the hiring out of his enslaved laborer. It is from this account book that we learn the identity of this laborer: his name was Will. Here we also learn that Jacob Dunham typically received about a dollar per day for Will's labor. Thus, we might estimate that Will put in about a month and a half's worth of labor on the construction site of the college building.[81]

Jacob Dunham's ledger allows us also to reconstruct some of Will's other movements and experiences as an enslaved laborer who was frequently hired out by his master. Will performed various tasks for individuals in and around New Brunswick. This work included things like "tending mason," "casting work bench," "carting loads," "ringing bell" at auctions and sales, and "breaking sugar." The ledger begins in 1816, but Dunham carried over balances from a previous book, confirming that Will labored outside of Dunham's household before 1816. For instance, on October 1, 1816, Dunham recorded that Thomas

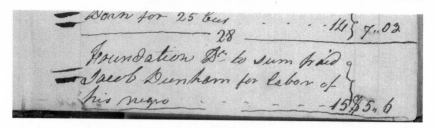

FIGURE 3.2 "Foundation [*sic*] to sum paid Jacob Dunham for labor of his negro ... " Entry recorded by Abraham Blauvelt in the Queen's College Building account book, September 28, 1808. Special Collections and University Archives, Rutgers University Libraries.

Hill owed $7.23 for "Balance due for my negro mans work as per bill rendered by book."[82] Dunham did not specify the type of work Will performed for Thomas Hill, though he likely recorded this information in the previous ledger. Thomas Hill was actually a slave owner himself and held several women in bondage.[83] Will may have been hired to perform arduous tasks that required a male slave or the specialized trade in which he was trained.

It appears that Will possessed both specialized and ordinary skills. Jacob Dunham charged Benjamin Frazle, "the coachmaker," $0.31 for "casting your work bench."[84] However, there were also sordid jobs to do as well. Additional charges to Frazle included $2.00 for "carting 8 loads for you (3 manure and 5 goods)" on March 24, 1817, and April 5, 1817.[85] Since it is highly unlikely a prominent doctor possessed metalworking skills or would personally transport manure, we can reasonable assume that Will performed this labor. From August 4 to 13, 1817, Will worked for William Jones, earning $8.00 for Jacob Dunham. This included construction work: "1 days work of Will tending mason yesterday and all this day with Mr. Chapman" on August 5th.[86] This labor was similar to the work that Will had performed at the Queen's College construction site in 1809. Mr. Chapman—the mason who hired Will for the day in 1817—was most likely James Chapman. He was a local builder who had provided Queen's College trustees with estimates for masonry work before the construction of Old Queen's began.[87]

Will did a variety of endless work for which Jacob Dunham received payment. Dunham, for example, charged Robert M. Boggs $2.00 for "ringing bell by my negro Man for sale of grass" in July 1818 and "ringing bell by my blk man for sale of boards & planks at Rob Morris's farm" in October 1818.[88] Robert Boggs was a prominent lawyer in New Brunswick and a Queen's College trustee for over thirty years from 1800 to 1831.[89] Boggs was a slaveholder who owned a number of slaves, including a man named Benjamin who would have been about twenty-four years old in 1818.[90] Thus, it is unclear why Boggs decided to hire Will as a bellman for the day. Nonetheless, Will frequently performed work as a bellman at sales and auctions around New Brunswick to earn money for Jacob Dunham. In 1821, G. Nevins paid $2.00 for "bellman's fee." William Schenck owed $2.00 "Bellman's fee for twice ringing for sale of your property in Albany Street."[91]

Will sometimes worked for an individual once or twice. Other times, he labored for extended periods at another master's business or construction site. Over the course of a month (March 27 to April 29, 1820) Will went to work for John C. Dunham doing various tasks. On March 27 Jacob Dunham charged John C. Dunham $4.00 for "3/4 days work of Will, my blk man, tending mason" and four loads of sand. The total charge for Will's labor over the month was $20.13.[92] Similarly, Will worked frequently for Richard Duyckinck from August through December 1821, earning a total of twenty-four pounds, eleven shillings, and six-pence for Jacob Dunham. The next year Will continued working for Duyckinck and earned a total of thirty-five pounds, nine shillings, and sixpence for his owner in 1822. This included a half day that Will spent "breaking sugar" for Duyckinck in October 1822.[93] Unfortunately, Will did not own the rights to his own labor and lacked the legal power to keep the money he earned.

Will disappears from the record after August 20, 1823. On this date, Will spent half a day working for Robert M. Boggs. In 1830, the U.S. Census reported eleven individuals living in Jacob Dunham's household.[94] Two in the household were black: a free black female between the ages of ten and twenty-three and an enslaved male between fifty-five and ninety-nine years old. The woman (or girl) was most likely a domestic servant. It is impossible to know whether the aging enslaved man enumerated in the census was Will, but it seems unlikely because we know Will performed physically strenuous labor in the 1820s. If the man listed in the 1830 census was a different slave, there are several possibilities for what could have happened to Will after 1823. A review of the manumission records for Middlesex County suggests that Will did not attain freedom. He may have died, been sold to another owner, or run away.

In all likelihood, Will was not the only enslaved laborer who toiled on the Queen's College construction site starting in 1808. Ironically, Abraham Blauvelt's building account book records Jacob Dunham's "negro's services" precisely because Dunham was a physician and not actually a building contractor. When white masons and carpenters brought enslaved laborers with them onto the construction site, there was no need for Blauvelt to note the presence of black workers in his ledger. For example, when John P. Sandford received over $3,000 "for himself and sundry masons," the chairman of the Building Committee did not record the composition of Sandford's large team.[95] A number of building contractors were slaveholders, including James Dehart, Michael

Garrish, John Smalley, and Jacob Van Deventer.[96] And those who did not own able-bodied black men had every opportunity to hire another master's slave for construction work, as Will's life and labors amply illustrate. One man who may have brought enslaved laborers with him to the construction site was John Voorhees, who received payments "for himself and his hands." His numerous relations appear as slaveholders in county records and runaway slave ads in the 1810s.[97]

Three years after he finished work on the building, John Voorhees sold a thirty-one-year-old black woman named Luck to James Schureman, a prominent local politician who was a fixture at the college. Schureman graduated from Queen's College in 1775 and remained deeply involved in his alma mater, serving on the board of trustees for over forty years.[98] In February 1813, Schureman purchased Luck for a term of six years and paid her former master $50.[99] At the time of this transaction in 1813, Schureman was wrapping up his eighteen-year stint as treasurer of the college and getting ready to hand over the school's accounts to his successor, Staats Van Deursen.[100]

Luck and other enslaved individuals who toiled at James Schureman's house were not the only people who were treated as chattel by him. He acted as an executor to the estates of multiple relatives and associates. Schureman was among several Queen's College trustees who sold enslaved people as executors for deceased friends and relatives. Selling an estate often meant putting a group of enslaved people on the auction block (along with livestock and furniture) and selling them off one by one to the highest bidder—the worst possible scenario for an enslaved family and the surest route to traumatic family separation. In March of 1821, a group of black men and women and several children came face to face with James Schureman as he prepared to liquidate the estate of his late friend James Bennet.[101] Schureman managed to sell most of these black children and adults, but did not find a buyer for one of the men in the group. It seems that this enslaved man lived in the Schureman household for nearly a year until Schureman, once again, posted an advertisement promising to sell the unnamed man "at a reduced price."[102]

Similarly, longtime Middlesex County clerk William P. Deare auctioned off three black men, several women, a boy, and two girls as an executor of his friend's estate in 1818.[103] William P. Deare was a graduate of the Queen's College class of 1794, a trustee for over twenty years, and a slaveholder.[104] At the time of this auction, Deare served as the secretary of the board of trustees of the college, an office he held from 1807 to 1821.[105] His friend Captain George Farmer owned a farm of 300 acres on the Raritan River across from New Brunswick where he used slave labor (he also owned other buildings and land lots in New Brunswick and other nearby towns). However, George Farmer was deeply in debt when he died, necessitating the sale of every single thing and every single person that he had owned.[106] Deare arranged an auction at his late friend's farm, where buyers could inspect horses, cattle, hogs, and black people before they bid. Standing in front of the house and farm where they had toiled for some years, these black children and adults must have trembled because 1818 was a terrible year to be on the auction block in New Brunswick. No doubt these individuals had heard how others in their community had recently been torn from their families and shipped down South. Deare was also well aware of the flow of enslaved people from Middlesex County to Louisiana and Mississippi. As the county clerk, his job required him to make a record every time an enslaved person obtained manumission from slavery or was taken away from the state of New Jersey. Records of manumissions and removals for Middlesex County—preserved in a bound volume at Rutgers Special Collections and University Archives—provide an important window for tracing the history of slaveholding around Queen's College.

Why was the year 1818 so terrible for black people in and around New Brunswick? National and local events converged to create an exceedingly dire situation: U.S. law had prohibited the transatlantic slave trade in 1808, the invention of the cotton gin prompted a boom in cotton production in the South, and the recently acquired Louisiana Territory beckoned would-be planters with opportunities to get rich through exploiting slave labor. As a result, the interstate slave trade proliferated in this period. Although New Jersey adopted a gradual abolition law in 1804, the law did not provide enough protection against the interstate movement of slaves. According to the law, enslaved individuals were supposed to be questioned in court and had to give their consent to move out of the state, and parents had to give such consent for enslaved children under the age of twenty-one. Of course, the issue of "consent" was complicated by the reality of power dynamics between slave and slaveholder: masters had many tools for eliciting obedience and manufacturing such consent, not the least of which was violence.[107]

By 1818, Jacob Van Wickle, a local judge in Middlesex County, took advantage of his judicial powers to develop a sinister slave-trading ring shipping black people out of Perth Amboy to Louisiana and Mississippi. The business was incredibly profitable because the market price of enslaved laborers in Louisiana was far higher than in New Jersey.[108] In 1818, Van Wickle's colleague William P. Deare recorded the removal of seventy-eight black women, children, and men from the county, almost all of them headed for Louisiana (and a few to Mississippi) as part of Van Wickle's slave-trading operation.[109] Several historians have noted that concern and outrage over Van Wickle's operation led to the tightening of New Jersey's abolition law in order to stymie the slave trade.[110] But the full impact of these sales on the black community in New Brunswick and the surrounding areas is not yet fully understood. Van Wickle, however, was not the first person to send enslaved people from Middlesex County to Louisiana.

In the fall of 1817, two young black women appeared before the Court of Common Pleas in Middlesex County with their masters. Their names were Phillis and Dinah.[111] Phillis was enslaved to Staats Van Deursen and Dinah to his younger brother Dr. William Van Deursen. The Van Deursen brothers both graduated from Queen's College and went on to serve as trustees. They were part of a prominent New Brunswick family that maintained close ties to the college for at least three generations beginning with their father, William Van Deursen the elder. The older brother, Staats Van Deursen, sent his son to Queen's in the early 1810s and was deeply involved in the college's affairs.[112] At the time of his appearance in court with Phillis in 1817, he was serving as the treasurer of the college, an office he held for ten years.[113] The brothers Van Deursen decided to sell Phillis and Dinah to a man named Jacob Klady, a New Brunswick landholder who divested his holdings in New Jersey seeking an opportunity to go to Ouachita, Louisiana, and establish a cotton plantation.[114] Jacob Klady knew that he could buy a number of slaves at a bargain price in New Jersey, and the Van Deursens were eager to sell the two women.[115]

Phillis and Dinah had to appear before the court and "consent" to move out of the state of New Jersey with their new master, Jacob Klady. The women likely understood that they were headed for a hard life of backbreaking labor on the cotton plantation. Notably, Dinah attempted to negotiate with Jacob Klady and only consented to go with him after he promised to manumit her after fifteen years of faithful service. This nonbinding agreement held no legal weight, but the judges recorded it nonetheless. Phillis and Dinah were both approximately twenty-two years old. According to New Jersey law, these women were slaves for life, but their children would be considered "slaves for a term" and would gain freedom after twenty-one (females) or twenty-five (males) years of service. The move to Louisiana would have devastating consequences for these young women: Louisiana's laws would ensure that their children (and their grandchildren and so on in perpetuity) would become slaves for life, depriving the next generation of the freedom promised by New Jersey's gradual abolition law for those born after 1804.

In this way, Staats Van Deursen and William Van Deursen inaugurated the movement of enslaved people from Middlesex County to Louisiana, and Phillis and Dinah became the first victims. Phillis and Dinah's plight illustrates the danger facing young black women in New Brunswick at this moment. The traffic in human beings affected men and women as well as boys and girls in every age group. Yet young black women and their children were particularly vulnerable. Targeted for their reproductive capacity, some of these young women departed with infants in their hands, like twenty-two-year-old Rachel, who left with her six-week-old daughter, Rozenah.[116] Or Nancy, age twenty-two, who gave birth to a baby boy and two days later carried him to court to "consent" to move with

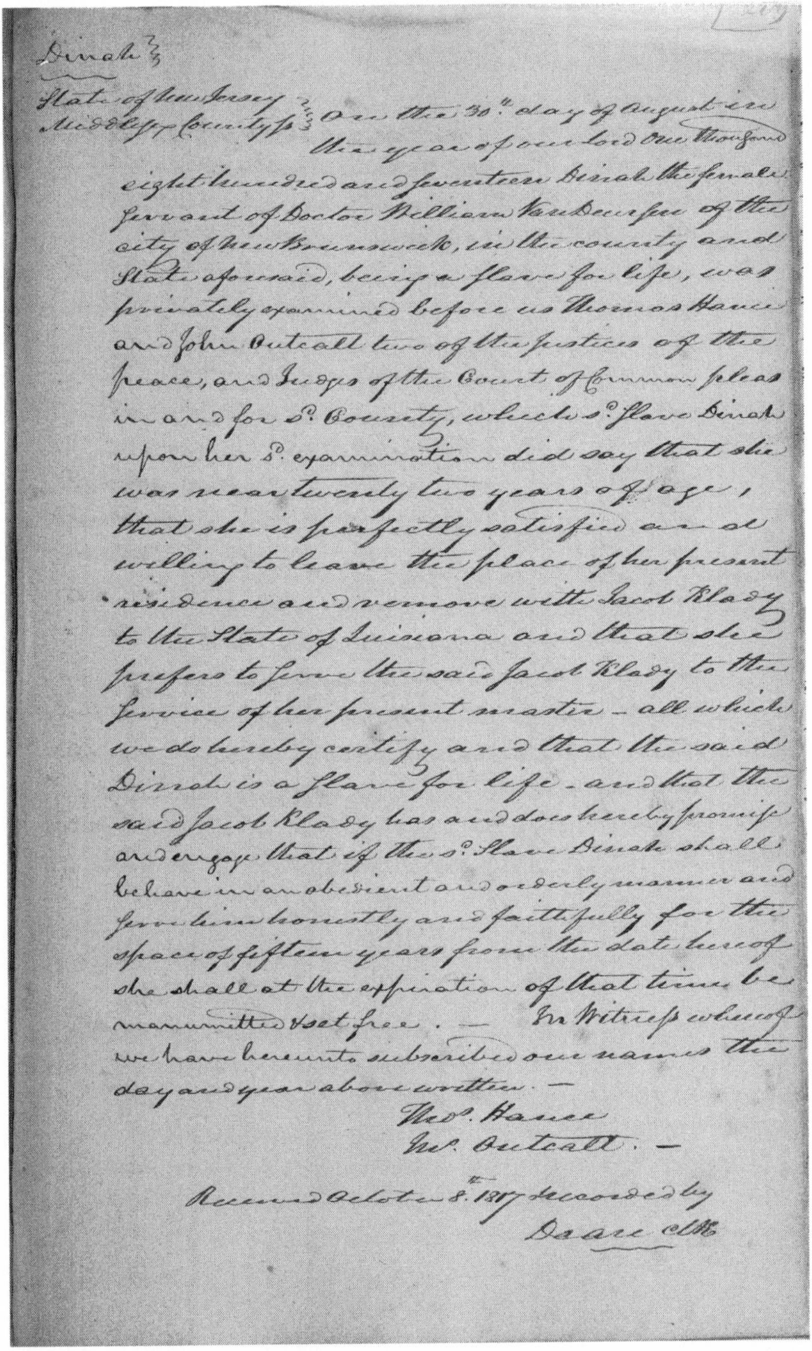

Dinah

State of New Jersey
Middlesex County } On the 30th day of August in
the year of our Lord one thousand
eight hundred and seventeen Dinah the female
servant of Doctor William Van Deursen of the
city of New Brunswick, in the county and
State aforesaid, being a slave for life, was
privately examined before us Thomas Hance
and John Outcalt two of the justices of the
peace, and Judges of the Court of Common pleas
in and for said County, which said slave Dinah
upon her said examination did say that she
was near twenty two years of age,
that she is perfectly satisfied and is
willing to leave the place of her present
residence and remove with Jacob Klady
to the State of Louisiana and that she
prefers to serve the said Jacob Klady to the
service of her present master — all which
we do hereby certify and that the said
Dinah is a slave for life — and that the
said Jacob Klady has and does hereby promise
and engage that if the said slave Dinah shall
behave in an obedient and orderly manner and
serve him honestly and faithfully for the
space of fifteen years from the date hereof
she shall at the expiration of that time be
manumitted & set free. — In Witness whereof
we have hereunto subscribed our names the
day and year above written. —

Thos. Hance
Jno. Outcalt. —

Received October 8. 1817 Recorded by
Da___ Clk

FIGURE 3.3 "Dinah" Manumission of Slaves, 1800–1825, Middlesex County (NJ) Records, 1688–1929, Vol. XI: 209, Rutgers Special Collections and University Archives.

him to Louisiana.[117] Staats Van Deursen also helped Jacob Klady sell his land in New Brunswick so he could buy land in Louisiana. In addition to serving as the treasurer of Queen's College, Van Deursen was also a public servant in New Brunswick and sat on a committee for establishing a poorhouse farm. This was an institution where impoverished individuals would be confined and put to work on the farm (or sometimes rented out from the farm). Towns throughout New Jersey were at work establishing such institutions in this early period of gradual abolition as white residents began raising concerns about controlling the growing free black population. On behalf of the township of North Brunswick (which included New Brunswick in its boundaries), Staats Van Deursen purchased Jacob Klady's land on George's Road for use as the new poorhouse farm, paying Klady $50 per acre for approximately 139 acres.[118] By 1823, the younger brother, William Van Deursen, would be elected to the City Council of New Brunswick and join a committee charged with "ascertain[ing] the residence of Free Negros, Vagrants and paupers in this city, with authority to take such steps for their removal as to them appears to be right and lawful."[119] This committee's mission illustrates how "free negro" and "vagrant" were categories intertwined in the eyes of white residents of New Brunswick. William Van Deursen and his committee were then authorized to "employ such number of men, in conjunction with the Marshall of the city, as they may deem advisable, to take up any negros or blacks they may find out after ten o'clock on Saturday evenings."[120] Free black people breaking the curfew risked being arrested and sent to the poorhouse farm.

As the institution of slavery in New Jersey evolved after the adoption of the gradual abolition law in 1804, enslaved individuals increasingly pressed their masters for concessions.[121] In the early nineteenth century, a number of black people in and around New Brunswick gained manumission from several Queen's College officers and benefactors. Although we have access to the records of their manumissions, the precise way they gained their freedom was usually not recorded. Many enslaved individuals married free people of color, and some people obtained manumission when their free relatives managed to save enough money to buy their freedom. Others managed to negotiate for their liberty after serving faithfully for a certain number of years. This allowed slaveholders to use the promise of freedom to compel obedience.[122] Whatever the route to freedom for these individuals, it certainly involved a complex negotiation with their masters which evidences their resistance to the institution of slavery. The possibility of gaining one's freedom through manumission was, unfortunately, rare. Only about eleven black people gained freedom each year in Middlesex County in the early nineteenth century.[123]

A woman named Sarah, for example, gained her freedom from Andrew Kirkpatrick in 1802.[124] Her age was not recorded by the court, only that she was between the ages of twenty-one and forty years old—the requisite age range for manumissions. Her master, Andrew Kirkpatrick, was a prominent judge and a strong supporter of Queen's College.[125] He had taught for a time at the college's grammar school in the 1780s before he embarked on a career in law. His family maintained a connection with the college for generations, sending their sons to the school, serving as trustees, and making generous gifts to build the Kirkpatrick Chapel on campus.[126] Andrew Kirkpatrick helped revive the college in 1807, but he stepped down from the board of trustees in 1809 to focus on his work as the chief justice of the New Jersey Supreme Court. That same year he appeared in the Court of Common Pleas declaring to manumit "his slave called Glasgow, but who calls himself Abraham Glasgow."[127] Similarly, in 1818, Kirkpatrick recorded the manumission of "Sam, but who calls himself Samuel Lane," according to Kirkpatrick's certificate.[128] These men insisted on their identities as Abraham Glasgow and Samuel Lane, and their names give us a clue as to something that might have helped them gain their freedom. Enslaved people in New Brunswick did not have legal family names, but sons born to an enslaved mother and a free man of color typically insisted on using their father's last name. Thus, Abraham Glasgow and Samuel Lane probably had free relatives who worked to help pay for their freedom.

An unusually detailed manumission was recorded in 1822 by James Parker. A longtime trustee who served for over fifty years, Parker was a prominent state legislator from Perth Amboy. He convinced his siblings to give a piece of land to the college from his late father's estate, and the Parker family donated land to the college in 1807—the land where Old Queen's would soon be constructed.[129] That same year, James Parker purchased a black boy. Fifteen years later, on August 8, 1822, twenty-five-year-old John Annin appeared in court with James Parker to receive his manumission. Parker explained to the judge that he purchased John Annin from Joseph Annin of Somerset County in 1807 when John Annin was a boy of ten. The fact that John Annin shared a last name with his previous master evidences a close relationship to his master or perhaps to Joseph Annin's former slave or another person in the Annin household. At the time of the sale in 1807, the boy, his old master, and his new master made an agreement: even though young John Annin was born seven years before the gradual abolition law of 1804 and did not qualify for its benefits, Annin would gain his freedom at the age of twenty-five, just like the boys who were born after 1804. In explaining this to the court, James Parker explicitly made reference to the law, compared Annin's lot to those who were born after 1804, and made good on his promise to release John Annin from slavery on his twenty-fifth birthday.[130]

Other individuals who gained their freedom from Queen's College trustees included Phillis, who was manumitted by John Neilson in 1822.[131] She was most likely the child he purchased in 1787, and by the time of her manumission, she would have been a woman in her mid-to-late thirties.[132] The same year, twenty-eight-year-old Benjamin gained manumission from trustee Robert Boggs, and a woman known as Betsey or Eve was manumitted by Boggs a year later, as well as a man named Nicholas in 1825.[133] Robert Boggs continued to hold people in bondage, however, reporting in 1829 that an enslaved woman in his household gave birth to a boy named Harry.[134]

Slaveholders sometimes rushed to manumit slaves who were nearing their fortieth birthday—the maximum age allowed for manumissions after 1798. Some masters saw manumission as an opportunity to relieve themselves of the burden of caring for aging black people whose labor productivity was on the decline.[135] This may have been the case with a woman named Patty who was thirty-nine years old when Queen's trustee John Croes manumitted her in 1820.[136] John Croes had been the principal of the Queen's grammar school from 1801 to 1808 (although the undergraduate classes were suspended during this time, the grammar school continued in operation and had about seventy pupils when Croes resigned in 1808).[137] Patty probably served Croes during his years at the grammar school—she would have been twenty years old when he began his tenure as principal.

Similarly, Abraham, who was enslaved to Dr. Charles Smith, experienced a late manumission. Smith served as the senior tutor at the college in the 1790s until the college closed its doors, and when the college reopened in 1807, he returned to teach once again.[138] At this point, Abraham was twenty-three years old and may have accompanied Smith to campus. Charles Smith's teaching at the college seems to have been short-lived, but he served as trustee for thirty-five years from 1804 until 1839.[139] In 1823, Smith released Abraham from service. Abraham was now thirty-nine years old and had already spent his most productive years laboring uncompensated for his master.[140] Around the time Abraham gained manumission from Charles Smith, Queen's College trustees renewed their fundraising zeal in order to save the struggling college. Donations from slaveholders like Henry Rutgers breathed new life into the school, and in 1825 the college was renamed in his honor.[141]

In the 1740s when a Dutch school for ministers was only a dream in the home of the Reverend Frelinghuysen, enslaved Africans served the Church leaders who would go on to establish Queen's College. By the 1820s, when the college finally gained a measure of financial stability—and a new name—yet another generation of African Americans labored uncompensated for their white masters, experiencing violence and trauma in the process. From Ukasaw Gronniosaw to Abraham eighty years later, black people dreamed of freedom and of reuniting with their families. At times they vacillated between desperation and hope that faithful service might earn them freedom (a yearning that was rarely fulfilled). Some, like Claus, Jack, Sam, and Dick, ran away hoping to start a new life in another state or simply to flee from unbearable violence. Others, like Abraham and December, may have found themselves in the position of human ransom or "confiscated property" during the Revolutionary War. Even as New Jersey moved toward gradual abolition in the early nineteenth century, people like Phillis and Dinah became victims of the interstate traffic in human beings. And when the college accepted generous land grants from slaveholders, enslaved workers like Will dug into the ground and labored to build the physical structures that continue to house the university's most prestigious offices to this day. The stories of these black individuals are in no way exceptional, because the institution of slavery was an ordinary part of life "on the banks of the old Raritan." How we remember their lives, their hopes, and their sacrifices is a question that Rutgers University now must address.

Acknowledgments

We would like to especially thank Thomas Frusciano, Erika Gorder, Albert C. King, and David J. Fowler for their assistance with our research.

4

"I Hereby Bequeath . . ."

Excavating the Enslaved from the Wills of the Early Leaders of Queen's College

Beatrice Adams and Miya Carey

One of the most voluminous source bases for reconstructing the relationship between the leaders of Queen's College and the institution of slavery are wills. Legal documents that provide instructions about the management of people's estates, the wills of the leaders of Queen's delineate their possessions, including enslaved persons, and provide a general picture of the material wealth of a person or a family. Alongside more traditional ways of making use of wills, these documents are also useful for uncovering details about slaving culture in New Jersey and New York, and the lived experiences of the enslaved. Often excluded from formal means of creating and saving knowledge, locating and narrating the lives of the enslaved within the historical archive can prove to be a challenging task.

To be sure, slavery was ubiquitous in and around Rutgers. The leaders of Queen's College owned enslaved people and when Rutgers's founding fathers died, they bequeathed their slaves to their wives, daughters, sons, and grandchildren. Some indicated that their slaves be freed after their spouses had died. Even a person who did not own slaves may have hired slaves from someone else, attended church with enslaved persons, or have been called to be an executor for an estate that included slaves. Thus, the practice of slavery was part of the social reality of Queen's College's early leaders and the development of Rutgers was intertwined with the history of slavery in America.[1]

This essay analyzes the wills of five trustees and one contractor, covering the period from 1786 to 1825. The wills illuminate key characteristics about the institution of slavery as practiced by the trustees and the lived experiences of the enslaved persons whom they owned. Somewhat extraordinary because of the thorough descriptions they contain, the wills can be read alongside each other as a way to construct a composite description of the enslaved persons whose lives helped to ensure the growth and development of Queen's College.

The Reverend Simeon Van Artsdalen

The will of the Reverend Simeon Van Artsdalen reveals the way that religion shaped ideas about the enslaved and how slaves could potentially use religion as a way to negotiate their circumstances. Van Artsdalen was born in Bucks County, Pennsylvania, in 1753 and graduated from Queen's College in 1780.[2] Upon graduating, he served on the faculty and as a trustee until his death in 1786. Van Artsdalen was also the pastor of the Readington, New Jersey, Dutch Reformed Church from 1783 until his death.[3] In addition to being a minister, a trustee, and a faculty member at Queen's College, Van Artsdalen was also a slave owner. He referenced two slaves in his will: "black Toney and his wife Peg."[4] According to the inventory, Toney and Peg had two children, but their names, ages, and genders were not listed. Van Artsdalen outlined his plan for Toney and his family in his will when he said, "That they may be as happy as their circumstances can permit as especially as my black man Toney makes profession of our Christian Religion, it is my will if circumstances will possibly admit . . . that he may be placed to his own liking and at such place where he may not be interrupted, but encouraged in the Religion he professes."[5]

It is unclear who Toney selected as his new owner, but his case demonstrates the complexities of agency among the enslaved. By the mid-seventeenth century, the Dutch Reformed Church "mandated slave baptism and encouraged masters to establish pathways to freedom for slaves."[6] While it is possible that Toney chose to follow Christianity out of a sincere desire to embrace the faith, it is also possible that Toney's choice was motivated by a belief that doing so might improve his family's circumstances, even if they remained unfree. While choosing Christianity did not equal immediate manumission for Toney and his family, it did offer him some leverage in determining his future. On the one hand, if the will was honored he had the ability to choose his new owner; on the other hand, this opportunity may have been predicated on a personal choice that Toney otherwise would not have made.

Van Artsdalen's will also raises the issue of the relationship between the Dutch Reformed Church and slavery and racial thought within the Church. In this post–Revolutionary War period, New Jerseyans grew increasingly wary of abolition and what that would mean for relations between blacks and whites in the state. Van Artsdalen's thoughts on abolition are not clear, but John Nelson Abeel, another clergyman in the Dutch Reformed Church and a Queen's College trustee, believed that the social mingling of blacks and whites brought on by abolition would disrupt the social order. In a sermon delivered in the 1780s, Abeel declared that "those negroes who are as black as the devil and have noses as flat as baboons with great thick lips and wool on their heads," along with "the Indians who they say eat human flesh and burn men alive and the Hotentots who love stinking flesh," could prove dangerous if freed.[7] Abeel's characterization of blacks and Indians as sinister and barbaric suggests that those in the Church believed that maintaining slavery was a fulfillment of Christian duty. It is unclear if Van Artsdalen shared Abeel's sentiments, but he might have believed that introducing Toney to Christianity and making provisions for him to continue on his spiritual growth was an act of benevolence. However, Abeel's comments point to the notion that benevolence actually often resulted from the belief that people of African descent and Native Americans were subhuman and needed enslavement for their own good.

John Schuneman

Embracing Christianity was not the only possible pathway for a slave to choose his or her master. Consider the circumstances of Criss, an enslaved woman named in John Schuneman's will. A founding trustee of Queen's College, John Schuneman had numerous ties to the early school. In addition to being in attendance at the first meeting of the trustees in Hackensack in 1767, he served as a trustee for the college until his death in 1794.[8] Additionally, Schuneman was a clergyman for the Dutch Reformed Church in Coxsackie and Catskill, New York, between 1753 and 1794. He studied under the senior Theodore Frelinghuysen as well as the Reverend John Henry Goetschius, the latter of whom played a key role as early advocate for the establishment of a college by the Dutch Reformed Church.[9] In his will, Schuneman left several enslaved persons to different members of his family after the death of his wife, Anna Maria Van Bergen. Specifically, his "old negro wench" Criss should have "the privilege" to choose to live with any of "his children."[10] He also directed that whichever child she picked "shall have her and keep and maintain her."[11]

The circumstances described in the will and Criss's "privilege" suggest that Criss may have had a key role within the family, such as a house or family servant. Furthermore, the reference to her as old suggests that his directive may have functioned as a way to ensure that someone would actually care for Criss when she was no longer able to care for herself. Since older enslaved persons were often freed to avoid the added expense of caring for an infirm person, Schuneman might have included this order in his will to ensure that someone would care for the person who had helped to care for the family's development. The idea that Criss's age played a key role in his order is supported by the fact that a seemingly younger enslaved person listed in his will as "girl" who shares the name Criss is not given the "privilege" to pick a new owner but is bequeathed to his granddaughter after his wife's death.[12]

His order may have also been fueled by the emerging discussion around the burden infirm emancipated slaves posed to Northern states who would have to provide freed people with food and shelter if they were unable to work.[13] Thus, for Criss, the ability to choose a master may have been seen as a privilege since it was not given to her fellow enslaved persons. However, her choice did not necessarily ensure her a better quality of life or freedom.

Colonel Johannes Hardenbergh and Charles Hardenbergh

The Hardenberghs, one of the most prominent families in the early history of Rutgers, with various members serving as trustees and even a president, owned both Sojourner Truth and her parents, Bomefree and Mau-Mau Bett. Their story also illuminates the ways that age shaped slavery and freedom, and how material possessions did not necessarily improve an enslaved person's quality of life.[14] Truth, who was born Isabella Baumfree, is well known for her work as an abolitionist, religious leader, and early women's rights activist. Truth is possibly best known for her "Ar'n't I a Woman" speech, in spite of the fact that historical work has demonstrated that Truth never actually uttered the now famous words.[15]

Colonel Johannes Hardenbergh, who served under General George Washington in the Continental Army and was a member of the Colonial Assembly (1743–1750) and New York State Legislature (1781–1782), owned Truth's parents.[16] Colonel Hardenbergh was one of Queen's College's founding trustees and served in this capacity until his death in 1786.[17] Alternatively, based on Truth's recollection published in her life narrative, Colonel Hardenbergh died shortly after she was born in approximately 1797.[18] Nonetheless, based on either date, Truth would have had no memories of Colonel Hardenbergh, as she plainly states in her narrative.[19]

However, she did have memories of his son Charles Hardenbergh, brother of the then president of Queen's College, Jacob Rutsen Hardenbergh, who removed her parents from their cottage and moved them into the basement of his great stone house.[20] Because of the detailed recollections found in Truth's autobiography, her experiences as an enslaved woman, and those of her parents, can be read alongside Charles Hardenbergh's will to illuminate the broader realities of their day-to-day lives. For example, in her autobiography, Truth provides a detailed account of the living conditions provided by Charles. Housed in the basement of the hotel, Charles's slaves slept on the mud and board floor with minimal straw and blankets. The room was mostly dark since there were few windows, and both sexes slept together. Charles, like many colonial masters, required that his enslaved people provide their own subsistence.[21] Truth remembered that before Charles's death, Bomefree and Mau-Mau Bett had been allotted a small plot of land to grow their own food as well as additional crops which they sold to buy other essentials.[22] This was hardly a show of benevolence or generosity on Charles's part. Inasmuch as Bomefree and Mau-Mau Bett worked for free, insult was added to injury when Hardenberg failed to provide subsistence.

Like Johannes's death, Charles's death illuminated other widespread disturbing practices, particularly the manumission of elderly slaves as a way of getting rid of them. For example, when Charles died Bomefree became a burden because he was infirm and blind and could no longer provide valuable labor. None of Charles's heirs wanted to take on the burden of caring for him.[23] As a solution to this problem, Charles's siblings decided to free Mau-Mau Bett, presumably so that she could care for him. Unfortunately, Mau-Mau Bett died shortly after they were freed. Having no way to sustain himself, Bomfree died alone in a cabin from either the cold or starvation.[24]

When read alongside Sojourner Truth's narrative, the deaths and wills of Colonel and Charles Hardenbergh are, therefore, quite revealing. The callousness embedded in the way Bomefree was left to die directly challenged choosing one's own master as a "privilege," as seen in the lives of Toney and Criss earlier in the essay. Only allotted a small measure of dignity well into her old age, Criss's ability to benefit from freedom was clouded by her likely inability to sustain herself. No doubt this was something all enslaved persons fretted about and something that scrutiny of slaveholders' wills sheds light on.

John Smalley and Peter Vrendenburgh

Connected to Queen's College because of his work as a contractor during the building of Old Queen's, both John Smalley and his son, John Smalley Jr., appear in Middlesex County records noting both the birth and manumission of several enslaved persons. Born in 1736, the elder Smalley died at the age of eighty-six in 1822, leaving a wife, son (John Smalley Jr.), and brother (Benjamin). Smalley's will is extraordinary for the detailed instructions he leaves for the maintenance of his enslaved woman named June and her daughter Dinah. He manumitted June upon his death and instructed that Dinah be set free upon the death of her mother. Still the property of Smalley until the death of her mother, Dinah was excepted from Smalley's stipulation in his will that all of his property be liquidated "as soon as convenient."[25]

Unlike Bomefree, June was left with more to sustain herself. Smalley did not just manumit her but left her $300 for "giving aid," which if not expended by the time of June's death would be returned to his estate and divided among his heirs. In addition to leaving June money, Smalley also provided her with a place to live and specifically stated that June should have use of the kitchen, the room above it, her current bedroom, and a room used as a weaver's shop. Smalley stipulated that June's access to these spaces depended on her ability to keep a "decent and orderly house." He also stated that no one else, black or white, could live at the house besides June and her daughter. Smalley mandated that his executors see that June followed these regulations or she would lose access to these spaces. He granted June as much furniture from his estate as needed to maintain a "comfortable" house. In particular, the bed and bedding used by both June and Dinah, unlike the rest of the furniture, was to be given to Dinah after June's death. Lastly, Smalley granted June access to a plot in the garden, the privilege to keep a pig, and as many apples as needed from the orchard for familial use. While Smalley framed the right he gave June to raise a pig as a privilege, it was also a way to ensure that she, not his estate, would have to provide subsistence for Dinah, who remained family property until June died.[26]

Besides the unusually detailed instructions left for the care of June and her daughter, Smalley's will is also remarkable for the use of "black woman" as the main descriptor for June and "black girl" for Dinah.[27] Ordinarily, the derogatory term *wench* was used to denote black women. Smalley's language, read alongside his wish for them to live "comfortably," raises the question of why he made these stipulations and forces us to interrogate the relationship that existed between him, June, and Dinah.

While the exact reasons for Smalley's actions are not clear in the will, historical contextualization can provide a few suggestions for probable reasons for his actions. First, Smalley may have been led by his faith to manumit Dinah. Second, he might have been complying with New Jersey legislation regarding emancipation. In 1786, a New Jersey law was passed that required masters who wanted to manumit their slaves between the ages of twenty-one and thirty-five without a bond to be observed by two overseers of the poor and two justices of the peace. The purpose of these observations was to ensure that the slave would not be impoverished. The law also mandated that owners provide support for their former slaves if they required relief. The age requirement for manumission was rooted in fears about a growing free black population that could become dependent on the state.[28] New Jersey then passed a slave code in 1798 which stated that slaves between the ages of twenty and forty could be manumitted.[29] In 1804, the New Jersey Legislature passed the Act for the Gradual Abolition of Slavery.[30] With the legalization of gradual emancipation, Smalley might have felt compelled to free June and provide her with the necessary essentials to start a life as a freed woman and mother.

However, a sexual relationship between Smiley and June, coerced or otherwise, cannot be ruled out. It was not uncommon for slave owners to leave their formerly enslaved black women with property, money, and other material possessions in their wills. It has been argued that these acts signaled a sexual relationship between the male slave owner and his female slave.[31] This possibility is supported by Smalley's attention to Dinah, who may have even been his child. Moreover Smalley's mandate that no one live with June and Dinah can be read as a way to ensure that June did not take a husband or another lover.

Peter Vrendenburgh

The will of Peter Vrendenburgh, a merchant, county treasurer, and trustee of Queen's College, raises questions similar to those that emerge from Smalley's attention to June and Dinah. Vrendenburgh was a merchant in New Brunswick and in 1772 became the treasurer of Middlesex County. Ten years later, he became a trustee of Queen's College.[32] Vrendenburgh named two slaves in his will: Tom and Margaret. It is not clear whether or not they were married or related in some other way, but both were twenty-eight years old at the time of manumission in 1823.[33] Vrendenburgh manumitted both Tom and Margaret in his will, but made an extra provision for Margaret. He requested that Margaret receive $25, to be disbursed in installments "for her fidelity."[34] Like June, Margaret's manumission raises more questions than answers. Was Vrendenburgh's decision to compensate Margaret an act of kindness? Why were no extra provisions made for Tom? What was the nature of the relationship between Margaret and Vrendenburgh?

We do not know how Margaret used the funds, but we do know that because blacks were not afforded the full privileges of citizenship, it was easy for former slaves—particularly women—to slip into poverty.[35] The money that Margaret received would have given her the ability to start on a better footing than most recently manumitted blacks. Consider again the sexual customs of racial slavery. Did a sexual relationship exist between Vrendenburgh and Margaret? Or was Margaret Vrendenburgh's child? While the historical record may never reveal what motivated Smalley and Vrendenburgh to make such provisions in their wills for June, Dinah, and Margaret, their decisions point to the particularly complex relationships between slave owners and their female slaves.

James Schureman

As seen in the lives of Bomefree and Criss, age impacted blacks' experiences with slavery and freedom. James Schureman's 1824 will also highlights the ways that age impacted manumission. Schureman graduated from Queen's College in 1775 and became a trustee and member of the faculty in 1782. He also served as the treasurer of the college from 1795 to 1813.[36] In his will, Schureman bequeathed his servant girl Jane to his daughter Ann. He then added that Jane was supposed

FIGURE 4.1 James Schureman, Queen's College Class of 1795. Rutgers Alumni Biographical Files, Special Collections and University Archives, Rutgers University Libraries.

to be manumitted on August 12, 1828. He bequeathed his servant boy Anthony to his son William. He was to be manumitted March 1, 1829.[37] Jane and Anthony's ages are unknown, but the fact that they are referenced as a girl or a boy, rather than a man or woman, suggests that they were under the age of twenty, which is the youngest that one could be in order to qualify for manumission.

It is also possible that Jane and Anthony were "slaves for a term." As part of the Act for Gradual Abolition passed in 1804, children born to slaves after July 4,

1804, would become slaves for a term, so they were bound to a term of service to their mother's master. For males, this term of service lasted until twenty-five years of age; for females, service ended at twenty-one years of age. Their service was seen as an exchange of labor for freedom.[38] Although we do not know their ages, it is quite possible that Anthony and Jane were born after 1804. This would explain why they were to be manumitted on specific dates. In addition to Anthony and Jane, an enslaved woman named Bekky was bequeathed by Schureman to his son James. According to Schureman, her "age precludes [James] from manumitting her."[39] Bekky's age is unknown, but she was most likely over the age of forty at the time of her owner's death. That would explain why Schureman did not include any plans to manumit her in his will. New Jersey's law meant that Bekky probably spent the entirety of her life enslaved.

Conclusion

This essay provides a limited but important glimpse at the ways trustees and leaders of Queen's College were active participants and beneficiaries of the slaving culture of New Jersey and New York. Though some directions suggest benevolent practices, the wills betray slavery's harshness and the total control that whites had over enslaved people. The lives of Toney, Peg, Criss, June, Dinah, Tom, Margaret, Jane, Anthony, Bomefree, Mau-Mau Bett, and even Sojourner Truth may never be totally clear to us, but reading between the lines of the wills allows us to begin to imagine and reconstruct the experiences of the enslaved. What is clear is that the same men who shaped Rutgers helped frame the institution of slavery. Rutgers did not stand apart from slavery, but like other early American colleges, its history is intricately intertwined with the abominable institution.[40]

Acknowledgments

I would like to acknowledge Catherine Stearns Medich from the New Jersey State Archives for helping me locate the trustees' wills and offering guidance on how to navigate the massive collection of wills.

5

"And I Poor Slave Yet"

The Precarity of Black Life in New Brunswick, 1766–1835

Shaun Armstead, Brenann Sutter, Pamela Walker, and Caitlin Wiesner

Blessed by its prime location at the navigable high-tide limit of the Raritan River and midway on the thoroughfare between Philadelphia and New York, New Brunswick, New Jersey, served traders and travelers advantageously in the late eighteenth and early nineteenth centuries. New Brunswick earned the nickname "Hub City," which it retains to this day, largely independent of its relationship to the budding Queen's College, which would later become the flagship campus of Rutgers University.[1] It is indisputable that many, if not most, of the trustees of Queen's College through the eighteenth and early nineteenth centuries held slaves. Their names endure emblazoned on the academic buildings and surrounding streets: founding trustee Philip French (1697–1782), Colonel John Neilson (1745–1833), Jacob R. Hardenbergh (1736–1790), and James Schureman (1756–1824). Many of Queen's College's most illustrious alumni from this period, such as Jasper Farmer, John Bray, and Alpheus Freeman, underwrote advertisements in the local New Brunswick papers for the disposal of unwanted slaves.[2]

Each day, African Americans in New Brunswick shared space and crossed paths with people attached to Queen's College. They trod the grounds of the contemporary College Avenue campus en route to their households of employ on resplendent Water Street and on their way to the Samuel Holcomb and Ayres-Freeman general stores at the north end of town (Figure 5.1).[3] Yet while the black residents of New Brunswick lived and worked near Old Queens, the vast majority of them lived lives divorced from the daily happenings at the college. Instead, they spent their time as domestic workers within the impressive homes that dotted Albany and Water Streets, gambling and laughing in the tumble-down

Halfpenny Town neighborhood or running errands outside the bustling Market-House near the Raritan.[4]

It is a poignant testament to the oppression of slavery that our understanding of humans in bondage most often derives from the documents white observers left behind. Indeed, remarkably few names of black residents—enslaved or free—in New Brunswick have survived in the historical record. The few exceptions are piecemeal: those who earned a notorious spot in the local newspapers as runaways, those who caught a fleeting mention in the ledger books of local elites (like Dr. Jacob Dunham's slave Will), or those preserved in the baptismal records of the First Presbyterian Church. Noteworthy free blacks who left more substantive records behind, like Caesar Rappleyea of the African Association of New Brunswick, and Silvia Dubois, who dictated her biography to a white physician, can be counted on one hand. And as no one source could ever paint a complete picture of what enslaved persons felt, thought, hoped, or desired, it is crucial that we use all the documents—no matter how fragmentary—we have at our disposal. These limitations in and of themselves bring the precariousness of black life into sharp relief.[5]

Lacking a detailed archival record, we can cautiously commence a partial reconstruction of the world that Will, Caesar, Silvia, and thousands of others

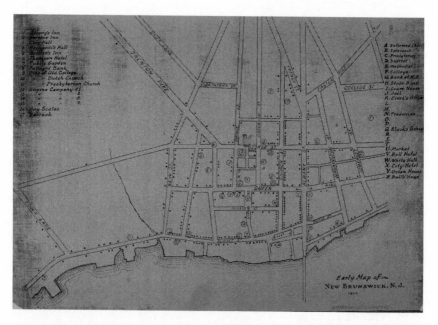

FIGURE 5.1   Early map of New Brunswick, [Middlesex County], New Jersey c. 1800–1820. Retrieved from http://dx.doi.org/doi:10.7282/T39G5N48. Rutgers, The State University of New Jersey Special Collections and University Archives.

navigated and survived each day. Marrying the tools of geography with the fragments offered up by runaway slave and slave sale advertisements in New Brunswick newspapers, several annotated maps from the early nineteenth century, church records, the ledgers of prominent New Brunswick citizens, and the minutes of the African Association of New Brunswick, it is possible to produce a rudimentary portrait of African American life in late eighteenth- and early nineteenth-century New Brunswick.

The overarching theme that encompasses this two-part investigation of the diverse experiences of enslaved and free African Americans living in New Brunswick between 1766 and 1835 is the pervasive precariousness of black life. The slippage between the categories of "free" and "unfree" during the "slow death" of New Jersey slavery in the early nineteenth century had a centrifugal effect on enslaved and free black existence in New Brunswick, dispersing both groups throughout the city while keeping them within the orbit of white power structures.[6] The first section will examine how, despite the city's reputation as a stop on the New Jersey leg of the northern Underground Railroad, the geographical layout of New Brunswick underscored the conditional nature of black freedom in the city. It will also analyze the advertisements for the private sale of slaves that appeared in New Brunswick's newspapers between 1785 and 1835. Although deceptively simple in their formulaic constructions, these documents offer important details on the daily existence of enslaved Africans in the city. In particular, they illustrate the extent to which the local character of New Brunswick slavery was heavily gendered. The second section will more deeply consider the ways in which prominent free blacks in the city contested their precarious position in the larger society of New Brunswick. While the African Association was in many ways still a space circumscribed by white stakeholders, this study reveals how blacks negotiated for greater freedoms and made meaning of exclusively black spaces in a community where racial segregation in public spaces was relatively relaxed. The African Association of New Brunswick provides a compelling case study as to how New Brunswick's free black population overcame the limitations placed upon it and constructed a coherent black identity through a limited, but potent, public sphere. Furthermore, this section considers how African American women in particular might have utilized familial and kinship networks to navigate early black public institutions.

Codifying Precariousness: Runaways, Free Blacks, and the Local Character of New Brunswick Slavery

Although local census data is sporadic prior to the 1820s, we can ascertain that eighteenth- and nineteenth-century New Brunswick was home to a relatively robust community of slaves and free blacks. According to the minutes of the

New Brunswick Common Council, a census conducted in April of 1828 noted that in addition to the 4,435 whites who resided within city limits, there were 374 free blacks. New Brunswick also claimed 57 slaves for life and 127 slaves "for a term." Slaves for a term were those born after the 1804 Act for the Gradual Abolition of Slavery, which required female children born to slaves to serve their mother's master until age twenty-one. Male children born under the same circumstances had to serve until age twenty-five. In all, 558 persons of African descent lived in New Brunswick in 1828, comprising a significant 11 percent of the city's total population.[7] In comparison, the entire state of New Jersey had a black population of only 6.5 percent in 1830.[8]

With its sizeable free black population and easy access to road, water, and later rail travel, New Brunswick provided relatively favorable conditions for runaway fugitives heading farther north. By the mid-nineteenth century, the city was an instrumental terminal in New Jersey's northern network of the Underground Railroad. Runaways traveling through Delaware, Pennsylvania, and south New Jersey typically converged in New Brunswick on their way to New York City or Canada.[9] However, New Brunswick was also widely regarded as one of the most dangerous legs of the journey. Self-appointed slave hunters enforcing the controversial Fugitive Slave Act of 1850 mercilessly patrolled the footbridge that stemmed from Albany Street eastward across the Raritan River.[10] The perceived safety of the Raritan dictated the final stages of a runaway's route: those who managed to cross the Raritan safely headed to Rahway and then Jersey City before ultimately arriving in New York; those unwilling to risk the river and its notorious slave hunters took an alternative route through Perth Amboy.[11] While New Brunswick served a vital role for many African Americans in search of freedom, a focus on the city's role in the Underground Railroad risks obscuring those who ran from, and not just through, New Brunswick.

Not all runaways headed north. Some attempted to stay in New Brunswick, unwilling to sever kinship and social ties. When a black girl known as both Charlotte and Brook ran away from her owner, George D. Fisher, on a Saturday, she stayed in the area, reportedly burglarizing Fisher's home Sunday night. Charlotte/Brook did not take any food or valuables from the home, only "one light colored gown and one cravat." The theft of the cravat in particular is a compelling curiosity. As a piece of men's apparel, it is possible Charlotte/Brook traded the cravat to someone else in the community in return for assistance or accommodations. Or perhaps she intended to wear the cravat herself to disguise her identity while remaining in the local community. It is clear that Charlotte/Brook felt no immediate desire to leave New Brunswick, for as Fisher complained in a runaway advertisement printed nearly two weeks after her escape, "She has been seen running the street almost every day or night," always managing to elude capture.[12] Ironically, despite Charlotte/Brook's dangerous decision to remain in a community cognizant of her fugitive status, staying in New Brunswick allowed her to make use of her social ties and knowledge of the local geography—vital resources that certainly prolonged her freedom.

While Charlotte/Brook's familiarity with New Brunswick allowed her to avoid capture, Silvia Dubois's unfamiliar black face attracted white harassment. After Dubois received her manumission in Great Bend, Pennsylvania, near the turn of the nineteenth century, she went in search of her mother, who she eventually learned was living in New Brunswick. Dubois traversed nearly 200 miles, walking most of the way carrying her infant child. Just outside of New Brunswick, she was stopped by a white man who demanded to know, "Whose nigger are you?" Dubois audaciously responded, "I'm no man's nigger—I belong to God—I belong to no man." He pressed her, "Where are you going?" To which she retorted, "That's none of your business. I'm free. I go where I please." In recalling the interaction, Dubois remembered that she then "sat down my young one, showed him my fist, and looked at him; and I guess he saw't no use. He moseyed off, telling me that he would have me arrested as soon as he could find a magistrate. You see in those days the negroes were all slaves. . . . But he didn't arrest me—not a bit."[13] In a fierce display of autonomy, Dubois elected to show her fist and not her manumission papers as evidence of her right to travel.[14] Aware that her supposed guilt was predicated only on her blackness, she recalled with great pride her ability to reverse the power dynamics in that brief, but potentially disastrous, interaction.

Although New Brunswick offered Charlotte/Brook and Silvia a degree of security to live freely, their stories ought to be read as exceptional. For the thousands of anonymous African Americans who dwelled in New Brunswick in the late eighteenth and early nineteenth centuries, the prospect of personal freedom was much less sanguine. An examination of New Brunswick's geography during this time can help to account for these lives. It also quickly disabuses us of the notion that urban life promised enslaved and free African Americans greater control over their lives and destinies.[15] In practice, the structure of the city blurred distinctions between these two groups, a reflection of the permeability between the legal categories of "free" and "unfree" codified in the 1804 Act for Gradual Abolition. In some cases, the slippage between enslavement and freedom in New Brunswick had positive ramifications for the city's African Americans, such as the relaxation of racial segregation in public places. This was especially true in places of worship like the First Presbyterian Church. However, this same slippage also impeded the critical mass required to carve out substantive autonomous free black communities within the city. In 1823, a socially prominent free black man named Caesar Rappleyea established the African School in his home at the "upper end of Church Street" with the financial assistance of the local African Association and the First Presbyterian

Church.[16] It quickly evolved into an important node of African American life in New Brunswick where free blacks and the enslaved (should they obtain the permission of their masters to attend) received an elementary education side by side. However, this site in which enslaved and free blacks could share in a relative freedom was just a few blocks south of the city's most potent symbol of their shared precariousness: the city gaol, or jail. In this way, a critical element of freedom for African Americans—the pursuit of education—was bound in notions of unfreedom.

For local African Americans, the New Brunswick gaol loomed large as a space of punishment and imprisonment.[17] Located on Prince Street (now Bayard Street) between George Street and Queen Street (now Neilson Street) and less than a half mile from Old Queens, the gaol stood near the center of the city (Figure 5.1.) New Brunswick served as a regional hub for the incarceration of both runaway slaves from surrounding counties and states and local free blacks found in violation of the city's various racially targeted ordinances.[18] The gaol held in intimate confinement black, white, male, and female prisoners on charges ranging from petty theft to murder. Many antebellum gaols functioned practically as warehouses for runaway slaves awaiting retrieval by their owners.[19] New Brunswick was no exception to this rule. Thanks to New Brunswick's reputation as a stop on the Underground Railroad, the gaol was, if nothing else, a convenient and somewhat secure repository for intercepted runaways. The sheriffs for Middlesex, Somerset, and Mercer Counties regularly apprehended blacks who were unable to produce papers proving their free status on the highways and thoroughfares that flanked New Brunswick and committed their charges to the gaol in New Brunswick.[20] From there, the sheriff or gaoler would announce the arrest in a local newspaper, sometimes giving slave owners as little as ten days' notice to travel to New Brunswick to "come and prove their property, pay charges, and take them away."[21] If the allotted time elapsed without a slave owner's paying restitution and proving his ownership, the imprisoned individual would be put up for sale. The common practice of selling unclaimed runaway slaves in order to compensate the city for their keep directly implicated the capture and sale of slaves in New Brunswick's municipal finances. In this way, the city of New Brunswick could never claim neutrality in relation to slavery.

While most black prisoners languished in the gaol in passive awaiting of their fate, some found their surrounding walls penetrable. Between 1808 and 1814, at least thirteen individuals escaped and absconded from the New Brunswick gaol. A massive jailbreak in April of 1812 sheds light on those most susceptible to imprisonment in New Brunswick. Nine individuals escaped at once "by piercing a hole through the wall of the south wing of the prison." All nine were black men, but only one appears to have been a local resident. The other men hailed from Somerset, Mercer, Essex, Salem, and Cumberland Counties, and as far away as northern Maryland, suggesting considerable movement of black individuals within New Jersey and the surrounding region. Only one man, Thomas Somers, was noted to be "born free." Tellingly, gaol keeper Francis K. Labau offered a reward for the return of Somers equal to the bounty that would be paid for the return of Somers's enslaved collaborators.[22] He made no distinction between free and enslaved status in his ward—literally quantifying their worth as equal.

While Silvia Dubois successfully managed to avoid the New Brunswick gaol, others found that their free status could not ensure their protection from arrest. In 1768, two black men, London and Robert, were committed to the New Brunswick gaol despite their insistence that they were free men. Presuming their guilt, the gaoler described the situation as such:

> They pretend to be free, say that they did belong to a Gentleman a Merchant from St. Christopher's that they came with their Master to New-York, who lodged with the Widow Richardson on Rotten-Row, that their Master died there last Spring and before his Death gave them free. The chief Cloathing about them was contained in a good Ozenbrig Bag, marked P.R. #19, viz, a white Fustian Coat, lined with Shalloon, a pair of Leather Breeches, one White Linnen Jacket, 5 white Shirts, one pretty fine, marked W.I., 2 pair of cloth breeches, 2 pair of Trowsers, one a pair of Yarn, and 2 pair of Worsted ribb'd Stockings, one White Handerkerchief, one Duffields Great Coat, had on each a Beaver Hat, one about half-worn; Jackets, coarse Shirts and Trousers, pretty good and in Appearance belonged to a Gentleman. Whoever claims said Negroes are desired to be speedy in taking them out. Or if Mrs. Richardson or any other person knows them to be free, are desired to give Notice thereof, that upon paying charges, they may be set at Liberty.[23]

The men's possessions are deeply incriminating in the eyes of the gaoler, who is unable to fathom any innocuous reason for "good" and "fine" clothing worthy of a gentleman to be in the possession of black men. Although the gaoler prods their presumed master "to be speedy in taking them out," he concedes the possibility that Mrs. Richardson "knows them to be free," while dissuading her from coming forward by placing upon her the burden of payment. Confined in the gaol of an unfamiliar city, London and Robert are dependent upon the word of a woman from New York for their freedom. The precarious case of London and Robert reveals how easily a free black person of the North could leave New Brunswick an enslaved person of the South.

Free blacks stood to be imprisoned just as capriciously as their enslaved kin for a variety of racially specific offenses, including violating curfew, distributing alcohol at illicit "tippling houses," vagrancy, or even on mere suspicion of having the propensity to commit a crime. The arbitrary and informal nature of justice for blacks in New Brunswick is apparent in the New Brunswick Common Council's offhanded mention in 1801 that "Mr. Phillips was appointed to take the proper steps for committing to jail a free negro named David, *supposed* to be a dangerous person."[24] The New Brunswick Common Council's enactment of a racially specific curfew in 1824, which empowered "the committee heretofore appointed in relation to paupers, Vagrants and Free Negros. . . in conjunction with the Marshall of the city, as they may deem advisable, to take up any negros or blacks they may find out after ten o'clock on Saturday evenings," also made use of the city gaol in the persistent struggle to constrict the mobility of free blacks.[25] The council ostensibly intended for the curfew to contain the "riots and other great disorders particularly at night, and on the Sabbath day," of which New Brunswick residents had complained to the council since 1821. The date and time of the curfew also suggest a desire to curtail any traces of free black recreation within the city. In the eyes of the Common Council, it was unseemly, if not downright dangerous, for blacks to congregate and use their bodies for something other than productive labor.[26] For it was not only in the South that whites feared slave insurrection. In 1779, in nearby Elizabeth-Town (now Elizabeth), the *New York Packet, and the American Advertiser* reported that "it was discovered that the negroes had it in contemplation to rise and murder the inhabitants of Elizabeth-Town. Many of them are secured in gaol."[27] Such accounts, no matter how vague, amplified white suspicion and surveillance of the black community. In New Brunswick, the advent of gradual abolition, in particular, spurred Common Council ordinances designed to discipline free black existence within the city. They peaked in number and severity between 1821 and 1824, just as the first generation of "slaves for a term" born after the 1804 Act for Gradual Abolition approached the age of manumission.[28] The intensification of antiblack ordinances in the city may have indicated collective anxiety among New Brunswick's slaveholders over the growth of the free black population in the city and the imminent reality of widespread manumission.[29]

While the New Brunswick gaol systematically reduced free blacks to the marginality of slaves, it was not necessary for free blacks in New Brunswick to be physically confined within the prison walls in order to experience the gaol as a site of subjugation. They would have been required by daily necessity to crisscross the city landscape, invariably drawing them into the downtown commercial districts that were riddled with reminders of their nominal freedom.[30]

Enslaved persons would have lived in households scattered throughout the city, but the data on where exactly free blacks resided within antebellum New Brunswick is murky at best. Historian James Gigantino correctly points out that New Jersey's Act for Gradual Abolition stymied the formation of free black households and coherent free black communities comparable to those in Philadelphia or New York for much of the 1810s and 1820s. Free blacks who wished to remain in close proximity with family members who were still in bondage were forced to remain within the orbit of slaveholders. As a consequence, they faced severe handicaps on their mobility and ability to bargain for higher wages, two factors that were instrumental to the formation of autonomous black communities.[31] The fact that late eighteenth- and early nineteenth-century New Brunswick never developed its own black church, the cornerstone of antebellum free black communities, attests to the dispersed nature of black life in the city.

Nevertheless, five mentions in the historical record provide us with clues as to the location of free black homes within the city. First, a 1790 map of the properties owned by Philip French, a founding trustee of Queen's College, indicated one "Negroes house near ye mine" at the extreme north end of the city where King Street met the Raritan River (Figure 5.2).[32] Historian Richard L. Porter reports that this northernmost stretch of the city was known as "the Mines" as late as 1825, in reference to the copper mining that took place there in the early eighteenth century. By the early nineteenth century, however, it was more readily recognized as a community of white and black fishermen and boatmen who either rented or squatted on the land.[33] Second, the diary of white slave owner Rachel Van Dyke, recorded between the years of 1810 and 1811, makes reference to "Halfpenny Town" along the banks of the Raritan on the eastern edge of the city toward Queen Street. A disreputable neighborhood of squatter cabins occupied by poor white fishmongers and some free blacks, Van Dyke described Halfpenny Town as a lively spot where, she observed, "the negroes . . . all assembled in their Sunday clothes, as happy and as merry as Lords and Ladies. Some were gambling with Cents, some dancing to the violin others talking and laughing—and all appeared to be without care—only regardful how they might enjoy the passing moment."[34] While Halfpenny appears to have been a space of leisure for the black community, it was not removed from white scrutiny, as evidenced by Van Dyke's very own observations. Third, the 1821 minutes of the New Brunswick Common Council mention that the "negro disorders" against which they were legislating occurred in "houses kept by free negros" in the "upper part of the City." These were the broader streets toward the west and south of New Brunswick that lay at a higher elevation than the narrow streets closer to the wharfs, like Burnet Street and Water Street.[35] These disturbances likely occurred in the vicinity of French Street, which was rocked by a violent racially fueled uproar in 1815.[36] Fourth, Dr. Jacob Dunham mentions in his ledger that in 1825 he treated the wife of Jasper, a free black man in New Brunswick, at her home "at the Landing," near the Raritan Bridge.[37] Finally, one 1835 article from the *Fredonian* compiled a list of the damage wrought on New Brunswick by a catastrophic tornado. It mentioned fleetingly that on Schureman Street, the penultimate southernmost street in the city, one property rented out by

John W. Stout to free blacks had been unroofed in the whirlwind. According to Rachel Van Dyke's diary, this southernmost point in town was known as the "Goose Pasture," as it was mostly woods and cleared meadows with a sprinkling of ramshackle houses.

Based on the composition of these fragmentary clues, it is difficult to pinpoint the exact locus of a free black community in late eighteenth- and early nineteenth-century New Brunswick. However, we can safely assume that while free black residences were somewhat dispersed, they mostly dwelled on the periphery of the city, huddled along the Raritan River, the southernmost streets, or the westernmost edge of the city. We can therefore envision how free blacks living under the shadow of slavery in late eighteenth- and early nineteenth-century New Brunswick would have been compelled by the daily necessities of purchasing food and finding work to navigate what historian Marisa Fuentes has described as the "punitive architecture" of urban slavery.[38] The city gaol would have been an inescapable feature on the daily commute from the designated "black" pockets and outskirts of town to the downtown commercial districts. The free black family that dwelled in the rented home on Schureman

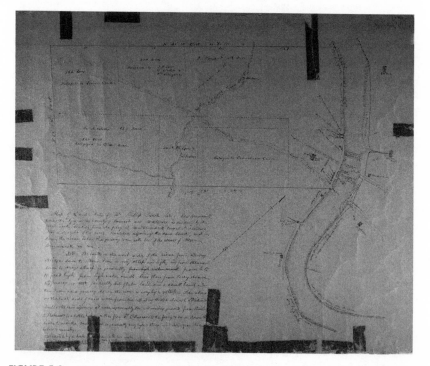

FIGURE 5.2   Benj. H. Manning, "Map of Land late of Mr Phillip French late of New Brunswick deceased ... " 1790, Manuscript Map #20,015, Special Collection and University Archives, Rutgers University Libraries.

Street would have surely passed near the New Brunswick gaol as they ventured north on George Street or Queen Street toward the hawkers outside the Market-House, the services at the First Presbyterian Church, or the general stores along Church Street. Free blacks lodged near French Street would have performed a similar trek, first eastward down Church Street and then southward down George Street or Queen Street. Any black inhabitants of "the Mines" also would have ventured down what was then King Street and continued onto Queen Street, drawing them ever southward until they eventually reached its fateful intersection with Prince Street. Even those cramped into somewhat centrally located Halfpenny Town or Raritan Landing would have regularly passed near the gaol in order to take part in the smallest modicums of freedom, like visiting the well-to-do households in which their spouses and parents continued to be held in slavery or attending Caesar Rappleyea's African School. Indeed, even Caesar Rappleyea, who was exceptionally privileged by his ability to live in moderate comfort along Church Street and engage regularly with the African Association, could not escape the shadow of the city gaol, in which imprisoned runaways languished awaiting sale. His alcove of black freedom was circumscribed by hostile white surveillance.

Nor would the visceral daily reminders of their proximity to slavery cease once they had passed the gaol or if they took roundabout routes to avoid it. As much as it was a utilitarian space marked by mundane chores, the Market-House was a constant backdrop to slave sales in New Brunswick and a consistent reminder of the precariousness of free black life in late eighteenth- and early nineteenth-century New Brunswick. The Market-House, which stood immediately adjacent to the wharfs along the Raritan, at the corner of Hiram Street and Queen Street, was at the heart of New Brunswick's commercial life. It was a venue for New Brunswick's denizens of both races to purchase daily necessities, sell their wares, and partake in a swarming social scene. Of course, among these transactions, visible to all passersby, was the regular auction and sale of slaves. In 1784, Robert Hude proudly proclaimed that his recently opened "Vendue Store Near the Market-House" was both "centrical and in every respect well calculated for the business" and "ready for the reception of every species of goods intended for public and private sale." He listed slaves among his stock, alongside horses, small boats, and household furniture.[39] In 1784, Jasper Farmer utilized Hude's store in order to dispose of his "sundry Male and Female Negroes" alongside his husbandry and farming utensils, as he intended to quit farming and take up a new trade.[40] A similar scene played out in 1823 when Thomas F. Sergent punctuated his advertisement for his writing and conveyance business located "opposite to the Market-House" with an offer to sell "the time of a Black Girl, Seventeen years old, for five years."[41] As nearly four decades elapsed and gradual abolition chipped away at New Jersey slavery, the Market-House retained its reputation as a site for the exchange of slaves. Even an ostensibly neutral space served as a lifetime symbol of terror for free blacks and reinforced the conditional nature of their freedom.[42]

Even in death, geography informed the ambiguous status of free blacks in New Brunswick. In 1822, amid the flurry of anti-free-black city ordinances in New Brunswick, the *Fredonian* printed a notice "to THE coloured people of New Brunswick" to alert them that the city had appointed a black sexton, William Coryell, to bury the city's dead African Americans. The disclosed intention of the notice was to ensure that "the funerals would be conducted with decency and decorum."[43] But in effect, the appointment barred the black community's practice of performing the job at their own discretion, thus wresting control of funerary rites from local blacks. While black funerals remained, strictly speaking, in black hands following the 1822 notice, the funerary rites were ultimately subject to white supervision and white approval by the city leaders.[44] White New Brunswickers did allow blacks to be interred alongside them in integrated denominational cemeteries, but this ostensibly benevolent gesture only contributed to the circumscription of autonomous black space within the city. Just as there was no independent black church, there was no independent black graveyard free from white gaze.

Whereas the geography of nineteenth-century New Brunswick imparts clues as to how free African Americans navigated the city, it conveys little about the character of life for New Brunswick's sizeable population of slaves who were not runaways. To put it another way, geography marks routes that Jacob Dunham's slave Will may have taken in his daily travels across New Brunswick and what may have accosted him along the way, but geography remains mum on the daily expectations that confronted Will and his kin as enslaved persons in an urban space in a Northern border state in the late eighteenth and early nineteenth centuries. To this end, the advertisements for the sale of slaves that peppered local New Brunswick newspapers assist in the partial reconstruction of enslaved life in New Brunswick. Historian Graham Russell Hodges soundly warns that printed advertisements for slaves represent only the "tip of the iceberg" of a slave-trading market that thrived on informal transactions.[45] Taking Hodges's warning to heart, the following analysis is not intended to be an exhaustive study of New Brunswick's slave-trading economy and culture. To their credit, these admittedly preliminary findings extracted from advertisements for the sale of slaves in New Brunswick between 1780 and 1835 continue to dismantle any extant binary between "slave" and "free" status in New Brunswick.[46] More to the point, these underutilized sources clarify elements of the local character of slavery in New Brunswick that are obscured in other sources. For instance, they confirm the acknowledged female majority on both sides of the color line in late eighteenth- and early nineteenth-century New Brunswick and how this predominantly female society led to a distinct gendering of the practice of slavery in New Brunswick.

Due in large part to its commercial importance and connections to Queen's College, New Brunswick quickly developed into a hub for the production of newspapers that were distributed both locally and in neighboring counties. Consequently, by the early nineteenth century, New Brunswick's newspapers were vibrant regional forums for the private sale of slaves. Far from serving as impersonal go-betweens for prospective slaveholders, the local newspapers were well integrated into the city's commercial life and, by extension, its slave-trading economy. The office of the *Fredonian*, New Brunswick's long-running Federalist newspaper, was situated at the corner of Church and Dennis Streets less than a block away from the Market-House. Often, its printed advertisements for slaves requested that interested customers "enquire of the printer" directly, a practice that implicated the newspaper in the exchange and worked to obscure the identity of the subscriber who placed the advertisement.[47] The integral role played by the city's newspapers in facilitating the sale of slaves renders these sources a reasonably reliable barometer for the slave sale economy in nineteenth-century New Brunswick. The fact that the majority of the enslaved advertised in the New Brunswick newspapers were sold individually in private sales, as opposed to being auctioned off in large lots, offers a unique glimpse into the particular expectations that individual New Brunswick slaveholders held for their slaves and the ways in which these individual slaves interacted with white power structures.

While advertisements for the sale of enslaved persons are an unparalleled source for the examination of trends in slaveholding in late eighteenth- and early nineteenth-century New Brunswick, the halting pace of abolition in New Jersey complicates the discernment of trends. While the majority of the slaves who changed hands in New Brunswick between 1780 and 1835 were slaves for life, the 1804 Act for the Gradual Abolition of Slavery created a new category of servitude: "slave for a term." Because their parents had no legal right to forbid the transaction, slaveholders in New Jersey regularly sold children born to slaves after 1804 out of state before they reached the deadline for manumission in order to recover their financial investment. This legal loophole was expertly exploited by Jacob Van Wickle, a judge of the Middlesex County Court of Common Pleas who lived in South River, just six miles southeast of New Brunswick. In 1818, Van Wickle turned a steady profit by selling hundreds of Jersey-born slaves who would soon be rendered worthless by the looming threat of manumission to the eager markets of Louisiana. There they could be sold for nearly triple the price they could fetch in New Jersey.[48] However, this "backdoor" to the Deep South did not completely extinguish New Jersey's intrastate slave trade, as demonstrated on the pages of New Brunswick's newspapers. While advertisements

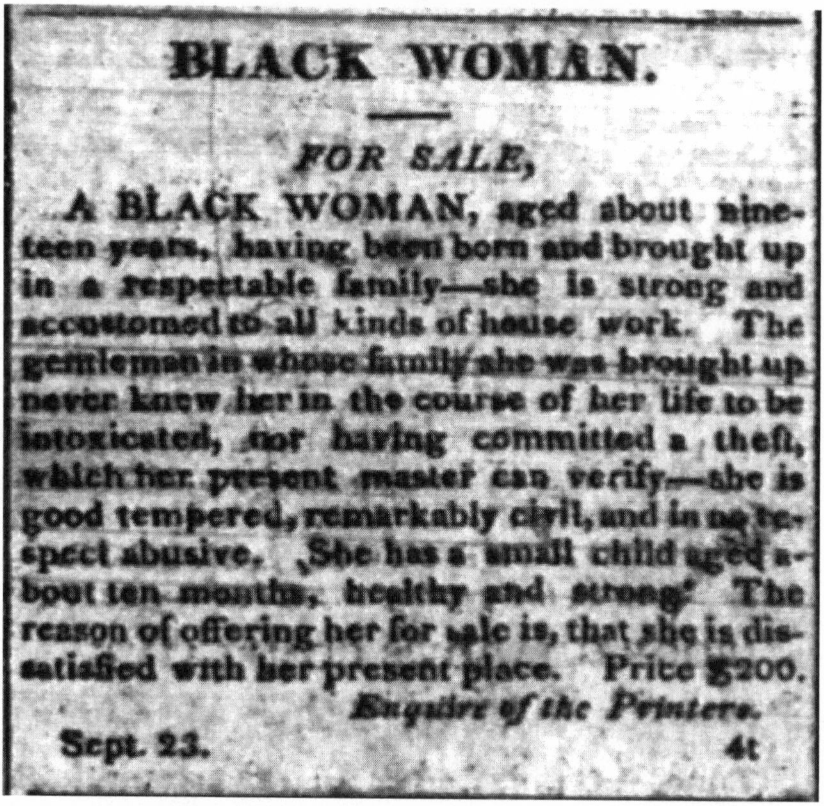

BLACK WOMAN.

FOR SALE,

A BLACK WOMAN, aged about nineteen years, having been born and brought up in a respectable family—she is strong and accustomed to all kinds of house work. The gentleman in whose family she was brought up never knew her in the course of her life to be intoxicated, nor having committed a theft, which her present master can verify—she is good tempered, remarkably civil, and in no respect abusive. She has a small child aged about ten months, healthy and strong. The reason of offering her for sale is, that she is dissatisfied with her present place. Price $200.

Enquire of the Printers.

Sept. 23. 4t

FIGURE 5.3 "Slave Sale—Black Woman" *Fredonian* (New Brunswick), 7 October 1813, microfilm image, *Fredonian (New Brunswick)* June 26, 1811–April 27, 1820, Alexander Library, Rutgers University Libraries.

rarely set a firm price for the slaves they marketed, relying instead on vague modifiers like "cheap" or "moderate terms," one advertisement printed in the *Fredonian* in 1813 for a nineteen-year-old woman and her ten-month-old child listed a specific price of $200.

Evidently, an enslaved woman still in the prime of her childbearing years and an infant who would require manumission in its early twenties could still demand a decent price in the local New Brunswick market. Gigantino reports that 17 percent of all bound black labor advertised for sale in New Jersey newspapers between 1804 and 1824 were to be sold "for a term."[49] New Brunswick slightly edged this figure, with 18.5 percent of their slaves sold via newspaper between 1780 and 1835 billed as serving "a term of years," although this statistic is slightly inflated by the practice of temporarily selling of slaves "for a term" with no promise of manumission in the years prior to 1804. The somewhat common practice of hiring out slaves for a "term of years" prior to 1804 allowed New Brunswickers to transform slaves into independent commodities and muddy the categories of "free" and "unfree" well before the legislative advent of gradual abolition. Among those in New Brunswick who opted to cash in their depreciated assets on the local market after 1804 were those who attempted to sell their slaves on average four years prior to their date of manumission. Not surprisingly, advertisements for the sale of slaves in New Brunswick dropped off precipitously after 1835. This was most likely due to the fact that any remaining "slaves for life" would have been at least thirty years old and therefore no longer attractive to prospective buyers seeking able-bodied laborers. Also, by 1835 the majority of slave children born after 1804 would have already outgrown their obligation to their mothers' masters. The New Jersey Supreme Court formalized this knowledge when in 1836 it ruled that blacks were no longer prima facie slaves, and therefore presumed to be free unless proven otherwise.[50]

Despite these fluctuations in the precise meaning of bondage for slaves sold through New Brunswick newspapers between 1780 and 1835, one trend remained constant. The most striking and consistent feature of advertisements for the sale of slaves in New Brunswick through the late eighteenth and early nineteenth centuries is the gender imbalance. Of the sixty-four individual slaves with specified genders offered for sale across fifty-five articles published in New Brunswick newspapers between 1780 and 1835, 59.4 percent were female. More importantly, the majority of slave sales listed in New Brunswick newspapers were for women, both before and after the Act for Gradual Abolition in 1804. They respectively comprised 66 percent and 57 percent of sales listed in New Brunswick newspapers.[51] In New Brunswick, women predominated in the advertisements for both term sales and full title transfers. The median and average age for these women was between nineteen and twenty. Gigantino concludes that this figure is simply a reflection of the higher proportion of female slaves of childbearing age than males in the overall state slave population. After all, this rate is consistent with statewide trends between 1804 and 1824, during which 60 percent of all advertisements for the full title transfer of slaves in New Jersey newspapers marketed women.[52] Additionally, Gigantino argues that the gender imbalance in the New Jersey slave pool was exaggerated by the 1804 Act for Gradual Abolition. Because the law renewed emphasis on the reproductive capabilities of New Jersey's enslaved women in the hope of replenishing slaveholders' dwindling supplies of slaves, masters were much more loath to manumit their female slaves.[53] This would explain why most female slaves sold in New Brunswick went to market around the apex of their childbearing years.

Gigantino's explanation for the market preference for female slaves of childbearing age in early nineteenth-century New Jersey is certainly correct in emphasizing the importance of female reproduction to the maintenance of local slave markets.[54] Although slaveholders in New Brunswick often sold their women in tandem with their infants and small children, this custom was not based on sentimental reverence for the slave family but for economic expediency. For instance, in 1780 when John Bray offered for sale an enslaved family consisting of a thirty-two-year-old man, a twenty-four-year-old woman, and a fifteen-month-old child, he admitted a preference to keeping the family together but concluded that "a few miles separation will not prevent a sale."[55] In any case, enslaved women in early nineteenth-century New Brunswick certainly labored under the heartbreaking knowledge that any children they might bear would likely be sold away from them prior to their promised date of manumission. In New Brunswick, however, the slave advertisements printed in newspapers express a conscious preference for young female slaves that cannot be completely explained by market supply or reproductive ability. In addition to the advertisements offering slaves for sale, New Brunswick newspapers in the late eighteenth and early nineteenth centuries also featured printed requests from individuals in the community seeking to purchase slaves. Of these printed requests, the majority called for female slaves, with ages ranging widely between fifteen and thirty.[56] The few that requested male slaves sought them as assistants for businesses conducted by the subscriber, as in the case of Jacob Chowell's dry goods store on Albany Street.[57] A conscious gender preference also permeated articles advertising the sale of specific individuals. One 1813 *Fredonian* article offering an eight-year-old boy for sale noted that in lieu of a cash payment the subscriber would gladly accept "an exchange FOR a black girl."[58] This apparent preference for female slaves in New Brunswick cannot be reduced to a simple desire for breeders. According to historian Steven Deyle, the close quarters in which white slaveholders and black slaves lived in the urban North actually brought some slaveholders, unlike their counterparts in the rural South, to lament the excessive fertility of their slave women well into the nineteenth century.[59] In 1795 a subscriber to *Arnett's New Jersey Federalist* offered his sixteen-year-old female slave, who had been "carefully brought up to do all kinds of housework," for sale because she "promises to be too great a breeder of children for the convenience of the family." Crucially, rather than simply replacing his fecund female slave with an equally young and able-bodied male, the subscriber included the caveat that "she will either be sold or exchanged for an elderly woman."[60] In other words, the New Brunswick denizen specifically sought an enslaved female that was devoid of any troublesome fertility that might strain his finances. Or he may also have sought a slave that was devoid of any sexual allure that might strain the peace of his household.[61] In either case, he anchored his desire for an enslaved woman not in the children she could produce but in the labor she was ready to perform. Scholars like Daina Ramey Berry have identified support for this particular rationale of slave ownership. She has argued convincingly that while the going rate of bondswomen certainly peaked during childbearing years, her value was not solely dependent upon her reproductive capacities.[62]

Based on these evidentiary clues drawn from slave advertisements, New Brunswickers may have based their vocalized preference for female slaves on the work they expected of their slave women's hands more so than slave women's wombs. In other words, the overwhelming desire for female slaves may have reflected slaveholders' expectations that these women would perform feminized domestic labor rather than the expectation that they would reproduce. Indeed, Graham Russell Hodges points out that this overrepresentation of female slaves serving as domestics in the urban spaces of New Jersey and New York mirrored an overrepresentation of agriculturally skilled male slaves in the more rural regions of both states.[63] This is not to suggest that enslaved women bought and sold in New Brunswick never touched a sickle or hoe. Northern and Southern slaveholders alike had no reservations about black women's ability to perform demanding agricultural labor.[64] Many New Brunswick slaveholders, like Rachel Van Dyke's father Frederick Van Dyke, pursued agriculture in the outlying areas of the city and readily tasked male or female slaves with tending to their fields and orchards.[65] Nevertheless, advertisements for the sale of slaves in late eighteenth- and early nineteenth-century New Brunswick newspapers displayed greater interest in, and reserved their highest praise for, the domestic skills honed by female slaves. In 1784, Jasper Farmer boasted that his fifty-year-old female slave was an "excellent cook."[66] A 1792 listing in the *Brunswic Gazette* assessed a twenty-year-old slave woman to be "well calculated for doing the business of a kitchen."[67] Another from the *Guardian; or, New Brunswick Advertiser* in 1799 proclaimed that the sixteen-year-old female slave in question "understands housework perfectly well."[68] From the same publication in 1815, an advertisement announced that the twenty-five-year-old slave woman listed for sale happened to be "an excellent spinster of flax, wool and tow."[69] Meanwhile, the advertisements described male slaves only as being "acquainted with farming."[70] Runaway slave ads from the same period bear out the fact that antebellum New Jersey's diversified economy produced male slaves who possessed the specialized skills of shipbuilding and blacksmithing. However, the only other skills that New Brunswickers desired for their prospective male slaves besides farming was waiting tables. This occupation was largely reserved for prepubescent boys and was often annexed by female domestics.[71] Interestingly, the intensification of interest in female slaves' domestic skills in slave sale advertisements in early nineteenth-century New Brunswick newspapers coincided with the turn in New Jersey agriculture toward less labor-intensive crops that required fewer slaves for cultivation.[72] Whether they were cynically attempting to entice a prospective buyer or were genuine in their praise of their bondswomen's housework,

New Brunswick slaveholders in the late eighteenth and early nineteenth centuries nonetheless expanded the definition of *skill* beyond its traditional application in the trades and desired that their female slaves be particularly skilled in domestic labor.[73]

The domestic work enslaved women were expected to perform was rigorous, unrelenting, and tremendously devalued. Rachel Van Dyke's diary offers a telling glimpse into the quotidian dynamics between a white woman and her enslaved female domestic in a New Brunswick home. Van Dyke's family owned at least four enslaved individuals, and she frequently and confidently delegated domestic chores. Once a week, Van Dyke would "set Sylvia to work scouring my room."[74] On one occasion, Van Dyke decided to clean her room herself, with Sylvia only assisting. Afterward, Van Dyke recounted, "I don't think I have ever worked so hard in my life," noting that she could "scarcely move hand or foot" due to her exhaustion. She described the physical toll the chore took on her body, noting that "my hands burn, my feet are in pain. Foolish girl!" In retrospect, Van Dyke wished she had left the chore for Sylvia to perform alone. But then on second thought, she admitted, had Sylvia done the work, "perhaps it would not have pleased me quite as well as it does now."[75] Even as she wallowed in agony from performing domestic work, Van Dyke remained oblivious to the overwhelming pain and exhaustion Sylvia was forced to endure on a daily basis. This insensitivity on the part of Van Dyke is all the more remarkable considering a woman she enslaved (most likely Sylvia) repeatedly voiced her arduous condition in front of her mistress. According to Van Dyke, her "old woman who came from Africa" often told her, "'I worked, Miss Achel dis thirty years—worked hard—and see now, what better are I—I old and stiff—and I poor slave yet.'"[76] Though captured in the confines of her mistress's diary, this African American woman's quote speaks to the anguish of decades of work without reward or respite. Over the years, this woman probably saw friends and family move from bondage to freedom—whether it be from running away, receiving or earning manumission, or through the Act for Gradual Abolition—and yet her status always remained the same. Irrespective of the blood, sweat, or tears that she poured into her domestic labor, this African American woman, and many others like her in New Brunswick, remained enslaved.

The anecdotal evidence from Rachel Van Dyke's diary implicates New Brunswick's white women in the hands-on management of slaves within their household.[77] Importantly, unlike the rest of the state, New Brunswick enjoyed a steady white female majority in the early nineteenth century, seemingly granting white women greater power and autonomy in conducting household affairs.[78] One New Brunswick local named Mary Keyworth even published slave sale advertisements in her own name in the *Fredonian* in 1820.[79] In order for these women to perfect their household managerial positions within the

FIGURE 5.4 "Sylvia Dubois." Photograph from the Women's Project of New Jersey Records, MC 833 (Box 13), Special Collections and University Archives, Rutgers University Libraries.

antebellum "cult of domesticity," New Brunswick's upper- and middle-class white women in the early nineteenth century, like their counterparts in other locations of the slave holding United States, would have relied increasingly on black slave domestics.[80] This demand may have led black female domestics to supplant other forms of slave labor in the local market. This should not give the faulty impression that female domestic slaves in New Brunswick somehow fared better under the tutelage of white mistresses than their field-hand sisters in other parts of the state. Historian Thavolia Glymph has summarily discredited the myth of the benevolent white mistress, holding white women culpable for inflicting violence comparable to their patriarchal husbands.[81]

Nor did the apparent feminization of the New Brunswick slave market imply that enslaved life in New Brunswick was devoid of the notorious violence inherent to the South. Although Van Dyke did not make any reference to explicit violent confrontations with slaves in her diary, one instance suggested that nineteenth-century New Brunswickers did not hesitate to treat their slaves violently. After her maternal grandfather died, Van Dyke described how benevolent he was to a young enslaved boy, Edward. Van Dyke's heightened attention to her grandfather's kindness implied that kindness toward slaves was not the norm for nineteenth-century New Brunswick. Having bought Edward "when he was almost an infant," she wrote, her grandfather was "always . . . more like a father to him than a master."[82] Indeed, her distant cousin, Margaret, took pains to describe the upstanding manner in which her grandfather cared for his slaves. In 1906, Margaret compiled her recollections of her childhood during the 1820s and 1830s. She declared with certainty that her "Grandpa, tho' so severe, and I so young, was a priest in his own family and sacrificed for his children and 'retainers' daily, invoking God's care for the household."[83] These effusive remarks suggest that white slaveholders in New Brunswick paid little mind to violence—physical or otherwise—committed against the enslaved. The descriptions of slaves' bodies in runaway advertisements, replete with mentions of scarification and lameness, cement this contention.

Aside from the description of skill, other elements of slave sale advertisements between 1780 and 1835 spoke for the actively gendered nature of slavery in New Brunswick. In particular, statements on white expectations of slave personality and performance suggested a conscious effort to cultivate a feminized slave market based on domestic labor. Whereas the advertisements qualified the personalities of slaves directly with promises as to their sobriety, honesty, and industriousness, they reserved the term "respectable" to describe the selling family. The term was used to clarify that the family in which the slave had been raised was stable and had raised the slave in question to perform assigned tasks competently. More accurately, it was a coded acknowledgment that the seller's family had maintained the proper lines of authority over the chattel within their household. Thus, they had reared a slave who was, above all else, obedient and unlikely to cause problems for prospective buyers.[84] For example, an advertisement placed in the *Fredonian* in 1813 for a nineteen-year-old black woman proudly proclaimed that "having been born and brought up in a respectable family, she is accustomed to all kinds of housework. The gentleman in whose family she was brought up never knew her in the course of her life to have been intoxicated, or to have committed theft, which her present master can verify."[85] In this case, the respectability of the original slaveholder's family directly informed her ability to perform housework and indirectly informed her demeanor. Another advertisement from 1793 in the *Guardian; or, New Brunswick Advertiser* emphasized that the "Negro wench" in question was "brought up in the Rev. Van Dyke's family" in order to attract potential buyers.[86] The notion that a slaveholding family's respectability shaped the disposition of their slaves smacked of the paternalist ethos that apologists for slavery often attributed to the master-slave relationship. However, it is worth noting that in New Brunswick the question of a slaveholder's respectability is only brought to bear on advertisements for enslaved women. In this way, slave sale advertisements in late eighteenth- and early nineteenth-century New Brunswick applied "respectability" in order to specifically guarantee the behavior and performance of female slaves who had been purchased primarily to serve well-to-do white women as domestic servants. White slaveholding women in New Brunswick, as the closest point of contact between female domestic slaves and the white family, would have been directly responsible for the transmission of this respectability. Thavolia Glymph details how plantation mistresses in the South, aspiring to antebellum domestic perfection, regularly attempted to educate their domestic slaves to impart to them a kind of respectability based on work ethic and good manners.[87] More research is needed to determine more precisely the extent to which gendered expectations of female domestic slaves by white slaveholding women in the plantation South mapped onto the urban antebellum North.[88] It nonetheless stands that the question of familial respectability was irrelevant to transactions involving male slaves. A guarantee of compliance and moral soundness was of little importance for New Brunswickers purchasing males who would labor at a distance in fields. It was essential for female slaves intended for domestic labor who would experience the most spatial intimacy and interpersonal interaction with their prospective purchasers, especially considering the well-documented sexual threat that white mistresses felt female slaves posed to their potentially errant husbands and sons.[89] In this way, the investment of New Brunswick slave purchasers in the respectability of slaveholding families evinced the predilection for female domestic labor as the basic unit of New Brunswick slavery in the late eighteenth and early nineteenth centuries.

Another compositional element of the slave sale advertisement in New Brunswick newspapers—the "reason for sale"—similarly evinced the local orientation toward a feminized slave market. Typically, slave sale advertisements in late eighteenth- and early nineteenth-century New Brunswick did not list a specific reason for sale. One can assume from the naming of administrators and executors that the former owners of the slaves involved had died, prompting the sale in order to settle their estates.[90] Among those that did list a specific reason, the most common reason was for "want of employ," a bland but telling statement on the growing redundancy of African slave labor in early nineteenth-century New Jersey agriculture.[91] However, one unusual reason for sale was referenced solely in transactions involving female slaves: "dissatisfaction with current residence." It would be incorrect to assume that enslaved black women in early nineteenth-century New Brunswick were nothing but hapless pawns shuffled between New Brunswick households. Some took a page out of

Silvia Dubois's book and turned gendered expectations of their behavior on its head in order to achieve greater mobility, however limited that mobility may have been. An advertisement placed in the *Guardian; or, New Brunswick Advertiser* by Jacob Hardenbergh for the sale of a female domestic slave in New Brunswick quipped that she was "sold for no other reason other than being dissatisfied with her master's place of residence."[92] Hardenbergh was not completely alone in his rationale to sell his slave. Another advertisement placed in the same publication in 1815 similarly indicated that the twenty-five-year-old enslaved woman was "for sale at her own request."[93] It is tempting to read Hardenbergh's offer of sale as acquiescence to his slave's personal desires, perhaps instigated by the greater leverage afforded slaves after the enactment of gradual abolition.[94] However, this is unlikely considering Hardenbergh placed this advertisement in 1801. It is more probable that Hardenbergh, like many others, used the phrase euphemistically to disguise his own inability to control his slave's sullen and discontented behavior.[95] While life within the confines of slavery could easily emotionally compromise a woman and interfere with her ability to adequately perform her work, others may have deliberately donned and exaggerated discontented attitudes. This mundane, but apparently effective, form of resistance removed them from households that they disliked. But by the same token, this modicum of agency afforded to New Brunswick's enslaved female domestics came with a considerable inherent risk—they still retained no control over where, or to whom, they would be sold.

Challenging Precarity: Navigating Space and Negotiating Black Freedom in the African Association of New Brunswick

On November 12, 1825, John Bartley gathered with the congregants of New Brunswick's First Presbyterian Church to joyfully witness the baptism of his new bride, Ann Upshur Bartley. Two years later, the pious free black couple gathered again in the biracial church to dotingly watch the christening of their first daughter, Emily. The annotation "colored" followed both listings in the church registry, indicating their African ancestry as it did for the dozens of other black communicants of the First Presbyterian Church.[96]

The appearance of the Bartleys in the church ledger offers a fragmentary sketch of the family's important milestones—weddings and baptisms, and recordings of deaths. Indeed, this outline is more than we have for most African Americans, free or enslaved, in New Brunswick. Noteworthy, then, is the fact that Bartleys resurface in another set of New Brunswick records, this time in the African Association of New Brunswick, placing them in a predominantly black public space. The African Association, founded in 1817 for free and enslaved people of color to gather and discuss education, religion, and racial uplift in the United States and Africa, actually served as Ann and John's introduction to one another. In 1822, Peter Upshur, the president of the African Association and also Ann's father, invited John Bartley, Philadelphia native and student at the African School of Parsippany, New Jersey, to serve as primary teacher of the soon-to-be-established African School of New Brunswick. Accepting the invitation, John moved to New Brunswick in 1823 and joined the association, serving as secretary while funds were raised for the school. With meetings held regularly in the Upshur family home, the twenty-one-year-old Bartley inevitably met Ann Upshur, a woman eight years his senior and a member of the organization from the very beginning. The two were married by the time of Ann's baptism in 1825.[97] Subverting the persistent attempts of New Brunswick society to restrict the city's free black population and reduce them to the status of slaves, the African Association was foundational to the strengthening of black social ties in New Brunswick and is uniquely situated as a crucial space for black identity formation and the development of a black public sphere in the early nineteenth century.

As previously noted, relaxed policies on segregation made shared space, particularly in times of pleasure or reverence, not uncommon for New Brunswick. Whites and blacks, both free and enslaved, often gathered for baptisms in the First Presbyterian Church, attended weddings officiated in the home of the Reverend Joseph Clark, or partook in merriment at Halfpenny Town.[98] The lack of exclusively black spaces like churches made New Brunswick unique in this regard. While Newark, New Jersey, and Philadelphia were veritable hubs for the African Methodist Episcopal Church, the absence of any strong black church caused African Americans to gravitate toward New Brunswick's white congregations, among them First Presbyterian, First Reformed Church, and Christ Church (First Episcopal).[99] On one hand, the relative acceptance of integrated church space might be observed as a sign of progress, especially during the period of gradual emancipation. Blacks and whites worshipped and wed in the same space. They even mourned and buried their dead in the same cemeteries. On the other hand, exclusively black churches have long been considered linchpins of the antebellum African American community. Indeed, as scholar Eddie Glaude notes, black churches were "sites for a public discourse critical of white supremacy and the American nation-state as well as the spaces for identity construction."[100] Thus, the nonexistence of exclusively black spaces, particularly black churches, meant that New Brunswick was missing a crucial arena for black identity construction. Moreover, the absence meant that virtually all public spaces, even houses of worship, were subject to white surveillance and could be used as mechanisms for the social control of black New Brunswickers.

An investigation of the African Association of New Brunswick, then, offers a distinct window into the development of an exclusively black space (with some critical caveats) and the construction of black identity during the first three decades of the nineteenth century. Under the advisement of purportedly benevolent white men, some with unsavory ties to the American Colonization Society, the African Association of New Brunswick, which had originally been constructed to help finance an African School, became an interstitial space of freedom negotiated by free and enslaved blacks. Sure enough, the complicated and often paradoxical network associated within the African Association indicates that blacks were willing to ally with a multiplicity of characters in order to assert a modicum of freedom. Distinguished by its extensive social network, the association was not simply a meeting place for people of color; it was perhaps the only exclusively black space in New Brunswick.[101] This section uses the African Association as the point of entry to explore negotiations of freedom and black identity formation in early nineteenth-century New Jersey despite the adversity and precariousness that attended black life in New Brunswick. Additionally, it offers a preliminary exploration of how women navigated black public spheres like the African Association in order to assert a shred of agency in early nineteenth-century New Jersey.

In 1822, the African Association decided to establish an African School in New Brunswick. They recruited John Bartley from the African School of Parsippany, "who came highly recommended," as a teacher.[102] According to an 1823 advertisement in a New Brunswick newspaper, the African School opened at the start of the new year and was held in the home of Caesar Rappleyea, a longtime leader with the organization.[103] Thus, at the upper end of Church Street in downtown New Brunswick, a school was established by free and enslaved blacks for the "reception of COLOURED CHILDREN," just two blocks from the prison that regularly housed escaped slaves.[104] The spatial proximity of liberation and oppression could not be more striking as virtually every black New Jerseyan during the first half of the nineteenth century occupied an ambiguous status of unfreedom.

At the turn of the nineteenth century, the antislavery movement was escalating in the North but so was black political exclusion. In 1804, gradual abolition went into effect after the New Jersey Society for the Abolition of Slavery "petitioned for the abolition of slavery for the unborn."[105] White anxiety over the imminent increase in the free black population led the New Jersey Legislature to enact a law in 1807 that disenfranchised free black men, removing a liberty they had had since the American Revolution.[106] As the antislavery movement made incremental breakthroughs, retrogressive policies were set on upholding a racially stratified society. Even with the official abolishment or reclassification of "all former slaves as 'apprentices for life'" in 1846, the legal status of black Jerseyans was precarious from 1804 until the end of prima facie slavery in 1835.[107]

With the emergence of the African Association of New Brunswick on January 1, 1817, came one of the earliest iterations of a black public sphere in central

New Jersey. Though it was constructed for the sole purpose of supporting an African School for the "educating of young men of Colour to be teachers and preachers to people of colour within these states and beyond," it quickly became a space of black identity formation and racial uplift as members engaged in discussions on black education, Christianity, abolitionism, and colonization.[108] Some meetings were held in the Sessions Room at the First Presbyterian Church while the majority were held in the homes of free black New Brunswickers. With close ties to the First Dutch Reformed Church of New Brunswick and the First Presbyterian Church, the association initially funded the African School in Parsippany, New Jersey. The Parsippany school was founded in 1816 under the auspices of the Synod of New York and New Jersey, with the New Jersey American Colonization Society auxiliary succeeding them in leadership of the school not long after it was initially established.[109] Promoting Christianity and a decidedly gradualist abolitionist formula, the Parsippany school was designed to "educate free black New Jerseyans and instill 'proper' behavior in future ministers and public officials for Liberia."[110]

The African Association operated from 1817 to 1824. Committee meetings were held each month, but the New Year's anniversary meeting drew the largest crowds for any given year. Open to the entire black community of New Brunswick, it was a momentous occasion consisting first of dues collection for the school followed by an address from an influential black gentleman, usually a student or teacher from the Parsippany school or an abolitionist from the area. Noticeably, women made up a fourth to a third of anniversary gatherings.[111]

Enslaved people were also a noteworthy demographic. Though typically no more than 10 percent of attendees, Article Five of the constitution required that the enslaved present a "permit from his or her Master or Misstress signifying there Approbation" upon arrival to the meeting.[112] That slave owners would allow their enslaved permission to gather in the homes of free blacks, in such close proximity to freedom, illustrates the degree to which whites were willing to negotiate freedom and mobility. Article Five also shows how willingly the association negotiated with slave owners to advance its goals. In general, whites viewed the African Association as a welcome addition to the New Brunswick community, praising its potentially pacifying influence on the town's black population.[113]

The association's reputation definitely benefited from close ties to esteemed white men who were members of the African Colonization Society (ACS) or leaders at the African School of Parsippany. For the most part, these men intended for the African Association to serve as a representative model of black behavior to be emulated by other African Americans in the area. The African Association's relationship with the Reverend Mr. Huntington appears to be foundational to the organization's existence. Although his ties to the American Colonization Society are not fully understood, the pastor of the First Presbyterian Church of New Brunswick appears to have served as the first trustee of the African Association of New Brunswick and as an advisor to the ACS-sponsored African School at Parsippany. Huntington served as the conduit for all monies that flowed from the association to the Parsippany school until his death in 1820.[114] Joseph C. Hornblower stepped in when Huntington died. A long-standing member and one-time vice president of the American Colonization Society, Hornblower went on to become chief justice of the Supreme Court of New Jersey. Prior to his term, he served as treasurer of the African School at Parsippany, ensuring that all of the funds raised by the African Association from 1821 to 1822 were siphoned through his hands.[115]

Samuel B. How is another peculiar figure related to the African Association. A Dutch Reformed minister and later a Rutgers trustee, the Reverend How likewise served in an advisory position, continuing the trend of white control over the association's donations to the African School in Parsippany. Of the three men most closely affiliated with the organization, his connection brings the most pause. A slaveholder himself, How also trained black teachers and ministers in the African Association and the ACS. Nearly ten years after the legal (albeit superficial) end of slavery in New Jersey, the ardent anti-abolitionist argued that "slaveholding was without sin."[116]

Organizational oversight by these three respected figures of New Jersey's white community should indeed be read as yet another example of white surveillance over black life in New Brunswick under the guise of benevolence. Though using language that encouraged black self-determination through education and religion, Huntington, How, and Hornblower clearly drew the line when it came to management of the association's finances. Furthermore, their paternalistic view of the African Association as a character builder and as behavioral education—training African Americans for future and perhaps permanent service in Africa—was in line with the ACS's gradualist approach to the abolition of slavery and the organization's espousal of African American removal. As affiliates of the American Colonization Society, these men believed in "mediated black freedom with white supervision" and as a consequence promoted a platform that lacked clear paths toward black liberation and self-determination in the United States.[117] As James Gigantino notes, members of the ACS thought that the "most serious obstacles in the immediate emancipation of slaves . . . is that they are not prepared for the enjoyment of freedom." From the standpoint of the ACS, education through the African Schools equipped "free colored children for their usefulness" not in the United States but "in Africa."[118] This less than sanguine approach to abolition through removal maintained that blacks were unfit for American citizenship and residence in the United States. Of course, black support for education and colonization as "the best option in a state that had largely rejected black freedom" adds even more complexity to this already convoluted period of gradualism.[119] On the whole, however, ties to the Reverends How and Huntington, along with Mr. Hornblower, gave assurance to whites in the community that this was a measured and safe organization to which one could send slaves.

Because whites superficially understood the African Association as one of many tools at their disposal for extending social control over African Americans, they neglected to see how the African Association could serve as a subversive space for black identity formation. By granting "full permission to become a member of the African Association" in the hope that the association's model "would be followed by the many sons of Africa," slave owners granted their enslaved not only a taste of freedom but unbridled access to a nascent black community engaged in conversations about the meaning of freedom and the value of education in black-controlled spaces.[120] Furthermore, while "freedom" for all blacks might have been nominal in the greater landscape of New Brunswick, the permission slip process gave the monikers "free" and "slave" an internal meaning in the predominantly black atmosphere. Alone, the mingling of free and enslaved in an exclusively black space distinguished the African Association as an anomaly in the established system of relative integration. Further undermining the idea that this was an entirely safe organization for instilling "proper" behavior was the fact that the majority of meetings were held in the private homes of free blacks devoid of white surveillance, making them ideal spaces for black identity formation in the early decades of the nineteenth century. The January 1 meeting in the Sessions Room at the First Presbyterian Church would have been the only meeting of the year with the semblance of a white presence, undoubtedly making all other meetings exclusively and permissibly blacks-only spaces.

Conspicuously dry, then, are the minutes from meetings held in the homes of Peter Upshur, William Coryell, Caesar Rappleyea, Francis Parker, Cuffe Steel, and a host of other leaders in the association. The rather terse and nondescript notes leave many questions regarding the content of these gatherings. What did free and enslaved blacks discuss in the absence of white advisors? How might black networks and involvement in the emergent black public sphere have encouraged rather than quelled black resistance to slavery? How could a space like this alternatively serve the black community and subvert white perceptions of the organization? The answers could in fact lie in the silence that permeates the meeting minutes where no white man was present. That numerous monthly meetings were consistency held though "no business was done" raise suspicions that there was more to the organization than simply white pacification.[121] It would be a mistake to think that all members in the association agreed with the gradualist approach of their white advisors or that they gladly welcomed

How, Hornblower, and Huntington as self-appointed treasurers of their money. It is almost implausible to think that conversations rejecting gradualism did not take place in the privacy of black homes, where blacks could speak candidly about the various experiences of unfreedom.

Simply put, the African Association of New Brunswick was an anchor for community development and networking for blacks in the city. Contrary to other spaces in New Brunswick, the African Association gave enslaved and free blacks exclusive and intimate proximity to one another. On another level, the African Association might have served as an early iteration of black nationalism. "Black nationalism," Eddie Glaude explains, "finds its initial place in the various schemes of colonization or emigration designed to escape this tyranny and feelings of desperation and alienation."[122] Black nationalism in the early nineteenth century was not directly concerned with the construction of a black nation-state but rather a uniting of black people. Moreover, as Glaude argues, black "nation language" does not necessarily "predicate . . . a rejection of America."[123]

Taking into account Glaude's understanding of early black nationalism, speeches and letters delivered to the African Association similarly reveal blacks grappling with their identity as "sons and daughters of Ethiopia" and as Americans.[124] For example, Gustavus V. Caesar, a student at the Parsippany African School, simultaneously embraced both colonization and a Black Atlantic identity. In 1821, he wrote the African Association praising the "union among us people of colour of this nature."[125] "You are the first united band of Africans," Caesar announced, "that has ever put forth their hands in the great work of sending heralds of the cross to your perishing brethren."[126] In the same vein, another speaker emphatically addressed the group, stating, "We ought to thank the god of heaven that we are so highly favored." Blessed with the opportunity of education and Christianity, he advised, "'Up you get back to the land of your fathers'—go carry light, liberty, laws and civilization."[127]

Indeed, educated blacks and abolitionists felt burdened with a responsibility to enlighten their kin across the Atlantic, who were "by all account many centuries involved in gross ignorance . . . our condition only a century ago."[128] Addressing those who gathered for the 1820 anniversary meeting, Jeremiah Gloucester asked, "But Brethern have you forgot that your fellow mortals, who have not the privaledge you enjoy; yea those that are destitute of both temporal & spiritual knowledge? . . . For your eyes have been opened in a country [the United States] . . . and soon we shall be the heirs of [public and social benefits]."[129] Admittedly, many of the black speakers deployed a "gradualist rhetoric of education and empowerment" much aligned with their white mentors. To this end, they simultaneously "influenced some Jersey blacks to see colonization as a viable option for their future lives as freedmen," while expressing black nationalist language that sought to unite disparate blacks across the Atlantic Basin.[130]

Understanding that freedom for blacks in America was not yet fully realized, many members of the African Association saw education and racial uplift as an avenue "to restore that liberty they have taken from us," as well as a way to spiritual liberation.[131] Thus, the early black nationalist ethos of the African Association, while locked in an intricate web of colonization and white paternalism, believed education would redeem a "hapless race who long have been/In darkness, slavery and sin" and, in doing so, unite the blacks in America and Africa.[132] Navigating uneven alliances with unpalatable, even racist, powerbrokers who attempted to circumscribe all areas of black life, members of the African Association were able to carve out critical space for black identity formation in early nineteenth-century New Brunswick. Black women—who significantly outnumbered the black men in early nineteenth-century New Brunswick—also used the African Association itself to acquire a modicum of agency that defied traditional interpretations of nineteenth-century gender norms. Article Three of the African Association constitution made clear the gendered order of the organization: "Officers shall be chosen by the Mail members from the male members only."[133] As such, the minutes books of the African Association reflect strict adherence to the internal policy of male enfranchisement. Officers as well as the standing committee—the decision-making body of the association that met monthly—could only be chosen by and from the male members of the organization.[134] However, despite their second-class positioning, women sustained a constant presence in the organization throughout its existence. The disenfranchisement of black men in New Jersey in 1807 caused black men to jealously guard their voting privileges in the association, but this privilege by no means meant that women were passive spectators at meetings.[135] At the inaugural meeting of the association, black women made up 28 percent of the initial subscribers—twelve of the forty-four attendees. Indeed, women maintained visibility in the organization. Never falling below 20 percent, their peak attendance occurred in July of 1822 at 42 percent.[136]

Women like Ann and Nancy Upshur, Sarah Ball, and Margaret Utt were consistent attendees and contributors to the organization for nearly eight years, paying their fifty-cent dues just like the men.[137] Additionally, a fair number of enslaved women took advantage of the circumscribed mobility granted by their masters to attend the almost uniformly black gatherings. For example, an enslaved woman named Phillis obtained a pass from her master, John Neilson, a Queen's College affiliate, to attend the January 1, 1820, anniversary celebration. "Phillis Nelson" joined the association for at least three more gatherings over the next three years, contributing her subsidized membership fee of twenty-five cents each time it met.[138] It is clear, then, that black women, free and enslaved, in the New Brunswick community found the African Association to be of great value. Despite its male-centric organization, they found ways to inhabit that space and contribute financially no matter their sociopolitical or economic status. While the records reveal little more than their presence, it is worth considering how black women might have navigated this space.[139]

The lives of Nancy and Ann Upshur offer some clues. This mother/daughter team, members of the organization at the time of its inception, were likely able to assert a degree of agency through their close relationship with Peter Upshur, an association president described by the white minister of Newark Presbyterian as a man with a "an intelligent eye . . . and a general physiognomy indicative of vigorous intellect."[140] To be sure, while this description cannot be divorced from its decidedly racist undertones, positive relationships with men of influence could mean unparalleled mobility and opportunity. Peter Upshur's actual profession remains unclear, but his standing in New Jersey is evident. Upshur was regarded with "much respect by the whites" and according to the Newark pastor, he "exerts a benign influence over his colored brethren" as well.[141]

The Upshur home was regularly open to free and enslaved black men and women in the New Brunswick community, ensuring the influence of not only Peter but also Nancy and Ann. When Peter Upshur died suddenly in July 1823, the location of the standing committee meeting was not moved but remained in what was then recorded as "the house of Mrs. Nancy Upshur." Association dues collected for the Upshurs were then listed under "Ann L. Upshur and Co.," indicating Ann's shift from daughter to head of household.[142] Sometime around 1823 or 1824, Ann entered a courtship with John Bartley, the African School teacher and newly appointed secretary; however, it would be an error to assume that she receded from influence. By the time John made his way to the organization in 1822, Ann had essentially apprenticed for six years under one of the most prominent leaders of New Brunswick's black community and organization—her father. Marriage to Bartley would only allow her to maintain her influence in the association and the New Brunswick community more broadly, especially after the sudden death of her father. It is quite plausible, given her long-standing membership and understanding of the association, that Ann assisted in, if not directly managed, the day-to-day administrative duties of the African School of New Brunswick. More familiar with the social landscape of black New Brunswick than her husband, Ann probably served as John Bartley's gateway to the New Brunswick community. Leveraging her position as wife and lifelong New Brunswick resident, Ann Upshur Bartley, and, undoubtedly, other black women in the African Association, were able to gain a degree of agency and influence through intergenerational familial ties as well as through marriages to educated and respected men from their communities.[143]

Because women maintained strong regular attendance, it is safe to assume that free and enslaved women valued the networking opportunities and missional focus of the organization. In addition to Ann and Nancy Upshur, Sarah

Ball and relatives Margaret and Rachel Utt were regular attendees whose dues contributed to the establishment of the African School in New Brunswick. Numerous other women were able to attend less frequently or just once due to the constraints of motherhood, enslavement, or both. Nonetheless, their individual donations, ranging from as much as one dollar to as little as six and a half cents, helped to make the African School possible.[144]

As evidenced from speeches delivered by male members and affiliates of the organization, many men saw education and the work of racial uplift as a communal effort to be taken on by the men *and* women of the black community. Speakers frequently addressed the "brothers and sisters"[145] of the assembled body, charging all with the responsibility of bringing culture, Christianity, and enlightenment to blacks in America and Africa. Black abolitionist and Philadelphia native Jeremiah Gloucester acknowledged the significance of "Africas sons and daughters . . . combining themselves into societies" for "the purpose of instructing her sons, into scientific knowledge, and to have a rank among the rest of mankind."[146] Speakers largely refrained from using gendered language that denoted a higher "moral" obligation for women and a greater educational incentive for men. Christian sentimentalism and morality was evoked to "inspire each one of us with a more ardent affection for the deplorable condition of our fellow Creatures so that others around us may be induced to follow our example."[147]

Though the association was designed for "educating young *men* of Colour to be teachers and preachers," women most likely saw their participation as contributing to the collective advancement of black people.[148] Perhaps some women like an Ann Upshur privately protested the male-centric educational emphasis while publicly supporting the organization's general cause. Others, based on their donations, considered the education of their men as a progressive step toward the liberation of the race. Unfortunately, the records are wanting and leave much to be desired regarding the internal gender politics of this black community organization. On the whole, more scholarship is needed to better understand how women navigated the early nineteenth-century male-dominated black public sphere. What is evident, however, is that black women were steadfast contributors to the cause of black education, Christian missions, racial uplift, and other causes of the African Association. Giving time, money, and, likely, their voices to this complicated yet influential organization, black women were vital supporters of a nascent black public sphere in spite of their secondary positioning in the organization.

Conclusion

At the outset, this essay was an attempt to encapsulate African American experience in New Brunswick during the era of slavery, stretching from the colonial era in 1766 to the death knell of the legal category of "slave" in New Jersey in 1835. Admittedly, it has fallen short. It is not possible to deliver a generalized pronouncement on the character of African American life in New Brunswick during the era of slavery. The archive sharply limits what is knowable about New Brunswick's enslaved thousands, refracting their lives through the calculating gaze of white slaveholders and the disinterested structure of newspaper columns and street maps. Even those possessing the same legal status of "free" cannot be seamlessly blended into a composite portrait of a "typical" free New Brunswick black. Daring runaways like Charlotte/Brook and Thomas Somers led lives that differed markedly from the quiet dignity displayed by Caesar Rappleyea and Ann Upshur. While precise details on individual lives continue to elude us (and perhaps always will), we have nonetheless succeeded in sketching some of the contours of African American life in antebellum New Brunswick, such as the gendered nature of New Brunswick slavery. Paramount among these contours was the pervasive precariousness that cut across the varying legal statuses of the African American residents of New Brunswick in the late eighteenth and early nineteenth century. Runaways who passed through New Brunswick en route to more promising locations, local slave women who served in the homes of wealthy white elites, and free blacks with a modicum of social mobility were treated with the same callous indifference by the law. They were subject to the same geography that systematically reminded them that very little separated the free from the enslaved. At the same time, codified precariousness was not an impenetrable wall that utterly entombed black life in the city in the early nineteenth century. In a society that enforced the precariousness of black life by dispersing black families and circumscribing the formation of black communities, the African Association flourished as a remarkable testament to the resilience and ingenuity of New Brunswick's African American population. If nothing else, we have continued the historiographical work of undermining the outmoded dichotomy that posits New Jersey as a space of limitless black freedom opposite the cruel repression of the slaving South. In closing, we admit that the findings of this investigation into African American life in late eighteenth- and early nineteenth-century New Brunswick are, in fact, preliminary. We have raised far more questions than we have answered. What compelled runaways like Charlotte/Brook or free people like Silvia DuBois to either settle in New Brunswick or leave the city behind? To what extent did the relationship between Southern white mistresses and female domestic slaves in the antebellum plantation South translate into the urban North? How exactly did free black women like Ann and Nancy Upshur, alongside their enslaved counterparts, contribute to their interstitial black public sphere on a day-to-day basis? We hope these questions will animate future research on the history of slavery in New Jersey.

6

From the Classroom to the American Colonization Society

Making Race at Rutgers

Beatrice Adams, Tracey Johnson, Daniel Manuel, and Meagan Wierda

"Citizens of New-Jersey," exhorted Theodore Frelinghuysen, a fellow New Jerseyan, at an 1824 meeting of the state's colonization society, "—we appeal to you—survey your cultivated fields—your comfortable habitations—your children rising around you to bless you. Who, under Providence, caused those hills to rejoice, and those vallies to smile?—who ploughed those fields and cleared those forests?" His answer may have come as a surprise to some, as he demanded that his audience "remember the toil and the tears of black men, and pay [their] debt to Africa."[1] According to Frelinghuysen, the people of New Jersey owed their prosperity, security—indeed, their very happiness—to African American men. Disregarding the often-invisible labor of African American women, New Jersey's attorney general then invoked the transactional language of debt to convey the urgency of his cause. This language was not neutral. If New Jerseyans—and Americans more broadly—were indebted to Africa, it was because they had plundered its shores, stealing untold numbers of men, women, and children to be monetized first and then later sold. Indeed, the moral debt to which Frelinghuysen gestured was that incurred by Americans as a result of slavery.

Serving as an ambassador for the recently formed American Colonization Society (ACS), Theodore Frelinghuysen went on to condemn the slave trade, the institution of slavery, and the Janus-faced idea of freedom that resulted from the American Revolution. "On the same breeze have been borne to the ear," he argued, "the grateful shouts of American Freemen and the heart-sickening groans of subjugated Slaves."[2] Frelinghuysen recognized, like many of his fellow colonizationists, that freedom in the United States was conditional upon the color of one's skin. In spite of this, he would not advocate for racial equality, nor would he advocate for a more capacious definition of freedom, one that would extend civil rights to African Americans. Instead, Frelinghuysen favored the removal of newly freed blacks from the United States. Sustaining the belief that freedom and blackness were antithetical to one another, he argued that the "exigencies of circumstance may properly prevent [slavery's] prompt abolition—yet the duty of *gradually* removing so tremendous a curse, presses upon us with all the weight of eternity."[3]

Gradual abolition—a politics that rejected the immediate and unconditional emancipation of slaves—was the guiding principle of the American Colonization Society. Indeed, it was the guiding principle of many antislavery advocates during the first third of the nineteenth century. This was in large measure owing to the influence of Protestantism on antebellum reform. Calvinist theology, in both its Presbyterian and Dutch Reformed guises, shaped the early intellectual and spiritual outlook of north New Jersey and the areas around Manhattan and the Hudson River Valley. Both denominations, particularly their congregations in New Jersey, generally opposed radical social change, a stand that placed them firmly against the immediate abolition of slavery. From the early seventeenth century through the nineteenth century, Dutch Reformed theology cleaved to doctrines of predestination. The Synod of Dordrecht in 1618–1619 became a cornerstone of Dutch Calvinism, as it refuted notions of human free will and affirmed the Church's belief in unconditional election, the idea that God ordained the salvation or damnation of each individual before the creation of the world. In an intellectual tradition that ascribed all meaningful decisions and outcomes to divine will, there was little room for decisive human action. The Dutch brought strong Calvinist sentiments with them when they colonized and settled in New Jersey and New York in the years immediately after Dordrecht, and Dutch theologians and ministers in the Americas continued to defend unconditional election as a guiding ideal through the mid-nineteenth century. Conservative Calvinists, and most branches of Protestantism generally, had little to say on the topic of slavery, but they often opposed abolitionism, favoring moderate reforms or amelioration of the system's most visible abuses. As late as 1855, Dutch Reformed minister Samuel How, a member of Rutgers's board of trustees, deployed thoroughly Calvinist thinking in his defense of slaveholding. Echoing ideas of divine predestination and abhorrence of free will, he declared any radical human action on slavery to be a grave mistake. Only God could right slavery, he argued, as it was a social evil that resulted from humanity's fall from grace.[4] Framing slavery as a preordained and divinely willed institution, Reformed ministers built theological arguments against abolition or virtually any other radical challenges to the social and economic status quo.[5]

In many respects, then, gradualism appeared as a natural outgrowth of the social and intellectual culture of the period. The conservative nature of Calvinism tempered the fervency otherwise associated with the Second Great Awakening, the Protestant revivalism that swept the country during the first half of the nineteenth century. In particular, the newfound emphasis on salvation demanded not only the repentance of personal sin but societal ones more broadly. With respect to the latter, perhaps none were more pressing than America's original sin: slavery. For many Protestants in New Jersey and New York, however, antislavery reform took a decidedly conservative bent, one that ultimately looked to preserve divinely ordained racial hierarchies.

Historians of New Jersey and the larger Mid-Atlantic, including New York and Pennsylvania, have argued for the region's peculiarity. From the colonial era through the antebellum period, the Mid-Atlantic colonies or states defied any effort at easy categorization with Puritan New England or the plantation South. Nearly four decades ago, historian Douglas Greenberg observed that the Middle Colonies' "social diversity and ethnic-religious pluralism" caused them to stand out from the more homogenous North and South. While the Middle Colonies never came to rely as heavily on slave labor as the South, Greenberg acknowledged a similarity in racial politics between the regions, as "race and racism were crucially determinative components not only of the slave system but of the law generally" in the Middle Colonies. James Gigantino noted the continuity of this sympathy with Southern slaveholders among New Jersey's legislators during the early national and antebellum periods, and Emily Blanck described New Jersey as "a liminal state." She suggests that in its position "as the fulcrum of balance between slave societies and societies with small populations of slaves," New Jersey "gives us insight into the nature of that intermediate status."[6] These mixed allegiances to North and South ensured a prolonged struggle, as New Jersey grappled with the antislavery impulses of the postrevolutionary period.

New Jersey, whose location in the Mid-Atlantic defied the ideological and political geography of the "North," thus found itself in the thorny position of shrinking from both the institution of slavery as well as the enslaved. Far from representing an ideological contradiction, this abhorrence of bondage and blacks was commonplace during the period. As gradual emancipation extended across the Northeast, the region's free black population not only began to increase but it also began to flourish. African Americans both joined and founded antislavery societies; established a black press; were ministers, doctors, artists, and educators; and against all odds, created the conditions for thriving free black communities. Not only did this produce resentment among whites but also overwrought fears about the consequences of the demographic increase of free people of color. Indeed, as society's boundaries became increasingly difficult to police, white Americans no longer looked to restrict membership to the

American Republic based on whether an individual was free or unfree. Instead, they increasingly turned to biology to answer political questions. As racial difference and fitness for citizenship were increasingly inscribed upon bodies, it became all but impossible for blacks to be recognized as citizens of the United States. If the ultimate goal was to create a white body politic, the appeal of the ACS—with its goal of excising the country's free black population—becomes all the more obvious.

It is important to note, however, that the process of race-making during the antebellum period was not solely the task of racial scientists. Indeed, the drawing of lines between whites and blacks occurred within courthouses, classrooms, and churches. These institutions were in constant conversation with one another and, together, provided a degree of authority to claims about racial difference. In particular, New Jersey's Rutgers College was perfectly poised to weigh in on these debates. Given its position in the Mid-Atlantic and drawing on the intellectual heritage of the Dutch Reformed Church, Rutgers was a bulwark for race-making and the ACS's brand of gradualism. Indeed, the dual imperatives of antislavery and antiblackness would prove formative for the college as well as her agents, as they tried to contend with antebellum demands for reform. By rejecting a radical politics of antislavery in favor of gradualism, men like Philip Milledoler and Theodore Frelinghuysen would ultimately betray the liberationist possibilities of Protestantism. Along with instructors in the college and medical school, they would demonstrate the extent to which universities and their representatives were arbiters of both race and freedom during the antebellum period. Their claims would not go unchallenged, however, as free blacks contested a reformism rooted in prejudice, assumptions about their perpetual degradation, and the belief that freedom and blackness were antithetical upon U.S. soil.

The Dutch and the Theological Roots of Rutgers's Slaveholding Founders

The Dutch staked their claims to present-day New York and New Jersey through the earliest years of the seventeenth century. In 1609 Henry Hudson, under the patronage of the Dutch East India Company, explored the river now named for him and planted the seeds of Dutch influence. Members of Hudson's exploratory party described Manhattan Island as land "as pleasant with Grasse and Flowers, and goodly Trees, as ever they had seene," and here the heart of the future colony would sit. By 1617, the Dutch had established several trading houses on Manhattan and established Fort Nassau on the future site of Albany, New York. The Dutch West India Company (WIC) received a charter for monopoly control of the Dutch colonies in the Americas in 1621, and, three years later, it began to move settlers into regions surrounding the Connecticut, Delaware, and Hudson Rivers. The most important settlement was New Amsterdam on the southern tip of Manhattan Island at the mouth of the Hudson.[7]

The New Netherland colony faced considerable challenges before finally falling into British hands. Historians have consistently cited mismanagement by colonial administrators. Moreover, ineffective policies, like the parceling out of lands akin to a feudal system, discouraged settlement and immigration. As late as 1650, roughly 2,000 populated New Netherland, while some 30,000 had settled in New England. When the Dutch surrendered the relatively short-lived colony to British forces in 1664, the population had attained 9,000 settlers and some 500 slaves.[8] Despite its lethargic growth and brief existence, the Dutch settlement radiating out from Manhattan left an indelible mark on the Eastern Seaboard.

As it established both economic and religious institutions, the Dutch West India Company shaped the tenor of life in the colony. After receiving its charter, the WIC governed the importation of slaves into New Netherland. For much of the period of Dutch control, the importation of slaves was relatively lethargic, but the company nonetheless viewed slaves as essential to the agricultural and overall development of the colony. Events near the end of Dutch control turned slavery into the prime economic concern of the colony. The Dutch captured Curaçao, a critical supply depot in the transatlantic slave trade, from the Spanish in 1634. The Dutch also took El Mina, the slaving "fort" off Africa's west coast, from the Portuguese in 1637. After the loss of colonies in Brazil in 1654, the company shifted its attention to making New Netherland into a market for slaves. Thus, the importation of enslaved Africans into the colony increased dramatically. There were fewer than 100 slaves in the colony in 1656, but between 1660 and 1665, 403 slaves arrived. While the Dutch surrendered New Netherland only days after the arrival of several hundred of these slaves, they had established the foundation of a slave society, and the British would only tighten the legal structures of slavery. Though it was hardly committed to supporting the Church, the WIC had also pronounced the Reformed Protestant Dutch Church the official state church in the colonies. The company employed the first minister, or *dominie*, Jonas Michaelius in New Netherland, although it only brought Michaelius to North America in 1628, some five years after the first settlers arrived. Succeeding ministers also depended on the company's support for their livelihoods, but the number of company-employed *dominies* remained small throughout the Dutch period.[9]

Financially and theologically, ministers of the Dutch Reformed Church had little incentive to challenge slavery in the New Netherland colony. The WIC saw slavery as essential to colonial development, and many company officials were slaveholders. This put ministers, who drew their salaries from the company, in an uncomfortable position if they wished to speak against slavery, yet few within the Reformed Church saw any moral conflicts between Christianity and slavery. The deep implication of the Dutch in the slave trade meant that religious officials in the Netherlands voiced little criticism, and for much of the seventeenth and eighteenth centuries, all Reformed Church ministers, even those serving in the colonies, received their training in the metropole. Among the few religious leaders speaking on slavery was Godfried Udemans, and his 1638 text, *On the Spiritual Rudder of the Merchant Ship*, merely encouraged good treatment and education for the enslaved, with eventual emancipation as an ideal. Finally, through the late eighteenth century, a number of Reformed Church ministers in the American colonies owned, sold, purchased, and accepted slaves as payment of debts. There was, thus, no pronounced, theologically grounded challenge to slavery in the colonies.

Even if they had not been dependent on the company, Dutch ministers evinced little consideration for enslaved Africans. Writing to a friend four years after the colony's establishment, Michaelius, the first minister in New Netherland, described his female slaves as "thievish, lazy, and useless trash." He condemned the women's alleged greed and lethargy, but he quickly went on to voice considerable complaints about the scarcity of resources and inadequacy of rations provided by the WIC. "Every one is short . . . and wants more," he noted, regarding the needs of Dutch settlers, who did not warrant the same condemnations as those of slaves. Many ministers referred disparagingly to blacks throughout the Dutch and English colonial periods. They often spoke of blacks' irresponsibility and compared them to children or dogs.[10] This language persisted for centuries after the arrival of Africans on the continent, and it shaped the welcome they received in the Reformed Church.

Freed and enslaved Africans and the first generation of blacks born in the Americas sought membership in the Reformed Church. In the earliest years of the New Netherland colony, black men and women were able to marry and be baptized within the Church. These religious institutions elevated the social standing of many Africans and lent social legitimacy to their families. Because Dutch society viewed marriage and households as foundational to a stable society and orderly community, it is possible that the blessing of black men and women's nuptials meant that they were viewed as part of the early colony-building enterprise. Moreover, many blacks strategically selected witnesses, or godparents, for their children during baptism. Because transatlantic slavery separated families, black parents worked to establish networks of kinship for their children—namely, through the selection of godparents. In this way, and by marrying within the Church, Africans and their creole children were able to use Christianity to create new types of families and ameliorate some of the most brutal aspects of the slave trade. Many of these networks overlapped and reinforced each other, as men like Cleyn Anthony van Angola served as witnesses for multiple children's baptisms in 1641, bridging distinct families and linking a new generation of black Americans through Christianity.

As slavery became increasingly important to the New Netherland colony, however, blacks' access to the church declined. As historian Susanah Romney has noted, the number of baptisms and marriages of blacks decreased in the 1650s and 1660s, the same years that saw sharp increases in the number of blacks in the colony. It was an early signal of whites' anxieties about growing numbers of blacks on the American continent. By denying enslaved and free blacks access to marriage and baptism, ministers not only denied these families and individuals considerable social capital but also blocked potential avenues to freedom.[11]

As slavery became central to the New Netherland colony, access to religious institutions probably withered because it potentially promised freedom. Writing near the end of Dutch rule in the 1660s, the Reverend Henricus Selyns explained to Church officials in Amsterdam why local ministers denied baptism to African slaves. "The negroes occasionally request that we should baptize their children," he began, "but we have refused to do so." Ministers doubted slaves' knowledge of the faith, but in the requests for baptism, they also suspected "worldly and perverse aims on the part of said negroes." "They want nothing else than to deliver their children from bodily slavery, without striving for piety and Christian virtues," he complained. On both sides of the Atlantic in the seventeenth century, there was considerable debate about whether baptism conferred freedom upon slaves and whether Christians could be enslaved. As late as the eighteenth century, British colonists, with no official guidance from the Church of England, assumed that baptism freed slaves. Thus, many seventeenth-century Dutch slaveholders dodged theological concerns altogether and forbade the baptism of their slaves, fearing that baptism potentially meant emancipation. While one historian has noted that blacks in New Netherland experienced "greater freedom" than those living in other colonies, she also admits that few were embraced as full communicants in the Church.[12] Colonial officials quickly delimited the bounds of freedom, like baptism and religious participation, when they threatened slavery.[13] For the most part, baptism remained out of the reach of most blacks until the end of the eighteenth century.

Only in the late eighteenth century did the Reformed Church affirm the spiritual equality of free and enslaved people, but it in no way challenged the institution of slavery on this premise. The Church's Constitution of 1792 declared: "In the Church there is no difference between bond and free, but all are one in Christ." Notably, equality existed only "in the Church." Legal and social differences were accepted social conventions, which the Church embodied. The constitution promised "full communion" to any "slaves or black people" who were baptized, and any minister who denied black church members "the privileges to which they are entitled, shall, upon complaint being exhibited and proved, be severely reprimanded."[14] The document could have led to an increased number of baptized blacks, but it more accurately illustrated the Church's racial outlook. Baptism in no way altered a slave's legal status.

Increasingly disconnected from its European roots, the Dutch Reformed Church in America pushed for greater autonomy. Since its arrival on American shores, the Reformed Church had depended on the Classis of Amsterdam to provide ministers. The Church in America lacked approved facilities for theological instruction and ordination, and thus had to send its would-be ministers to, or request clergy from, the Netherlands. In the 1740s, the First Great Awakening renewed enthusiasm in the Dutch Reformed Church, and the trickling supply of ministers proved inadequate for the growing number of congregations. Moreover, Amsterdam retained the authoritative word in the American Church's theological and internal disputes. By the mid-eighteenth century, American Church officials found this relationship "defective, fruitless, and disagreeable" and, in 1754, a body of ministers convened an American Classis, independent of Amsterdam. A year later, the body met again to request the creation of a college in the colonies to train ministers. After turning away the petitioners for a decade, William Franklin, the royal governor of New Jersey, granted the charter for Queen's College, the future Rutgers College, on November 10, 1766.[15]

With an undergraduate institution in place, the Reformed Church still needed a reliable source for theological training. The New Brunswick Theological Seminary's roots reach back to 1784, when the Reverend John Henry Livingston offered private theological instruction for students in New York City. Livingston received no compensation from the Church, but, in 1806, the Church issued an appeal for funds to pay for an established professorship. By 1808 the need had been well met, and the Church officially hired Livingston as professor of theology. The seminary moved to New Brunswick to share facilities with the undergraduate college at Queen's. Both institutions moved into the college's first permanent structure, Old Queens, in 1811. They shared these accommodations until the middle of the nineteenth century. The early histories of the college and the seminary were thus nearly inseparable. As historian John Coakley has noted, small slaveholding Dutch farmers in Bergen County provided many of the financial subscriptions. Thus, slaveholders' patronage provided the financial support to establish the college's facilities and the first professorship in theology at the seminary.[16]

Through the early national and antebellum periods, the Reformed Protestant Dutch Church remained relatively small, even while Methodists, Baptists, and Anglicans saw periods of tremendous growth. In part, the Church remained small by its own design. Though it had conducted services in English since the late eighteenth century, the Church continued to cater almost exclusively to people of Dutch descent. Moreover, only after the Civil War did it adopt a more Americanized name, the Reformed Church in America. Because of its exclusivity, the Reformed Church saw little growth in the early nineteenth century and remained tied predominantly to areas north of the Raritan River.[17]

Perhaps the Reformed Church's small size and fear of schism discouraged active debate about slavery. Clergy and church officials had seen the deep sectional and ideological lines that slavery carved in other churches. For example, congregants expelled one Presbyterian minister from his Bethlehem, New Jersey, parish during the 1840s for speaking against slavery. While Presbyterians divided over other theological concerns, slavery created additional internal divisions that lingered long after the Civil War. Similarly, Baptist churches split into southern and northern factions in 1845 over slavery. That same year, Southern churches withdrew from the national Methodist Episcopal Church, creating a regional division that lasted nearly a century. Until the 1850s, most Reformed Church ministers remained silent about slavery. Already divided over a doctrinal debate similar to the Presbyterians', about the compatibility of revivals and Calvinism, the Reformed Church steered clear of the divisive and provoking issue of slavery.[18]

In fact, like the Reformed Church, the New Brunswick Theological Seminary and Rutgers College approached slavery conservatively. Unlike more liberal churches in northern New York that as a result of the Great Awakening embraced both antislavery and black equality, the seminary and most Rutgers trustees embraced antislavery but also black inequality. On the one hand, their belief that slavery was a sin that God would punish them for led many to be abolitionists. But on the other, they rejected black equality because of their belief that God had ordained the prevailing social hierarchy that placed whites above blacks.[19] This made those associated with the seminary and college perfect advocates for the American Colonization Society.

New Jersey and the Meaning and Philosophy of the American Colonization Society

The American Colonization Society (ACS) was a self-proclaimed antislavery organization formed in 1816, whose ultimate goal was to facilitate the removal of the country's free black population to West Africa. Undeniably a product of the Second Great Awakening, the ACS believed that by participating in the slave trade Americans had accrued a moral debt that could only be discharged by reversing the flow of peoples across the Atlantic. Indeed, colonizationists were far more attuned to past wrongdoings than inequities that beset free and enslaved blacks in the present. Instead of advocating for immediate freedom and equality for individuals of African descent, the ACS campaigned on a platform of gradualism, whereby emancipation was contingent upon emigration. For colonizationists, to be truly free and black within the United States was an oxymoron.

It is not difficult to understand the allure of the American Colonization Society. Its gradualist stance evoked the humanitarian reform impulses extant in America during the first third of the nineteenth century. For many reformers, gradualism—if not colonization—was the preferred iteration of antislavery activism. In fact, well-known abolitionists like William Lloyd Garrison, Arthur and Lewis Tappan, and Gerrit Smith were all members of the organization during its formative years. By the early 1830s, however, they had ultimately rejected the ACS's gradualism in favor of the immediate and unconditional emancipation of blacks. Still, their affiliation with the ACS—however brief—demonstrates the extent to which the ideology of gradualism proved not only seductive but also legitimate to many Americans in the North and the South, as well as the liminal space of the Mid-Atlantic states.[20]

In part, the widespread, interregional appeal of the American Colonization Society derived from the changing social and political landscape of the antebellum period. With the growing commitment to emancipation came the concurrent growth of the free black population. In an historical moment preoccupied with the difficulties of establishing and acknowledging various social identities in a republic (theoretically) based on the infinite potential of each individual, social flux proved troubling to many.[21] Straddling the line between repentance for slavery and the maintenance of racial hierarchies, the ACS would ultimately satisfy both antislavery and antiblack impulses.

Though the ideologies animating the ACS were by no means unique to New Jersey, as Americans in both the North and South simultaneously harbored antislavery and antiblack beliefs, the Garden State proved to be especially fertile ground for the entrenchment of a gradualist politics during the first half of the nineteenth century. Indeed, New Jersey defied assumptions about the supposed ideological consistency and continuity of the "North," as the state legislature's comparatively late passage of the Act for the Gradual Abolition of Slavery in 1804 makes clear. This law was inconsistent with a radical politics of emancipation and equality. The absence of a large commercial center, the entrenchment of slavery in the eastern half of the state, and the dearth of powerful white allies all but ensured the timid advancement of abolition in New Jersey.[22]

Perhaps most glaringly, the 1804 law produced what historian James Gigantino has labeled "slaves for a term." The law compelled children born to slave mothers after July 4th, 1804, to labor for their masters for twenty-one years (females) and twenty-five years (males). Moreover, it failed to account for those individuals already enslaved.[23] The results of the Act for Gradual Abolition were enduring. Slavery was not abolished in New Jersey during the antebellum period, as at least eighteen "colored apprentices for life" were recorded in the state as late as 1860.[24] It is important to note that the use of the term *apprentice* was simply a metonym for "slave," a designation the state had abolished in 1846.[25] As this new nomenclature serves to demonstrate, however, the half-life of slavery in New Jersey was lengthy. Furthermore, New Jersey was the only Northern state to vote against the Thirteenth, Fourteenth, and Fifteenth Amendments, respectively abolishing slavery, granting citizenship and equal protection under the law to formerly enslaved peoples, and prohibiting federal and state governments from prejudicially denying a citizen the right to vote.[26] Though the amendments were eventually ratified, slavery died a begrudging death in New Jersey. Moreover, because the 1804 law attacked slavery in piecemeal fashion, ultimately allowing for the maintenance of the prevailing social hierarchy, it was all but impossible for African Americans to dispel long-standing beliefs associating blackness with inferiority.

Though New Jersey's gradual abolition law ensured that slavery's demise would be protracted, vibrant free black communities increasingly began to dot the landscape in the decades leading up to the Civil War. In New Brunswick, home to Rutgers College, free and enslaved blacks laid claim to a district named Halfpenny Town. Passing by one summer evening in 1810, a young female diarist recorded that at "Halfpenny town the negroes were all assembled in their Sunday clothes, as happy and as merry as Lords and Ladies."[27] Continuing, she noted that "some were gambling with Cents, some dancing to the violin others talking and laughing—and all appeared to be without care—only regardful how they might enjoy the passing moment."[28] Although the diarist echoed centuries-old imagery of blacks as lazy, immature presentists, her recorded comments evidence a vibrant community, one that was a cause of concern to the white population.

Part of the concern had to do with the growth of the free black population. Just prior to the Civil War, free blacks in New Jersey numbered an estimated 25,336 out of a total population of 646,699, which was proportionally twice the size of the free black population of any other free state.[29] Perhaps for this reason it was unsurprising to find locally circulating newspapers, including the New York–based organ of the Dutch Reformed Church, the *Christian Intelligencer*, especially attuned to demographics. In an 1830 edition of the *Fredonian*, New Brunswick's Federalist newspaper, there was even the glaring juxtaposition of local census returns with an advertisement for the ACS.[30] Though we cannot necessarily ascribe intent to this layout, it nevertheless manages to evoke the suggestion that the increasing black population threatened white supremacy and that whites and blacks were better served if the latter were removed to Africa.

Concern with demographic increase among African Americans punctuates much of the literature produced by the society. According to a "Memorial to the Legislature of Virginia," published in the *Thirty-Second Annual Report of the American Colonization Society*, "The free people of color, now numbering not less than 60,000 in Virginia and increasing more than four hundred per cent in fifty years, will, without some action to prevent it, form a population of 240,000 in the year 1900, a period that will arrive during the natural life of our children."[31] Continuing this exhortation, the piece—drafted by a special committee—stated that "in 1950 our grandchildren will encounter this population increased to a numerical force of about one million—thirty per cent greater than our present white population—and our great grandchildren will see a free black population of 4,000,000 in Virginia."[32] Multiplying the sense of impending danger with each passing generation, it reminded legislators that "history furnishes no instance of one people residing in the midst of another people as a lower CASTE, and excluded from an equality of civil rights, that have stopped short of violence and rebellion so soon as their strength gave reasonable hope of a successful struggle."[33] Evoking the specter of Saint-Domingue (or Haiti), the watchword of antiblack alarmists during the antebellum period, the memorial reasoned that removal was the only valid option for this "indolent," "vicious," and "dishonest" population.[34] Though it would simultaneously acknowledge the degradation and disenfranchisement of free blacks in the United States, the memorial failed to interrogate the nature of the country's highly stratified society. Instead, the report played on the racism of its audience—the very same racism so integral to the ACS—by offering one final warning to its readers, noting that "while we delay, the evil is in progress. While we sleep, it gathers strength. While we stand still, time passes, children are born, grow into manhood, our free colored population multiplies."[35]

These sentiments were not reserved for the slaveholding states of the South alone. Antiblackness flew in the face of perceived ideological and political geographies. Certainly, eight out of thirteen of the ACS's original vice presidents were Southern slaveholders, including Henry Clay of Kentucky, William H. Crawford of Georgia, Andrew Jackson of Tennessee, and George Mason of Virginia—men who would continue to play important roles within the organization throughout the antebellum period. And yet the American Colonization Society would garner members throughout the Northeast and Mid-Atlantic, as auxiliary societies popped up in places like New York, Massachusetts, Connecticut, and Rhode Island, and, of course, New Jersey. In fact, though the ACS was formed in Washington, DC, in December 1816, Robert Finley, a Presbyterian minister born and educated in Princeton, New Jersey, who later settled and taught in nearby Basking Ridge, is generally considered to be the founder of the organization.[36]

Rutgers College, Its Leadership, and the
American Colonization Society

Rutgers College was deeply enmeshed within the culture and politics animating colonization. Not only was it situated in New Jersey, a state reluctant to carry out abolition as well as the ostensible birthplace of the ACS, but it was also the intellectual heir of the Dutch Reformed Church. As previously mentioned, the Dutch Reformed Church's position on slavery was conservative; it remained silent on the issue of slavery while it endorsed colonization. From the 1820s through the 1840s, the Reformed Church's governing body regularly reaffirmed its support for the American Colonization Society. Like the national leadership of the Baptist, Episcopal, Methodist, and Presbyterian Churches, officials praised "the value of the colonization enterprise, as conservative of the peace and harmony of our country."[37]

Rutgers College's fifth president, Philip Milledoler, expressed similar ideas. Born in upstate New York to Swiss immigrant parents, the importance of piety and of service to God were impressed upon him from a very young age. After graduating from Columbia College in New York City in 1793, he was ordained to the German Reformed Synod the following year. He was described as "a man of lovely spirit and unusually clear head" and was lauded as a successful pastor and an eloquent speaker.[38] It was said that "his preaching was adapted to instruct, to awaken and console; admirably fitted to arouse sinners to a sense of their condition, and point them to the Savior."[39] This ability to both rouse and rehabilitate congregants was at the heart of the Second Great Awakening's ethos. And so it is perhaps not surprising that Milledoler would play an active role in antebellum reform movements, including the American Bible Society, the United Foreign Missionary Society, and the American Colonization Society. Though he was vice president of New York State's auxiliary colonization society between 1824 and 1829, the clearest articulation of his colonizationist views came in 1831, when he delivered Rutgers's commencement address (Figure 6.1). In the first half of the address, he condemned slavery and warned his audience about the threat it presented, not only to individual virtue but also to that of the entire nation. "Despotism and slavery are the legitimate offspring of sin," he argued, suggesting that "no nation can long be free, that has ceased to be virtuous—and that to be virtuous, it must necessarily be intelligent."[40]

The second half of President Milledoler's speech changed course, however, and explicitly endorsed the American Colonization Society. Indeed, his speech conveyed the anxiety white New Jerseyans likely felt as they witnessed the growing number of not only free blacks throughout the population but also of African American–led abolitionist societies during this period. In particular, Milledoler praised the patriotism of the ACS. He noted that it "holds up to view

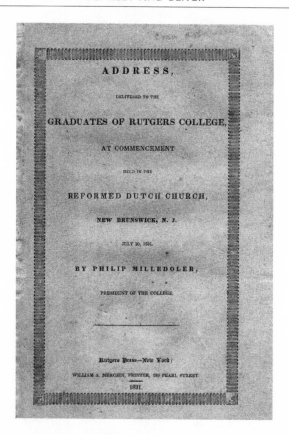

ADDRESS,

DELIVERED TO THE

GRADUATES OF RUTGERS COLLEGE,

AT COMMENCEMENT

HELD IN THE

REFORMED DUTCH CHURCH,

NEW BRUNSWICK, N. J.

JULY 20, 1831,

BY PHILIP MILLEDOLER,

PRESIDENT OF THE COLLEGE.

Rutgers Press—New York;

WILLIAM A. MERCEIN, PRINTER, 390 PEARL STREET.

1831.

FIGURE 6.1   Philip Milledoler, Address delivered to the graduates of Rutgers College at commencement held in the Reformed Dutch Church, New Brunswick, NJ, July 20, 1831 (New York: Rutgers Press, William A. Mercein, Printer, 1831).

the great principles for which our revolutionary worthies fought, and bled, and died."[41] More importantly, inasmuch as emigration of blacks back to Africa held the promise of increased manumissions here in America, Milledoler believed that the organization upheld the tenets of liberty in a way the Declaration of Independence failed to do—it granted freedom to all people, black and white.[42] Despite the fact that the freedom promised by the ACS was always conditional upon removal to West Africa, Philip Milledoler believed that the organization continued the Revolutionary War era tradition of liberty and freedom for all.

As a supporter of colonization, Milledoler believed free blacks—Africa's "own sons"—should seize and develop the continent of their ancestors. His commencement address exposed his optimism in the scheme, noting, "I think I see the Sun of Righteousness rising upon Africa, and pouring its cheering rays upon the hamlets of myriads of happy beings. . . . Emboldened by prophecy I repeat it—Africa will be regenerated."[43] Evoking the language of Rutgers's motto, which refers to *sol iustitiae* (or "sun of righteousness"), Milledoler tied Rutgers to the colonization enterprise.

As it turns out, Milledoler's speech inspired these eager students to recognize the importance of colonizing African Americans. A year later Rutgers students manifested a "lively interest" in the cause and formed a colonization society. According to ACS agents reporting from New Brunswick, the "propriety of the students forming themselves into a society, having it for one object to collect information respecting the free colored population of our land, was commended to their attention in a short address."[44] Indeed, their focus on acquiring information about the free black population was perhaps representative of the ACS's fixation on demographics, the population growth in New Brunswick in particular.

Like Philip Milledoler, these students could not envision an interracial America. They both feared and despised black people. "But cast your eye over the cities and plantations of the South," began the orator at a meeting of the New Jersey Colonization Society (NJCS), held in Princeton in 1824, "and ingenuously tell me, can you, in mercy to themselves, ask of our brethren to deluge their land with the horrid scenes that would certainly follow the liberation of a licentious, ignorant, and irritated population restrained by no principles, and with every bad passion of the heart inflamed." Anticipating the prejudice and fear-mongering of the above-quoted memorial to the legislature of Virginia by roughly twenty-five years, the orator argued that the liberation of enslaved men and women would "in effect, be to ask of them, after unsheathing the sword, to place it in the grasp of rapine and murder, and invoke their vengeance."[45] Demonstrating a similar concern with demography, he asked his audience to "look through New-Jersey." "We have long had on our rates a respectable number of Free blacks. The last Census rose to twelve thousand."[46] The rising numbers of free blacks continued to animate "the problem." The weight of both the past and of sheer demographic force presented too great a threat to whites, making the emancipation and equality of individuals of African descent impossible. Driving home his point, the orator reasoned that "as American citizens these men can never be free. And as American freemen, they never would be valuable."[47]

These were not the words of an apologist for slavery but rather the New Jersey–born Theodore Frelinghuysen, an ardent antislavery advocate, educator, lawyer, Whig politician, and member of the ACS for well over three decades, including a vice presidency that lasted between his appointment in 1832 and his death in 1862. He was also the seventh president of Rutgers College. Born to a prominent Dutch American family with ties to slaveholding and the son of Frederick Frelinghuysen, the first tutor of Queen's College, Frelinghuysen nevertheless condemned the peculiar institution. He, much like the college itself,

came of age of during the Second Great Awakening, when the idea that slavery was a sin infiltrated many Northern congregations. The Frelinghuysens had
important ties to the Dutch Reformed Church—extending all the way back to his
great-grandfather, Theodorus Jacobus Frelinghuysen, a Dutch Reformed minister—and so it follows that he was brought up in a pious household. Formative
also was the time he spent enrolled in the Reverend Robert Finley's classical
school for boys in Basking Ridge, New Jersey. It was there that Frelinghuysen
began a lengthy association with Presbyterianism and learned to think of life as
service to Christ.[48] "Because of such a Presbyterian and Reformed background,"
argues historian Robert J. Eels, "it is not surprising to find a man like Frelinghuysen on the vanguard of a crusade to transform not only the individual but the
whole society, to renew the moral foundation of the community itself."[49]

Popularly known as the "Christian statesman," Frelinghuysen's prominent
antislavery views tinged his political career as Henry Clay's running mate during
the 1844 presidential election. His long-standing advocacy of the ACS and the
donation of a building lot in Newark for the construction of an African American Presbyterian church would earn him the moniker of "Negro lover."[50] Elsewhere, reporting on a political cartoon meant to illustrate the character of the
Whig party that appeared in a Democratic-leaning newspaper, the *Whig Standard*'s readers were asked to imagine various scenarios comparing a coarse Clay
and a pious Frelinghuysen. For example, "Henry Clay shooting a fellow man in a
duel," while Frelinghuysen "was praying for sinners." The most interesting comparison, however, featured "Clay looking on while his overseer whips a negro
man" and "Frelinghuysen walking arm in arm with a black dandy [a stereotype
of an uppity black man]."[51] Although this last depiction attempted to emphasize
Frelinghuysen and Clay's diverging views on African Americans, it ultimately
obscured the ideological similarities that existed between the two men. Both
Clay and Frelinghuysen were members of the ACS, condemned slavery (though
Clay and likely Frelinghuysen owned slaves),[52] and advocated for the peculiar
institution's gradual end. Perhaps more importantly, both men espoused antiblack ideas. Much like the false dichotomy separating North and South, this was
a cleavage more mythic than real.

Men like Theodore Frelinghuysen (Figure 6.2) perfectly embodied the
ostensible tensions between antislavery and antiblackness during the antebellum period. Indeed, the very real racism that inflected his reformism did not
nullify his antislavery views. Frelinghuysen took almost every possible opportunity to critique the slave trade and slavery more broadly. "Conscience bears one
uniform conviction to the heart," he proclaimed in 1824, "that Slavery cannot be
justified."[53] "We have committed a mighty trespass," he later announced in an
address reproduced in the *Thirteenth Annual Report of the American Colonization
Society.* "Africa has a heavy claim against us—it is a long and bloody catalogue

of outrage and oppression—the report of our National crime has gone up to Heaven." Continuing, he declared that "it rose, Sir, upon the groans and tears of her kidnapped men—the infernal horrors of the slave ship have, in ten thousand instances, wrung from distracted bosoms the cry for vengeance, and there is a just God to hear and regard it!"[54] At times, he even expressed sincere dismay at the widespread assumption that individuals of African descent were incapable of "improvement." "We enslave, degrade, and oppress a people through many generations," he reasoned, "—shut out from them all the avenues to skill and science—and then we merely let them go, merely say to them, 'now live and breathe for yourselves, without our aid or countenance.'"[55] He concluded that this was as unjust as it was unreasonable and urged Christians to atone for their guilt and make reparations toward blacks. Ultimately, however, redress could only take one form: removal to Africa.

This was, at least in part, because Theodore Frelinghuysen believed that whites and blacks belonged to separate and distinct races. "But what are these unhappy men," he mused in his address to the members of the NJCS in Princeton in 1824, "and where are they after all the toils of benevolence?" "A separate, degraded, scorned, and humbled people," he concluded. "With a line of demarcation drawn deep and broad; and durable as time."[56] Ten years later, expounding on the plight of free blacks, Frelinghuysen argued that "they are a depressed and separate race; excluded from the privileges of freemen. . . . They enjoy no share of our political, and but a small part of our social privileges. We have seen these causes in constant operation for many years, and however we may and ought to deplore it, yet the depression exists, and the lines of separation are as deep and palpable as ever."[57] Talk of "deep" lines of "demarcation" and "separation" lent a biological justification to a political problem.

While the literature of the ACS did not overtly draw from the circulating science upholding racial difference, these views nevertheless managed to creep into their publications. In his 1816 pamphlet *Thoughts on the Colonization of Free Blacks*, the Reverend Robert Finley called for the removal of the country's free black population to a colony in West Africa, a place with a climate "congenial with their color and constitutions," which would allow for "their contracted minds [to] expand and their natures rise."[58] It is unclear if Finley was in any way influenced by natural history, but this environmentalist take on the relationship between race and climate was widespread during the first half of the nineteenth century.[59] Indeed, it dovetailed nicely with his belief that whites and blacks could not coexist. From the very beginning, Finley—Frelinghuysen's mentor—was looking for the "*gradual separation of the black from the white population.*"[60] Frelinghuysen's conclusion that there was an unbridgeable gap between whites and blacks—a separateness that was "deep," perhaps even biological— similarly evoked the racial science of the antebellum period. Difference, of

FIGURE 6.2   Portrait of Theodore Frelinghuysen (1787–1862), president of Rutgers College, 1850–1862, Special Collection and University Archives, Rutgers University Libraries.

course, is not neutral, nor is it exempt from subsequent hierarchicalization. In that respect, Frelinghuysen exemplified the ways in which antebellum reform perfectly accommodated the seemingly differing though ultimately compatible ideas of antislavery and antiblackness. This is perhaps why the ACS was able to achieve a modicum of interregional consensus on the question of slavery at a time when this was almost impossible.

African American Response to the American Colonization Society

Blacks resisted and refuted Frelinghuysen's and the American Colonization Society's growing emphasis on racial differences and the separation of whites and blacks. In an 1850 speech delivered in New Jersey, which supported the enfranchisement of African Americans, John S. Rock, a black abolitionist, dentist, and physician, challenged the ethnological claims of colonizationists. Rock underscored the one-sided relationship between African Americans and the American state. Blacks, who had given much to their country—in the form of taxes and military service—had received little to nothing in return; they bore all the responsibilities of citizenship but were exempted from its benefits. Echoing Theodore Frelinghuysen's 1824 speech at a meeting of the New Jersey Colonization Society, Rock asserted that "there is no just plea, and apology for you to shut every avenue to elevation, and then complain of degradation; what else can be expected, while we are looked upon as things, and treated worse than unthinking animals?"[61] Rock critiqued the legacy of dehumanization that had existed, virtually unchanged, since the earliest Dutch Reformed ministers in America had compared blacks to animals.

Switching gears, Rock then challenged colonizationists' arguments for removal. "Africa is urged upon us as the country of our forefathers," he observed wryly. "If this is good sophistry—and we think it will pass—then it follows that all men must go to the country of their forefathers: in this case, the blacks will go to Africa, and the whites to Europe." Following this reasoning to its logical conclusion, and to great effect, Rock then wondered where mixed-race individuals would go? "This sophistry is not designed to aggrandize any but the descendants of the European nations: Africa is the country for the Africans, their descendants and mongrels of various colors; Asia is the country of the Asiatics; the east Indies the place for Malays; Patagonia the country for the Indian; and any place the white man chooses to go. HIS country!"[62] In this spirited final section of his address, Rock, who also lectured on ethnology, showcased his familiarity with the current debates on racial difference. Moreover, he underscored the exceptionalism built into the colonizationists' logic, which suggested that people of color had designated homelands, unlike whites, who could lay claim to whatever territory they wished.

John S. Rock's pointed critique of the American Colonization Society represents but one among many during the antebellum period. From the very beginning, the vast majority of the country's free black population opposed colonization. Rejecting the politics of gradualism as well as the antiblack sentiments that sustained the ACS, free blacks actively challenged the assumption that within the United States their degradation was permanent, that justice was conditional, and that true freedom should be deferred. A typical refutation was expressed by free blacks in Trenton, New Jersey, in a resolution: "Forasmuch as the agents thereof, and its members who have petitioned the several legislatures, have unequivocally declared its object, to wit, the extermination of the free people of color from the Union . . . and to effect this they have not failed to slander our character, by representing us as a vagrant race; and we do therefore disclaim all union with the said Society, and, once for all, declare that we never will remove under their patronage."[63] Taking issue with the assumption that freedom and blackness were antithetical upon U.S. soil, the free blacks of Trenton made it clear that they would not leave. Indeed, against the urging of Theodore Frelinghuysen, many African Americans emphasized that the United States was their home.[64]

As the ACS's colonizationist discourse ramped up over the course of the 1830s, so, too, did abolitionists and free blacks protest against African American removal. In opposition to the city's colonization society, local ministers, and any number of Rutgers College affiliates, free blacks in New Brunswick, for example, sent anticolonizationist petitions to the state legislature in the 1840s.[65] With similar intent, *The North Star*, the abolitionist paper published by Frederick Douglass, listed the heads of the ACS to "place on record, for future reference, the names of those who fill the offices of President and Vice Presidents in this negro-hating society, that the colored people may know what and who are operating against their hearths, homes and happiness."[66] Among those names listed were Theodore Frelinghuysen (future president of Rutgers College), the Reverend Jacob J. Janeway (trustee and former vice president of Rutgers College), L.Q.C. Elmer (trustee of Rutgers College), and Peter D. Vroom (trustee of Rutgers College).

This was not the first time that Theodore Frelinghuysen had been singled out by black antislavery activists. In an 1840 open letter directed to Frelinghuysen and Benjamin F. Butler, entitled *The Colonization Scheme Considered*, Samuel E. Cornish and Theodore S. Wright, founding members of the American Anti-Slavery Society, Presbyterian ministers, and active members of New York's free black community, delivered a near-totalizing response to the claims made by the ACS in favor of removal.[67] "PREJUDICE! What is it?" inquired Cornish and Wright. "Lexicographers tell us, it is a decision of the mind formed without due examination of the facts or arguments which are necessary to a just and impartial determination." "And *prejudice against* COLOR!" they continued. "What does this mean?" Slowly building toward the crux of their argument, the authors considered whether it was possible to be prejudiced against things as ethereal as color, sound or sight, the air, and even light. Concluding that it was not, in fact, possible, they demanded to know how Frelinghuysen and Butler could connect their names and lend their influence to a national movement that rested on a "*philosophical absurdity*."[68]

At first glance, this argument appears tepid, but Cornish and Wright's argument was aimed at the reason, sensibility, and education of Frelinghuysen and Butler. By suggesting that "prejudice against color" was unjust, partial, and absurd, the authors of the letter were indicting their addressees for similar charges. That is not to say that Cornish and Wright denied the reality of prejudice against African Americans. Indeed, though they called into question the logic of prejudice they did not deny the very real ramifications of antiblack sentiment, such as disenfranchisement, poverty, and a lack of education.

Anticipating claims of innocence, Cornish and Wright then undercut any attempt on the part of men like Frelinghuysen and Butler to distance themselves from prejudice. "You, who do *not* hate us, by coöperating with those who *do*, encourage them," they argued. Indeed, prejudice, the emergence of which the authors attributed to slavery, continued to exist precisely because of the "coöperation of influential men at the North with Southern slaveholders." The ACS, with its interregional appeal and ranks swollen with presidential candidates, lawyers, clergymen, educators, and slave owners, helped to sustain antiblack prejudice. As long as men like Frelinghuysen and Butler assumed that the degradation of blacks was permanent and that "prejudice against color" was fixed, justice for African Americans would be deferred. "We suffer the *wrong*," maintained Cornish and Wright, "—and it ministers but little consolation, to be told that *you* feel none of the prejudice which others are pouring out in full profusion on our heads."[69] Morality, they argued, demanded more.

Samuel Cornish and Theodore Wright closed their open letter by asking their addressees whether they "ought to persist in a scheme which nourishes an unreasonable and unchristian prejudice—which persuades legislators to continue their unjust enactments against us in all their rigor [. . .]—which cuts us off from employment, and straitens our means of subsistence—which afflicts us with the feeling, that our condition is unstable, and prevents us from making systematic effort for our improvement, or for the advancement of our own usefulness and happiness and that of our families."[70] Finally, they asked for an answer from Frelinghuysen and Butler. They received none.

Ten years later, Theodore Frelinghuysen, vice president of the American Colonization Society, was inaugurated as Rutgers College's seventh president. In New Brunswick's First Reformed Church, before a densely packed crowd, the Reverend Doctor Samuel B. How (Figure 6.3) delivered the opening prayer. This convergence represented the collective accretion of decades' worth of antiblack sentiment strengthened by the cooperation between the Dutch Reformed Church, Rutgers College, and the American Colonization Society. The interplay of these forces had become familiar by the time internal debates about slavery within the Reformed Church reached a breaking point. In 1855 the North Carolina Classis of the German Reformed Church petitioned to join the Dutch Reformed Church, but the petition sparked controversy. A number of ministers objected to the German church's admission on two grounds. First, admission would provoke internal division on the issue of slavery. Second, many Northern ministers considered slaveholding sinful. In answering their concerns, the Reverend Samuel B. How, minister of New Brunswick's First Reformed Church and a member of Rutgers's board of trustees, objected to both claims.

FIGURE 6.3   Samuel B. How, Reformed minister and Rutgers College trustee, who was a staunch supporter of slavery. Special Collections and University Archives, Rutgers University.

In a sermon before the Church's governing body, How defended slaveholding as not only biblically sanctioned but also a divinely ordained social reality. If slavery was a lamentable evil, How admitted, it was certainly not a sin. He began with the New Testament, particularly the First Epistle to Timothy, to prove that scriptural support for slavery existed in the Christian as well as the Jewish, or Old Testament, tradition. In How's exegesis, scripture upheld property ownership over all other rights. He argued that "God therefore commands us to respect the right of property . . . even though it be a man-servant or a maid-servant," his scripturally sourced euphemisms for slaves. Moreover, slavery could not be easily undone. It was, in How's estimation, "one of the penal effects of the fall." The enslavement of others was deemed by God to be a burden borne by Christians. Finally, he warned, the consequences to ending slavery would be to "merely set loose a multitude of ignorant, unprincipled, immoral men" who would then act on "the promptings of their evil hearts." Slavery had degraded its subjugated masses, but he also declared that the enslaved were saved from heathenism and "spiritual darkness and hopelessness." Slavery was a consequence of humanity's fall from grace, and it was a divinely established convention, not to be undermined by human whim.[71] Even as the nation teetered on the brink of war over slavery, How embodied the Dutch Reformed Church's intransigence on the matter of earthly equality. He echoed the Revolutionary church's willingness to abide by spiritual equality, while refusing any alterations in blacks' social or legal status.

As he elaborated on the necessity of slavery, Rutgers trustee Samuel How drew upon age-old Calvinist doctrines that privileged divine will over human action as key to salvation. For humans to act against God's plans could lead only to discord and death, How urged. He offered an extended attack on abolitionism and all movements for change that were "so revolutionary, so subversive of the established order of society," including communism, Islam, and the radicalism of the French Revolution. He upheld the Haitian Revolution, a massive and successful slave revolt, as particularly disastrous and egregious for God's intent. For How, the liberal humanism of the Revolutionary era was incompatible with the conservative social order established by God. As he labeled "the inalienable rights of man" an "infidel abstraction" that "would bring ruin" to a prosperous nation,[72] he explicated a position of gradualist emancipation that appeared unchanged from the days of the Revolutionary church and New Jersey's 1804 Act for the Gradual Abolition of Slavery.

Conclusion: Race-Making on the Banks of the Old Raritan

Given Rutgers's heritage in the Dutch Reformed Church it is likely that slavery and race were topics of discussion in Rutgers classrooms. Certainly the early curriculum and public statements of Rutgers faculty members suggest this. Indeed, while enslaved labor was central to the construction, funding, and maintenance of college campuses, slavery also shaped knowledge production and America's "intellectual cultures."[73] Rutgers, like other early American colleges, was a space where intellectuals developed and debated ideas about race.[74]

There can be no doubt that Rutgers students learned about slavery. Starting in the 1830s, students were assigned Joseph Story's *Commentaries on the Constitution of the United States* during their senior year. Therefore, graduates of Rutgers would have been familiar with Story's discussion of the legal history of the slave trade and his argument that its continuance revealed "the barbarism of modern policy."[75] Additionally, students may have encountered the topic of slavery during their courses on moral philosophy. Like higher education more broadly during this period, these courses were focused on the training of

the mind as opposed to the direct study of specific problems. Students probably did not discuss current political issues such as the court case of *United
States v. The Amistad* (1841). However, they probably did discuss slavery when
they read Francis Wayland's *The Elements of Moral Science*. Like Story, Wayland
saw slavery as evil, not because of its barbarism but because it took away a
person's natural stimulus to perform labor. Wayland's criticism of the institution of slavery does not acknowledge the immorality of the daily terror and
violence of enslavement. He instead states that any means of violence used to
overthrow slavery would be more evil than slavery itself.[76] So while students at
Rutgers would have approached these texts through various regional, social,
religious, and cultural lenses, and had differing stances on the rationality of
the claims of Story and Wayland, we can reasonably conclude that the morality of slavery was, at the very least, an intellectual idea introduced to them by
their core readings.

As referenced in other chapters of this volume, Rutgers leaders maintained
strong relationships with the American colonization movement—for example, President John Henry Livingston, who also taught classes in theology, was
closely connected to the ACS. It is reasonable to assume that graduates of the
college were introduced to what we would now think of as racial ideology. Running parallel to the tensions embedded in Wayland's discussion of the morality
of slavery versus the morality of violent abolition, the men of the colonization
movement like Livingston, Milledoler, and Frelinghuysen also tried to create an
uneasy balance between calling for gradual emancipation while not arguing for
racial equality.[77]

In all likelihood, however, Rutgers College, like most early American colleges, was a space where ideas about the inequality of blacks and whites were
generated. Illuminating the reality that higher education played a key role in
the construction and maintenance of racial ideology in the United States, those
with an interest in using race difference to solidify positions of power looked
to the academy as a site where their questions could be answered. College faculty, specifically scientists and theologians, came to be responsible for sifting
through and refining all of this knowledge, and coming to definitive conclu-
sions about racial difference. However, scientific ideas in the academy did not
develop in a vacuum. Social experiences relayed in travelers' accounts, newspapers and Anglo-American stories and stereotypes of Native and African Americans influenced the development of scientific racism. Or as historian Craig
Wilder puts it, "Race did not come from science and theology; it came to science
and theology."[78] The rise of scientific racism occurred simultaneously with the
professionalization of medicine in America. The medical field was literally built
on the bodies of the poor and disenfranchised: blacks, Indians, and the Irish.
Doctors and their students used their exhumed bodies for experimentation and

anatomical study.[79] Furthermore, planters, land speculators, slave owners, and merchants provided the capital for scientific research to take place, using their financial and political power to establish medical schools and research facilities. By doing this, "they also imposed subtle and severe controls on science."[80]

The medical program at Rutgers at the start of the nineteenth century is illustrative of the ascendance of race science and the institutionalization of medicine. The involvement of Rutgers's medical faculty in the 1808 New York court case *Commissioners of the Almshouse v. Alexander Whistelo, A Black Man* makes this clear. In this New York City bastardy case, Lucy Williams, described as a mulatto woman, was first sexually assaulted by a black man, Alexander Whistelo. Later that same evening, a white man also assaulted Williams. She became pregnant and insisted that Whistelo was the father of the child, who was lighter in skin tone than both Williams and Whistelo. The case was called to decide who fathered Williams's child, but as Wilder notes, *Whistelo* "was about much more than paternity."[81] Reproduction was a central focus of race science. The court brought in expert witnesses to grapple with questions regarding complexion and heredity, how race shaped behavior, and when and why certain characteristics of race revealed themselves. These witnesses came from the most prestigious universities in the United States and Europe, and were founders and faculty members of medical programs, societies, and professional organizations in the United States.

Faculty members and medical professionals from and associated with Queen's Medical College testified as expert witnesses. David Hosack, then a slaveholding instructor of surgery, clinical medicine, obstetrics, and midwifery at both Columbia and Queen's College, and also Whistelo's employer (he worked as Hosack's coachman), testified that because of the baby's complexion, the father had to either be a white or light-skinned mulatto man.[82] William Moore, another affiliate of Queen's College who also taught at Columbia echoed Hosack's sentiments.[83] Dr. Samuel Mitchill, who was a New York senator at the time of the trial, offered a different opinion. Mitchill was also a slaveholding professor at Columbia and Queen's College. He was the founding vice president of Rutgers Medical College when it reopened under the leadership of Hosack, and along with Hosack, was one of the founders of the New York Historical Society. Mitchill also published the nation's first medical journal.[84] Countering the other testimonies, Mitchill argued that it was not unlikely that Whistelo was the father. According to Mitchill, the other witnesses treated complexion as an immutable characteristic, when it was actually something that was unpredictable. He went even further and argued that environment and behavior could affect biological characteristics.[85]

The *Whistelo* case illustrates the influence that the academy, Rutgers in particular, had on debates of the day. The arguments of Hosack, Moore, and

Mitchill shed light on the types of ideas about race that professors, particularly within the sciences, proposed to their students. Moreover, students' encounters with the works of Joseph Story and Francis Wayland no doubt made for lively conversation over the meaning and morality of slavery. As the years passed and the issue of slavery divided the nation, Rutgers students would be exposed to more than the philosophy of Story and Wayland and the scientific racialism of Hosack, Moore, and Mitchill. Indeed, over the course of their studies they would hear from Philip Milledoler, Theodore Frelinghuysen, and Samuel How, men who in addition to shaping and leading Rutgers College, were among the most ardent and articulate leaders of the American Colonization Society.

African Americans, however, pushed back on the racist discourses emanating from leaders of American universities. The *Colonization Scheme Considered* represents one of the most rigorous critiques of the American Colonization Society delivered by black abolitionists during the antebellum period. Perhaps more importantly, it is also one of the most radical. By focusing so centrally on the nature of prejudice, and by linking it to questions of complexion and color, Theodore Wright and Samuel Cornish cut to the heart of the antiblack sentiments vital to the ACS's aims. This is not to say that the organization's antislavery goals were not real. Indeed, the ACS counted among its members some of the most committed antislavery advocates of the antebellum period. Moreover, for reformers wedded to a gradualist politics of emancipation, the promise of freedom contingent upon emigration to West Africa made colonization one of the most realizable antislavery measures. This was evidenced by the number of moderate Southern slaveholders who agreed to manumit their slaves upon condition of removal.

This seemingly strange alloy of antislavery and antiblack views, however, was far from unconventional during the first third of the nineteenth century. To the contrary, it represented a rather typical approach to the changing social, political, and cultural orders of the early Republic. With the abolitionist movement making strides, and states in the Northeast beginning to pass gradual abolition laws, the corresponding rise in the free black population began to trouble those unprepared to live among former bondsmen and bondswomen. As Craig Wilder argues, "The intellectual cultures of the United States contained little space for the possibility of a heterogeneous society."[86] Within this context, it is not surprising that old colonizationist schemes looking to preserve the foundations of a white republic were revived. Capitalizing off of the religious revivalism that swept through the Northeast, colonization took on an air of reform with the inception of the American Colonization Society in 1816. With the dual aims of opposing slavery and ridding the country of its free black population the organization achieved a broad, interregional appeal. Given these realities, it becomes infinitely clearer how colonizationists were able to posit "degradation" as the primary cause for the removal of free blacks. Of course, this strategy also meant disregarding the innumerable successes of African Americans.

It follows, then, that a culture steeped in both gradualism and racial discrimination would produce some of the strongest bulwarks of colonizationism during the antebellum period, including the Dutch Reformed Church and Rutgers College. Though the latter's relationship to the American Colonization Society was typical of a college situated in the Mid-Atlantic region during the first half of the nineteenth century, we cannot overlook its concurrent relationship to race-making. In this case, the typical should not be confused with the benign. Deeming African Americans unfit for freedom—let alone citizenship—within the United States, many colonizationists were committed to the creation of a white republic. The exclusion of black people from American political life cannot be divorced from growing ideas about racial difference and its corollaries, racial hierarchy and white supremacy. "Public debate over the question of whether blacks were the equal of whites reflected political concerns in the new republic," argues Mia Bay, "as well as the new biological cast understandings of human nature [that] were beginning to acquire."[87] Indeed, one of the responses to an impermanent social order was to assert a permanent racial order. We see this impulse reflected perhaps most clearly with the rise of racial science in the decades leading up to the Civil War.[88]

Rutgers students were exposed to these ideas as race was made on the banks of the Raritan. In the classroom, from ACS lecterns, and from the pulpit, undergraduates learned that blacks and whites were different, that whites were superior to blacks, that America was for white people, and that for the nation's sake and that of African Americans, it was best that blacks go back to Africa.

7

Rutgers

A Land-Grant College in Native American History

Kaisha Esty

When Rutgers became New Jersey's land-grant college in 1864 under the Morrill Act of 1862, the state legislature had no indigenous community to answer to. It had been decades since the Lenni Lenape left their final footprints in the region they had known for centuries. Pried from their land through years of state-sanctioned violence, coercion, and trickery, the people the European settlers called the "Delaware Indians" met a fate of repeated removal and resettlement through the West.[1] The Morrill Act granted states the right to proceeds from federal lands to help fund schools for agriculture and the mechanic arts within their borders. As a proprietary state, New Jersey held no land within the public domain. Any lands that would help establish a scientific school for the state's industrial white classes were merely drawn from a vast faraway lottery. For many of the state's white inhabitants, the "Indian Question" was safely shelved as a distant memory.

Yet in becoming a land-grant college, Rutgers and the state of New Jersey were forced to revisit the "Indian Question"—even if their collective response was one of shameless silence, uninterest, and erasure. Indeed, the provisions of the Morrill Act demanded and protected this silence, while the Civil War consumed the nation's attention. Embroiled in a violent political climate that threatened to rupture New Jersey's racially stratified society, legislative officials rarely glanced at matters beyond the war effort. If there was a pressing question related to the state's non-European population, it concerned the movement and freedom of those of African descent.[2] For the faculty, and later the board

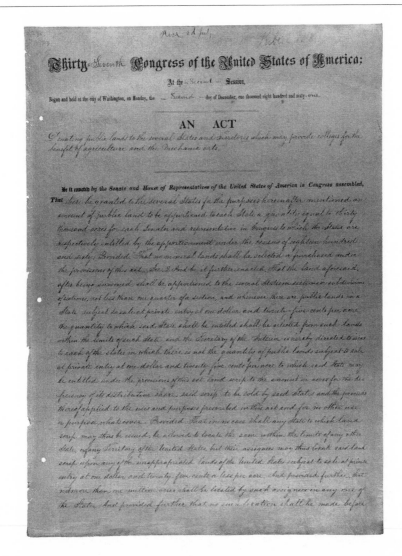

FIGURE 7.1 Morrill Act. Special Collection and University Archives, Rutgers University Libraries.

of trustees at Rutgers College, the time was ripe to take advantage of a federal endowment toward a scientific school. No thought was ever given to where that endowment would be drawn from.

What did it mean to bid for, win, and ultimately uphold the prestigious title of land-grant college within a broad national context of Native American land dispossession and Removal? In what ways could Rutgers be held morally culpable for benefiting from the proceeds of Indian land seized by the federal government?

When I began this project in spring 2016, I was kindly cautioned about the potential research difficulties that I faced. Supervising this project, Dr. Camilla Townsend, an expert in Native American history, counseled that I would either find something small (and still significant) or nothing at all. Regardless, investigating what could and could not be found was just as important as sharing a narrative.

It became clear early in my research that I would have to pursue a serpentine trail of archival silences in order to explore my questions. As a nineteenth-century African Americanist I felt somewhat familiar with the prospect of freeing a narrative from a constraining colonialist archive. Enslaved silhouettes often appeared in the archive in uneven, flat, and wholly violent ways. Reading silences befitted my training. But my relative privilege as a nineteenth-century African Americanist presented itself the more I struggled with the dead silence surrounding Native Americans, the Morrill legislation, and Rutgers College. For example, I realized that as property harnessed to white capital, slaves created at least *some* incentive for whites to pen a record. Whether they appeared in wills, court records, personal diaries, proslavery accounts, or abolitionist literature, they were, in some form, there. But in this case, Native Americans were nowhere to be found. Their presence simply problematized, challenged, and delegitimized the logic undergirding the Morrill Act. Their *erasure* was paramount to the establishment and growth of white capital. This core agenda manifested itself in different ways through federal and state records.

I started with the aim to find a tangible piece of evidence that would expose how Rutgers College benefited from proceeds under the Morrill Act at the expense of Native Americans. After some preliminary research, I visited the National Archives in Washington, DC, with the hope of locating the physical land certificate or "land scrip" that was paid to New Jersey by the federal government. Though the specialists at the National Archives were invaluably helpful, my progress hit multiple walls. Besides the draft of the actual Morrill bill, the National Archives held very few related records. This was the case for two main reasons: first, my research dates, which initially began in 1862, coincided with the incredibly turbulent period of the Civil War. Very few federal records survived the Civil War. As an archivist explained to me, missing federal documents between 1861 and 1865 were simply not uncommon. Second, the National Archives held few documents related to the Morrill Act and its implementation because the period in which the act was passed predated the establishment of the National Archives system.[3] Prior to then, there was no centralized federal record-keeping system. Surviving documents therefore rested on the whim of federal officials—what they deemed worthy of preservation. Original or duplicate copies of the federal land scrips issued to each state seemed to fall under this category.

Searching for federal land scrips proved incredibly difficult as the surviving documents were not consistently categorized. Land scrips were scattered across state and federal archives in boxes marked for agricultural colleges established following the second Morrill Act (1890), or in various land records. Refining my search down to a reasonable guess was deeply challenging. As one of the original thirteen colonies and a proprietary state, I learned that New Jersey's land records were not housed at the National Archives. This included the land certificate or scrip that was paid by the federal government in favor of the state of New Jersey. (It didn't matter that the scrip was for federal land somewhere in the West.) With the incredible help of the archival specialists, I was fortunate to view a land scrip issued to the state of Georgia for land in Utah. Leaving the National Archives, I visited the Bureau of Land Management in Washington, DC, where I confronted the same problems.

I left Washington feeling disappointed. My experience within the archives was very positive as far as assistance went, and the excuses for not housing certain records appeared reasonable. But I felt the frustration of wanting to share a piece of evidence as a small form of justice. It was a huge affront to Native Americans to be ignored as a factor in federal and state discussions of the apportioning of "public lands." After all, in a "two birds, one stone" kind of way, distributing vast federally held lands seemed to be a central component of the Morrill legislation.

At the New Jersey State Library and Archives in Trenton, I perused Senate journals, legislative documents, and reports from the Department of Agriculture, New Jersey Agricultural Society, Department of Education, and the Rutgers Scientific School. I noted down important dates and cross-checked them in the New Jersey Civil War newspapers collection at the state archives. Yet there was no discussion regarding land in the Western states/territories. Everywhere the "Indian Question" appeared to be comfortably settled by a deafening silence. Even the language of *disposing* scrips for "*unappropriated public lands*" seemed to augment a grotesque sense of waste and abundance, with no regard to the violence that this committed upon the Indians already inhabiting these vast regions. They were invisible.

The more I researched, the more I was forced to move the goalpost. From locating the federal land scrip issued to the state of New Jersey, I turned my focus toward the provisions of the act, the arguments presented by the Rutgers Board of Trustees to win the award, and finally the actual implementation of the act in the state. I read the records of the Rutgers Board of Trustees in the hope of adding characters and a human face to discussions around the act. Here I learned that Indians were really not part of the land-grant discussion. I decided to combine the silences of the archives with a broader reading of the Morrill Act as a *system*. In doing so, it became clear that the Morrill Act was itself legitimized by the lie of the "Indian Question" as a past, settled matter. Moreover, the legitimacy of the Morrill legislation rested on a national acceptance of Native American erasure. Though Indian erasure occurred at the national level, it was perpetuated at the state and local levels. When the faculty and Rutgers Board of Trustees entered the bid to become a land-grant university, they bought into this silently unethical system.

The Morrill Act and Its Implementation in New Jersey

The Morrill Act, also known as the Agricultural Colleges Land Grant Act, marked the "first federal aid to higher education."[4] Enacted in 1862, it was the first in a triumvirate of acts designed to provide federal help toward the establishment of agricultural and scientific schools.[5] Under the terms of the act, each state was entitled to a portion of "public lands" for "the benefit of agriculture and the mechanic arts" in at least one designated college.[6] Each state received 30,000 acres of "public land for each Senator and Representative in Congress to which the state was entitled."[7] Actual land was handed over to the states that could locate "public land" within its limits. For other states with no land within the public domain, such as New Jersey, "an equivalent amount of land scrip or land certificate" was issued.[8] The scrip authorized the selection of "unappropriated public lands" that, as Greg Bradsher notes, were generally "anywhere in the West."[9] Within five years of its passage, over 2.4 million acres of land was located under the Morrill Act.[10] According to a report by the Department of the Interior, General Land Office, this amounted to just under a third of the total "public lands disposed of during the year ending June 30, 1867."[11]

Though vague, the terms under which the scrip could be disposed revealed the underlying purpose of the act. Prohibiting states from owning land in another region, the responsibility fell on individual states to sell their land scrip to "private persons." Many states sold their scrip in full or part to individual wealthy white investors. Though the market was unfavorable, among the act's provisions was the stipulation that states establish or declare their institutions within five years of accepting its terms. Locating acreage thus fell on individual speculators who could choose any "unappropriated public land" that wasn't mineral land. Thus, the Morrill Act represented a federal scheme to transfer vast lands into the hands of white investors and settlers. The fact that many Indian tribes inhabited these lands was irrelevant. Their existence was systematically erased by the greater project of white Western settlement.

The Morrill bill was originally proposed by Justin Smith Morrill of Vermont to the House of Representatives in 1857. For Morrill and the bill's proponents, such legislation would be revolutionary in uplifting the nation's industrial classes, instilling in them an ideal character of robust innovation, physical vitality, and technological expertise on a world level. Most importantly, as Morrill argued, the legislation would bring the average white American man into greater synergy with the land he inhabited, setting the foundation for the survival of a free nation built from the ground up.[12] He argued, "If this bill shall pass, the institutions of the character required by the people, and by *our native land*, would spring into life, and not languish from poverty, doubt, or neglect."[13] Land-grant agricultural colleges, Morrill continued,

> would prove . . . the perennial nurseries of patriotism, thrift and liberal information—places "where men do not decay." They would turn out men for solid use, and not drones. It may be assumed that tuition would be free, and that the exercise of holding the plow and swinging the scythe—every whit as noble, artistic, and graceful, as the postures of the gymnastic or military drill—would go far towards defraying all other expenses of the students. Muscles hardened by such training would not become soft in summer or torpid in winter; and the graduates would know how to sustain American institutions with American vigor.[14]

Nature and the land, and man's ability to manipulate as well as live harmoniously within it, seemed to provide the blueprint for American progress, health, and civilization. What made this vision unique was the notion that this was the destiny of white America. It was a narrative that completely wrote over Native Americans' relationship to the land.

However, the bill was vetoed by President James Buchanan in 1859. In his very extended veto message, Buchanan critiqued the bill while exposing and ultimately endorsing its intent. Outlining six key objections, Buchanan contended that the bill was unconstitutional, ill-timed, and, in many ways, un-American. "The establishment of these colleges has prevailed over the pressing wants of the common Treasury," he stated. "No nation ever had such an inheritance as we possess in the public lands. These ought to be managed with the utmost care, but at the same time *with a liberal spirit toward actual settlers*."[15] Buchanan never mentioned the fact that such vast "public lands" were already inhabited, owned, cultivated, and settled by various Native American tribes.[16] Instead, in claiming that the United States "inherited" these lands, Buchanan subscribed to a dominant national myth that effectively whitewashed the violent truth of how these lands came under government possession. He continued:

> The United States is a great landed proprietor, and from the very nature of this relation it is both the right and the duty of Congress as their trustee to manage these lands as any other prudent proprietor would manage them for his own best advantage. Now no consideration could be presented of a stronger character to induce the American people to brave

the difficulties and hardships of frontier life and to settle upon these lands and to purchase them at a fair price than that to give to them and to their children an assurance of the means of education.[17]

Buchanan questioned the constitutionality of the federal government interfering in state matters such as the educational system. He was also unconvinced that selling "public lands" to wealthy speculators would later benefit those that he was most concerned about: actual white settlers. And, of course, Buchanan subscribed to an ideal of true American character rooted in a masculinized notion of strength, individualism, and self-creation. But in questioning the constitutionality of the bill, Buchanan never challenged its underlying ethics.

It was Buchanan's successor, President Abraham Lincoln, who signed the Morrill Act on July 2, 1862. At a time when the nation was consumed by a growing Civil War, Lincoln signed the act partly to fulfill the promise he had made while running for the presidential ticket. This is not to say that the act was a tangential matter in a society immersed in the Civil War. As historian Jean Wilson Sidar argues, "The law was passed partly because of the awareness of Northern leaders of the important of science, agriculture, and industry for the war effort, partly because the Eastern states were interested in getting a share of the public lands, and partly because land speculators hoped for personal profit."[18] In many ways, the Morrill Act was an integral component of a nation at war. It is no surprise, then, that the bill that was presented to Lincoln was almost identical to the original version presented to Buchanan. One important amendment was added: that students undergo mandatory military training as part of their education.

New Jersey accepted the provisions of the act on March 21, 1862. The state was endowed with a land scrip for 210,000 acres of "public lands." Faced with a declining "market for college scrip" and a looming July 2, 1867, deadline to establish their college, Governor Joel Parker along with the commission appointed to dispose the scrip began to release acres of scrip at far less than the minimum government value of $1.25 per acre.[19] By December 1864, the state had sold 36,000 acres at 70 cents. The buyer was James Bishop and Co., a New Jersey–based firm.[20] The remaining 173,920 acres were sold in October 1865 to New Yorkers Hiram Slocum and Francis Howland. The rate was a substandard 50 cents.[21] The total earnings amounted to $115,945.95, "to which the trustees of Rutgers College added $54.05 to make an even $116,000."[22] The state used the proceeds to purchase state bonds, out of which annual interest in the amount of $6,960 was paid to the trustees at Rutgers College. Neither Rutgers nor the state of New Jersey got their hands dirty by locating land in the West. The responsibility fell on the individual purchasers of the scrip, if and when they chose to redeem it.

Although New Jersey accepted the Morrill Act in March, "the first evidence of interest at Rutgers was not recorded until the minutes of the faculty meeting on December 8, 1862."[23] Revitalized by the new leadership of President William Campbell, the school desperately sought funding to realize the faculty's new visions. Along with his colleague David Murray, George Hammell Cook, the school's renowned geologist, drafted the proposal for Rutgers to be considered for the land grant. Cook was popularly known for his sympathy toward "the education of the sons of farmers and mechanics."[24] Despite his respect for agricultural sciences and the land, Indians or Indian land, however, did not figure into his campaign.[25] The concept of the Morrill Act merely coincided perfectly with Cook's educational "philosophy that science should serve men," as biographer Jean Wilson Sidar argued.[26] What Sidar failed to highlight was that "men" referred exclusively to *white* men. The Morrill Act's "system of education uniquely suited to the furtherance of the agricultural and mechanical arts and to the education of a democratic citizenry" was specifically furnished to a democratic *white* citizenry.[27]

Afterthought: Indians, Race, Citizenship, and the Morrill Act

The national violence committed against Native Americans continues through our largely uncritical celebration of the Morrill Act and traditionally white land-grant colleges such as Rutgers University. Indeed, the positive impact of the act cannot be doubted. It offered the first federal assistance to higher education, enabling millions of Americans access and upward mobility. It also set the federal government's responsibility to education more broadly—an area previously taken strictly as a state matter. Through the act's vague provisions, states were given a very attractive incentive to use the federal government's resources to build their educational systems. The legacy of the Morrill Act—with over 150 years of amendments and revisions—often precedes the violence of the original act of 1862.[28]

Even the process through which the act became diversified in its reach is worthy of exploration and critique. As Cynthia L. Jackson and Eleanor F. Nunn have noted, "The Morrill Act of 1862 had established land-grant schools for whites."[29] In 1890, a second Morrill Act was enacted to serve a racially segregated South: "The act required states with racially segregated public higher education systems to provide a land-grant institution for black students."[30] Funding to private institutions in states where there was no public institution was permitted.[31] Unlike traditionally white colleges such as Rutgers, black land-grant colleges navigated a hostile, racially tiered education system with limited resources and a segregated curriculum. Their position was tenuous and heavily circumscribed. Jackson and Nunn state that "although the concentration in agricultural and the mechanical arts was clear whether the institutions were a HBCU [historically black college or university] or historically white, the breadth, depth, and scope of their curricula were very different. HBCU land-grant schools would focus on vocations and technical training. Historically white land-grant institutions would concentrate on research."[32]

During the late nineteenth century, some Native Americans attended black land-grant colleges. Where they had been previously erased by the Morrill Act, they "appeared" in black colleges as recipients of the proceeds of the act. Yet the U.S. postbellum society constructed upon a black-white racial binary conspired to commit more violence on Native Americans. For example, when a group of Native Americans joined the historically black Hampton Agricultural and Normal Institute in Virginia, Helen W. Ludlow, one of the institute's teachers, interrogated "the cause of Indian education." Speaking as if Indian students were savages, she questioned: "Will Indians study? Can they learn? . . . Will Indians work? Can they be broken in to civilized pursuits?"[33]

Beginning in 1878, Native Americans joined Hampton Institute's Indian program as part of President Ulysses S. Grant's "Peace Policy," a "haphazardly implemented plan for 'civilizing' the Native American."[34] Led by Booker T. Washington, the emphasis upon race and education as a "civilizing" mission yielded ideological tensions that spoke to Native American students' refusal to reject their tribal cultural identification. As historian Donal F. Lindsey writes, Washington "knew that 'the average Indian felt himself above the white man and, of course, he felt himself far above the Negro.' He wondered whether a race thought to cherish freedom even more than the white would obey a former slave."[35] The agricultural pursuits of Hampton Institute—under the provisions of the Morrill Act—also failed to operate seamlessly among its Native American student body. The school's stock and grain farm became frequently used as a "reformatory or penal colony for refractory Indians." As Lindsey continues, "Indians sent there dreaded its stricter discipline and the exile from friends, and some may have also felt shame, because their tribes viewed farming as women's work."[36] The structure of a racially segregated education system neither respected nor considered what form an appropriate education for a student body of multiple Native American tribes should assume. The project of "civilization" meant assimilation and insertion into a racially stratified society. Thus, on the surface it may seem that Indians at Hampton benefited from the proceeds under the Morrill Act, but the reality was far more insidious. Invoking a reverberation of violence that had started generations earlier, "education" came at the price of cultural identity.

A glance at Native American attendance at Hampton Institute, a black land-grant college during the late nineteenth century, offers an afterthought to my questions and research findings. Throughout the nineteenth century, Rutgers was never forced to address the ethics of its prestigious position as a land-grant college. As a traditionally white college, its status as a land-grant college guaranteed that its students would pursue agricultural and scientific studies that would propel them into society's professional classes. As a traditionally white college in a state that had long since purged its Native population, Rutgers enjoyed a safe distance from Indians. Nobody gave a thought to the consequences of reaping the benefits of the Morrill Act. Silence around Native Americans reaffirmed the legitimacy of Rutgers College's land-grant status.

Epilogue

Scarlet in Black—On the Uses of History

Jomaira Salas Pujols

On behalf of the Committee on Enslaved and Disenfranchised
Populations in Rutgers History

In the fall of 2015, black students at more than seventy-seven colleges and universities in the United States organized to demand a series of institutional transformations aimed at addressing systemic racism on college campuses.[1] Many of their demands overlap with students pushing for greater faculty diversity, curricular changes, and expanded budgets for cultural centers.[2] Not unlike the black student movement of the late 1960s, students of color today are drawing from theories of liberation to push their universities to extend to them the same sense of belonging that white students have had since the founding of higher education in the North American colonies and later the United States. It is no secret that racial violence was a driving force behind the prosperity of many primarily white colleges and universities and this history continues to cast a long shadow on the lives of students of color today.[3] The Committee on Enslaved and Disenfranchised Populations in Rutgers History was born out of this context in an effort to ask difficult but important questions about the role of exploitation and dislocation in the founding of our university. Knowing this history allows us to move forward while creating a welcoming environment for all students. This first step should not be taken lightly, as it reflects a genuine commitment from committee members, graduate researchers, and the university as a whole to grapple with the scarlet stain that so many higher education institutions attempt to ignore. The preceding chapters laid out some of the history of how Rutgers University benefited from the institution of slavery and the disenfranchisement of indigenous populations. This epilogue suggests some of the ways we can make use of that history.

Though just a preliminary investigation, eight months of arduous archival research have confirmed our suspicions that Rutgers University and its founders and benefactors were prodigiously involved in the slave trade and the slavery economy. Albeit indirectly, we know the college benefited from Native American Removal, breaking ground in a land once occupied by the Lenni Lenape. We know that our namesake, Henry Rutgers, was a slave owner. We know the Livingston campus is named after William Livingston, whose family was involved in the slave trade and were well-known slave owners. We know that the early financial health of our institution was largely a result of monetary and in-kind contributions from individuals who made their wealth off of slaves. And we know that despite a struggling yet striving New Brunswick African American community, Rutgers's founding fathers supported schemes to send blacks back to Africa rather than build an interracial community. And yet the committee's findings demand even more difficult questions: How do we grapple with the fact that some of the people who literally built Rutgers were enslaved? What can the institution do to acknowledge and reconcile with its role in benefiting from slavery? Perhaps most challenging, how can it make this history accessible to students and other community members? It is with this last question that this epilogue asks us to engage: to think critically and creatively about the uses of history as a driver of institutional change.

First and foremost, we ask that plaques be placed around campus to literally mark the presence and work of African Americans. The first of these should be placed at Old Queens, for we have uncovered evidence that the slave named Will helped break ground on the campus building.

In an effort to ensure that our historical research becomes a central part of the Rutgers University experience, the Committee on Enslaved and Disenfranchised Populations in Rutgers History recommends the creation of a walking and digital tour, which we tentatively title the "Back in Black" tour. This initiative will bring to life our findings about the lives of African American and other disenfranchised populations at the university. With a focus on the seventeenth and eighteenth centuries, the tour will highlight the dispossession of lands from the Lenni Lenape and the role of slavery in funding, building, and sustaining Rutgers and the surrounding New Brunswick community. Additionally, the "Back in Black" tour will be an opportunity for Rutgers students, alumni, and faculty members to learn about how the university benefited from the removal of Native Americans, the slave trade, and gradual abolition. An important component of the tour will also be to center the lived experiences of black and Native Americans, as well as other students of color on campus. As such, participants will learn about important moments of dissent, including the 1960s campus protests and the subsequent push for diversity initiatives at the university.

We suggest that the "Back in Black" tour be offered throughout the academic year and that professors, student groups, and community organizations be invited to request free tours which will serve as an opportunity to connect the history of Rutgers University with legacies of oppression and resistance. We imagine that the tour will have at least three important consequences: first, by centering the experiences of marginalized populations on campus, the tour will lay the groundwork for the university to be honest, critical, and forthright about its slaveholding past. Instead of hiding its connections to slavery, Rutgers will be deliberately transparent about its role in building institutional wealth. We believe this acknowledgment is a necessary precondition for the university to move forward in creating a safe and welcoming academic space where students of color can thrive. Second, the tour will serve as a counter-narrative that contests notions of deficit in favor of a more complex understanding of the experiences and contributions of blacks and other people of color at the university. Because the tour will highlight both the history of oppression *and* resistance, we hope it will be a space where students of color can see their experiences and contributions reflected in institutional programming. Finally, we envision the "Back in Black" tour as a pedagogical innovation. It is a tool we hope professors and teachers in New Brunswick will utilize to bring history to life and connect it to the daily lives of students. This active engagement with scholarly work is a testament that academia and public outreach are not so far apart after all.

Besides a separate tour that highlights Rutgers's entanglement with slavery and dispossession the committee also recognizes the importance of centering this history in multiple spaces and places at the university. To this end we suggest that the Rutgers Admissions Office introduce elements of the findings on slavery and dispossession to the existing campus tours. By incorporating these findings into the traditional campus tours Rutgers will ensure that all visitors who tour the university have access to the history of slavery on campus. Perhaps most importantly, by talking candidly about the legacies of slavery on campus tours, the university will tell a more truthful story of its founding and prosperity; a story that is imperfect, but intellectually honest and necessary.

Like many other colleges and universities that are also grappling with questions of the legacies of slavery, it is important for Rutgers to think broadly about other institutional changes that are necessary to make the committee's findings widely available. Some institutions, like Georgetown University, have already undertaken much of this work, creating websites and digital archives aimed at bringing their findings to the public.[4] We expect Rutgers to do the same, creating a website with digital copies of important archival documents and developing a space for a digital version of the "Back in Black" tour, effectively making it a pedagogical tool available to educators nationwide. It is through this type of careful and engaging public scholarship that we hope to make use of our history.

Other colleges and universities have instituted new policies and programs to make amends with the residue of their slaveholding and prejudiced past,[5] and we expect Rutgers to do the same. In response to student-led protests about Woodrow Wilson's views on race, for example, a special committee at Princeton University recommended that the university invest money and resources to create a high-profile pipeline of underrepresented scholars.[6] Additionally, Princeton has planned an exhibition on the legacy of Woodrow Wilson on campus, with the goal of making information about his role in preventing the enrollment of black students at the university publicly and broadly accessible.[7] They did this because, while Wilson has been a revered figure on campus, his racist views and the way they impacted black student enrollment were more covert in the institutional memory. The Committee on Enslaved and Disenfranchised Populations in Rutgers History will follow in Princeton's steps to ensure that students, professors, and other community members learn about the uncomfortable facts of Rutgers's founding and prosperity. We expect to utilize public panels, invited speakers, and university professorships to facilitate discussions on critical scholarship and the creation of repositories of institutional memory. We hope to use public scholarship to both revisit the committee's findings and create additional research opportunities for undergraduates, graduate students, and scholars to pursue further research on the experiences of people of color at the university.

For too long now, the pursuit of scholarship in the classroom has followed a singular narrative that negates or ignores the history and lived experiences of underrepresented people in the United States. This can be addressed by including elements of Rutgers's history of enslavement, dislocation, and race-making within the core curriculum. While the extent to which professors will include this history will vary, doing so creates a unique opportunity for professors and students to engage in thoughtful dialogue about a history that took place in their own backyard and its impact on contemporary events. Again, we suggest that using our institution's history is not only a pedagogical tool but an exercise in intellectual honesty, one that extends to all corners of the university. As a result, along with the Task Force on Inclusion and Community Values, we have called for the university to establish a diversity course requirement for all students aimed at broadening their understanding of various issues of identity and belonging. Once inaugurated, we envision these curricular changes as pillars of Rutgers's commitment to acknowledging its role in the institution of slavery.

The committee positions its findings and the initiatives described in this epilogue as part of a long march toward acknowledgment and reconciliation.

We want to emphasize that the research presented in the foregoing pages is only preliminary and that we are committed to researching and writing a more complete story that includes all campuses of Rutgers University and that brings this history into the contemporary era. For now, we encourage students, faculty, and staff members to engage deeply with this difficult history—this scarlet stain—and to push for changes that will ultimately make Rutgers a more inclusive institution.

ACKNOWLEDGMENTS

This book required a Rutgers community effort and we would like to acknowledge all who made it possible. We would like to thank Chancellor Richard L. Edwards for initiating and funding the project. Without his unwavering support this would not have been possible. Dr. Karen Stubaus, vice president for academic affairs and administration, was also steadfast in her attention and dedication to this endeavor.

The Committee on Enslaved and Disenfranchised Populations in Rutgers History, which was composed of faculty, administrators, and students, met regularly to brainstorm ideas on how the research and writing should proceed. We would like to thank Carolina Alonso Bejarano, Sonia Brown, Paul Clemens, John Coakley, Thomas Frusciano, Wayne Glasker, Dionne Higginbotham, Denajah Hoffman, John Keene, Felicia McGinty, Richard Murray, Jomaira Salas Pujols, Karen Stubaus, Monica Torres, and Camilla Townsend.

Rutgers librarians were an indispensable resource. Their wisdom was only matched by their enthusiasm and without both this study would not have been possible. Special thanks go to University Archivist Thomas Frusciano, who worked with the aforementioned committee, helped guide our researchers (many of whom specialize in the twentieth century and were therefore unfamiliar with early American sources) through the maze of colonial Dutch and English sources, and read final drafts for accuracy. Librarian Erika Gorder, from the Special Collections and University Archives, also helped guide our researchers and commented on final drafts. Albert C. King and David C. Fowler, both of the Special Collections and University Archives division of Rutgers University Library, also helped direct our researchers.

As readers will see, the early history of Queen's College (later Rutgers) and the New Brunswick Theological Seminary cannot be separated. We are indebted to Professor John Coakley, the emeritus L. Russell Feakes Memorial Professor of Church History of the seminary, for his interest in this project, his suggestions for the organization of the research project, his service on the aforementioned committee, his leadership in getting the seminary involved, and his comments on final drafts. Librarians at the Gardner A. Sage Library of the New Brunswick Theological Seminary also provided crucial assistance. We would like to thank Bethany O'Shea, librarian for reference and access services, and Ondrea Murphy, librarian for technical services.

Various people in very different capacities also made this book possible. Catherine Stearns Medich from the New Jersey State Archives helped us locate the trustees' wills and offered guidance on how to navigate New Jersey's massive collection of wills. The History Department at Rutgers provided administrative and technical support. For this we thank Walter Rucker, Tiffany Berg, Matthew Leonaggeo, and Matthew Steiner. Amy Shockley, in the Sociology Department, also provided important administrative support. We would also like to thank Alexis Biedermann, senior executive associate to the chancellor, for coordinating the meetings and organizing the correspondence of the Committee on Enslaved and Disenfranchised Populations in Rutgers History.

NOTES

INTRODUCTION

1. Craig Steven Wilder, *Ebony and Ivy: Race, Slavery, and the Troubled History of America's Universities* (New York: Bloomsbury Press, 2013), 60–75.
2. Ibid., 74.
3. Ibid., 263–264.
4. Ibid., 29, 114.
5. Ibid., 12.
6. Rachel L. Swarns, "Georgetown University Plans Steps to Atone for Slave Past," *New York Times*, September 6, 2016, http://www.nytimes.com/2016/09/02/us/slaves-georgetown-university.html?_r=0.
7. Kate Zernike, "Slave Traders in Yale's Past Fuel Debate on Restitution," *New York Times*, August 13, 2001, http://www.nytimes.com/2001/08/13/nyregion/slave-traders-in-yale-s-past-fuel-debate-on-restitution.html.
8. Sven Beckert et al., eds., *Harvard and Slavery: Seeking a Forgotten History* (Cambridge, MA: Harvard University, 2011), http://www.harvardandslavery.com/wp-content/uploads/2011/11/Harvard-Slavery-Book-111110.pdf.
9. President's Commission on Slavery and the University, *Universities Studying Slavery* (Charlottesville: University of Virginia, 2013), http://slavery.virginia.edu/?page_id=157.
10. Swarns, "Georgetown University Plans Steps to Atone for Slave Past."
11. "Yale Retains Calhoun College's Name, Selects Names for Two New Residential Colleges, and Changes Title of 'Master' in the Residential Colleges," *YaleNews*, April 27, 2017, http://news.yale.edu/2016/04/27/yale-retains-calhoun-college-s-name-selects-names-two-new-residential-colleges-and-change.
12. Jalin P. Cunningham, Melissa Rodman, and Ignacio Sabate, "Harvard House Masters Now Called 'Faculty Deans,'" *Harvard Crimson*, February 25, 2016, http://www.thecrimson.com/article/2016/2/25/house-master-new-name/; Office of Communications, "Masters Change Their Titles to 'Head' of Residential Colleges," *News at Princeton*, November 18, 2015, https://www.princeton.edu/main/news/archive/S44/78/51S96/index.xml?section=topstories.
13. Kenneth P. Ruscio, "Remarks at the Introduction of the Historical Marker: 'A Difficult, Yet Undeniable, History,'" https://www.wlu.edu/presidents-office/about-president-ruscio/speeches/remarks-at-the-historical-marker-introduction.
14. "Gaol" is the eighteenth-century spelling for *jail*.

CHAPTER 1: "I Am Old and Weak . . . and You Are Young and Strong . . ."

1. John Heckewelder, *An Account of the History, Manners, and Customs of the Indian Nations, Who Once Inhabited Pennsylvania and Neighboring States* (Philadelphia: Historical Society of Pennsylvania, 1876 [1819]), 321–322. Heckewelder was a Moravian missionary who lived among the Lenape from the 1760s onward in the Ohio River Valley, where the majority of the Lenape had by then moved (see below). He became fluent in the language and his works provide the clearest view of Lenape culture in the colonial era available to us today.

2. There were three language families in the northeastern segment of what is now the United States: the Algonkian, the Iroquoian, and the Siouan. The Siouan were not well represented and will not be treated in this essay. The Iroquoians were the most highly politically organized at the moment of the arrival of the Europeans; the Five Nations in today's Canada and New York State conducted their business with outsiders as a bloc. The Algonkian speakers lived in mobile, self-governing communities scattered across the countryside, working as part-year farmers and part-year hunters. The Lenape of New Jersey, later called the Delaware, spoke varied dialects of the same language. The dialect in North Jersey is sometimes called "Munsee" and that of South Jersey "Unami"; however, there were no corresponding organized political entities. Tribes or local ethnic groups were relatively small, and almost all were interrelated through marriage. For an excellent recent study of the lifestyles they practiced, see Amy Schutt, *Peoples of the River Valleys: The Odyssey of the Delaware Indians* (Philadelphia: University of Pennsylvania Press, 2007). For an entrée into the archaeological studies that have been done, see the works of Herbert Kraft.

3. Jonas Michaelius to Adrian Smoutias, 1628, in Edwin T. Corwin, Hugh Hastings, and James A. Holden, eds., *Ecclesiastical Records: State of New York* (Albany: J. B. Lyon, 1901), 1:56–60. The early Dutch Reformed Church records were translated and edited by Edwin Corwin, an 1856 graduate of the New Brunswick Theological Seminary; the complete collection of these rare volumes is housed in the Gardner A. Sage Library at the seminary.

4. Ibid.

5. Ibid.

6. Ibid.

7. Seth Newhouse's relation in J.N.B. Hewitt, ed., "Iroquoian Cosmology," *Twenty-first Annual Report of the Bureau of American Ethnology, 1899–1900* (Washington, DC: U.S. Government Printing Office, 1903), 255–295. Hewitt provided a painstaking transcription and word-by-word translation parallel to his colloquial translation. He was interviewing a Mohawk man, and at first blush, it might seem that this text has nothing to do with Lenape religion. However, Lenape and Iroquoian religious traditions have long been known to be extremely similar (in the same way that Aztec and Mayan cosmologies are related, or French and German styles of Christianity). Scholars initially assumed that these tight linkages in religious stories were formed during the period of the Lenape's residence in Pennsylvania in the eighteenth century, as neighbors to the Iroquois (see below), but John Bierhorst has demonstrated that a similar creation story was told by the Lenape to the Dutch in the 1670s. See Bierhorst, ed., *Mythology of the Lenape: Guide and Texts* (Tucson: University of Arizona Press, 1995). Bierhorst lists all known texts and fragments of texts that tell the story. Note also that in the early 1650s, a Swede recorded a story that included definitely recognizable specific elements

of the narrative. See Peter Lindeström, *Geographia Americae*, trans. Amandus Johnson (Philadelphia: Swedish Colonial Society, 1925), 208–209. I use the Mohawk version here because it is the only one we have in an indigenous language, and thus the only one to include rich detail and subtlety.

8. David Zeisberger, *History of the Northern American Indians*, ed. Archer Butler Hulbert and William Nathaniel Schwarze (Columbus: Ohio State Archaeological and Historical Society, 1910), 147. Zeisberger was a Moravian missionary who arrived prior to Heckewelder, but despite his prodigious output, neither his language skills nor his cultural sensitivity ever matched Heckewelder's, and thus his numerous works are often misleading or confusing. They are useful only in limited regards. What he produced successfully are a number of works translating religious language into Delaware; these are of interest to people studying early indigenous versions of Christianity.

9. Lindeström, *Geographia Americae*, 208.

10. Versions of the Dido story appear in a number of indigenous accounts of the past around the globe—wherever, in fact, seventeenth-century missionaries were once present. On the European colonizers' love for the story, see Constance Jordan, "Jamestown and Its North Atlantic World," in *Envisioning an English Empire*, ed. Robert Appelbaum and John Wood Sweet (Philadelphia: University of Pennsylvania Press, 2005). For a thorough exploration of the phenomenon, see Andrew Newman, *On Records: Delaware Indians, Colonists, and the Media of History and Memory* (Lincoln: University of Nebraska Press, 2012). Newman believes the colonists probably liked to go through some sort of public ritual in which they actually enacted the story of Dido, but we find this highly doubtful. It is enough to know that the missionaries of the era loved the story and that they spent hours talking to Indians.

11. Only the barest outline of the story actually appears in the *Aeneid*. Vergil, *The Aeneid* (New York: New American Library, 1961), 16–17. However, a European folk tradition about the matter made its way into the study of mathematics from the Renaissance onward, possibly earlier.

12. Heckewelder, *History*, 71–75. This story lasted in Delaware oral culture into the twentieth century. See Bierhorst, *Mythology*.

13. Heckewelder, *History*, 71–75.

14. Ibid.

15. The most recent study of the era is Jean Soderlund, *Lenape Country: Delaware Valley Society before William Penn* (Philadelphia: University of Pennsylvania Press, 2015). See also Schutt, *Peoples of the River Valleys*.

16. Lindeström mentions these. None have survived, but we can assume that they probably resembled feather textiles created in Mesoamerica, in which the feather fibers are removed from the feather stalks and twisted into shimmering threads that are woven together. Lindeström, *Geographia Americae*, 222.

17. Ibid., 194, 198–199, 251.

18. This was Kieft's War, which has its own literature. See, for instance, Evan Haefali, "Kieft's War and the Cultures of Violence in Colonial America," in *Lethal Imagination: Violence and Brutality in American History*, ed. Michael A. Bellesiles (New York: New York University Press, 1999), 17–42.

19. For an excellent summary of these events and ensuing ones, see Maxine Lurie, "The Colonial Period: The Complex and Contradictory Beginnings of a Mid-Atlantic Province," in *New Jersey: A History of the Garden State*, ed. Maxine N. Lurie and Richard F. Veit (New Brunswick, NJ: Rutgers University Press, 2012), 33–63.

20. Augustine Herrman and W. Faithorne, "Virginia and Maryland as it is planted and inhabited this present year 1670" (London, 1673).

21. Lurie, "Colonial Period," 52.

22. Statement received by the Dutch Church, February 1665, in Corwin et al., *Ecclesiastical Records*, 1:578.

23. Peter Wacker and Paul Clemens, *Land Use in Early New Jersey: A Historical Geography* (Newark: New Jersey Historical Society, 1995).

24. Indentures, Indian Deeds, Drawer 1, Iroseheote and Lydia Bowne (Photostat), Rutgers University Special Collections and University Archives (hereafter cited as SC/UA).

25. Deeds and Land Conveyances, 1714–1721, Middlesex County Record Books, 6:234–236ff, SC/UA. Adam Hude was in the process of buying several tracts, the others being from white sellers. Indeed, the volume demonstrates that by this period, the area was largely in the hands of the settler population.

26. Ibid.

27. Indentures, Indian Deeds, Drawer 1, Andrew Wolle and John Peairs, SC/UA.

28. Samuel Smith, *The History of the Colony of Nova Caesaria, or New Jersey* (Burlington, NJ: James Parker, 1877 [1765]), 442–445. For more on Smith, see note 35.

29. Corwin et al., *Ecclesiastical Records*, 3:1609. For a full study on the wars in the American South that were creating the Indian slave trade, see Allan Gallay, *The Indian Slave Trade: The Rise of the English Empire in the American South, 1670–1717* (New Haven, CT: Yale University Press, 2002).

30. Corwin et al., *Ecclesiastical Records*, 3:1710.

31. Cited in Soderlund, *Lenape Country*, 197.

32. Moses Marshall, Overseer of the Poor, "Examination of Indian Hannah, alias Hannah Freeman" (July 28, 1797), appendix to *A Lenape among the Quakers: The Life of Hannah Freeman*, by Dawn G. Marsh (Lincoln: University of Nebraska Press, 2014).

33. There was at least one community of free blacks who had escaped the Dutch and welcomed such women as wives on a regular basis, making their contributions a part of their ongoing, distinct cultural life. See David S. Cohen, *The Ramapo Mountain People* (New Brunswick, NJ: Rutgers University Press, 1974).

34. A brilliant reconstruction of this man's life was accomplished many years ago by a Seneca historian. See Anthony Wallace, *King of the Delawares: Teedyuscung, 1700–1763* (Philadelphia: University of Pennsylvania Press, 1949).

35. Samuel Smith was a Quaker merchant from the Burlington area who involved himself in the series of conferences discussed here and later published the minutes he took in his *History of the Colony of Nova Caesaria*, 440–484.

36. Ibid., 459. This was actually preliminary to Teedyuscung's declaration that he would now side with the English.

37. Ibid., 458.

38. There is a vast literature on Brainerd, the production of which began at the moment of his death. See John Grigg, *The Lives of David Brainerd: The Making of an American Evangelical Icon* (New York: Oxford University Press, 2009).

39. Thomas Brainerd, *The Life of John Brainerd* (New York: A.D.F. Randolph, 1865), 230–239.

40. David Brainerd, *An Account of the Life of Mr. David Brainerd . . . pastor of church of Christian Indians in New Jersey* (Edinburgh: John Gray, 1765), 117. It was Jonathan Edwards who edited Brainerd's diaries and published them under this title.

41. He does not give a name, but this was probably Moses Tatamy, who worked as a translator for him for a long time. Little is known about him with certainty. He seems to have

been related to a number of chiefly families and was from the northwestern part of the state but lived mostly in Pennsylvania.

42. Ibid., 140.

43. Ibid., 181–182.

44. Ibid, 184.

45. The Royal Governor's Council received a complaint from white community residents that until then only Indian Andrew (Woolley) and Indian Peter (Tule) had lived there with their families; they feared the arrival of more. Cited in Soderlund, *Lenape Country*, 37.

46. Years later, Stephen Calvin's granddaughter told her minister this when she was living in Wisconsin. See Thomas Brainerd, *Life of John Brainerd*, 460–461. The story is substantiated by two facts: 1) other items mentioned match references to Weequehela found in English archival records that could not have been known to the granddaughter or the minister, and 2) Stephen Calvin in treaty negotiations listed his own involvement in Middlesex County land claims of sachems, without saying that he was a chief himself; see Smith, *History of Nova Caesaria*, 443. For more on Weequehela, see Soderlund, *Lenape Country*, 183–190.

47. Wallace, *King of the Delawares*, 458.

48. Early Land Records, 1650–1801, March term 1749: *Robert Hunter Morris v. Stephen Calvin [et al.]*, Box 479, file 26888; *Robert Hunter Morris v. Thomas Store*, Box 479, file 26886; *Robert Hunter Morris v. Philip Douty*, Box 479, file 26476; *Robert Hunter Morris v. Indian Andrew*, Box 479, file 24262; Supreme Court Minutes, November 1745–1752, Supreme Court Case Files, Box 6–7, book 4–5; Supreme Court Judgment Scrolls, November 1750, Supreme Court Case Files, Box 38, New Jersey State Archives, Trenton.

49. Steven G. Greiert, "The Earl of Halifax and the Land Riots in New Jersey, 1748–1753," *New Jersey History* 99, no. 1–2 (February 1981): 13–31.

50. For details, see Wallace, *King of the Delawares*; and C. A. Welsager, *The Delaware Westward Migration* (Wallingford, PA: Middle Atlantic Press, 1978).

51. For the complete listing see Smith, *History of Nova Caesaria*, 442.

52. The Swede whose name he bore was John Hans Stille (or Steelman), a merchant trader in the Great Egg Harbor area. See Soderlund, *Lenape Country*, 190–191.

53. John Brainerd to Eleazar Wheelock, March 23, 1757, in *Letters of Eleazar Wheelock's Indians*, ed. James Dow McCallum (Hanover, NH: Dartmouth College Publications, 1932), 29–31.

54. Ibid.

55. Smith, *History of Nova Caesaria*, 453.

56. Ibid., 456, 465.

57. Ibid., 470.

58. Ibid., 472.

59. Ibid., 474, 477.

60. Ibid., 483–484.

61. 1762 Indian Petition to the General Assembly stating that "their Mill is lately burnt which renders them utterly unable to pay their Debt," cited in George Flemming, *Brotherton: New Jersey's First and Only Indian Reservation* (Medford, NJ: Plexus Publishing, 2005), 59.

62. On this see Craig Steven Wilder, *Ebony and Ivy: Race, Slavery, and the Troubled History of America's Universities* (New York: Bloomsbury Press, 2013).

63. Indian Charity School Records, DA 403, Box 5399, Day Book 1765–1767, 18, and elsewhere, Dartmouth University Special Collections.

64. Jacob Woolley to Eleazar Wheelock, December 14, 1761, in *Letters of Eleazar Wheelock's Indians*, 251.

65. Jeremiah Halsey to Eleazar Wheelock, September 30, 1762, in ibid., 252.

66. Jacob Woolley's Confession, July 25, 1763, in ibid., 255.

67. Indian Charity School Records, DA 403, Box 5399, Ledger B, 21, Dartmouth University Special Collections.

68. Joseph Fish to Eleazar Wheelock, January 20, 1764, in *Letters of Eleazar Wheelock's Indians*, 260–261.

69. Joseph Woolley to Eleazar Wheelock, July 6, 1765, in ibid., 267–268.

70. Indian Charity School Records, DA 403, Box 5399, Ledger B, 14, Dartmouth University Special Collections.

71. Joseph Woolley correspondence and report of death in *Letters of Eleazar Wheelock's Indians*, 263–274.

72. Wheelock Correspondence, document 759619, Hezekiah Calvin's school work, Dartmouth University Special Collections.

73. Indian Charity School Records, DA 403, Box 5399, Ledger B, 16, Dartmouth University Special Collections.

74. Joseph Woolley to Eleazar Wheelock, n.d., positioned in collection as summer of 1765, in *Letters of Eleazar Wheelock's Indians*, 274.

75. Hezekiah Calvin to Eleazar Wheelock, February 19, 1766, in ibid., 49.

76. Hezekiah Calvin to Eleazar Wheelock, August 11, 1766, in ibid., 49–51.

77. Hezekiah Calvin to Eleazar Wheelock, August 14, 1767, in ibid., 57.

78. Hezekiah Calvin to Eleazar Wheelock, March 3, 1767, in ibid., 52–53.

79. John Secuter to Eleazar Wheelock, March 31, 1767, with notes enclosed, in ibid., 53–54.

80. Eleazar Wheelock to John Brainerd, July 8, 1767, in ibid., 55–56.

81. John Brainerd to Eleazar Wheelock, February 12, 1768, in Thomas Brainerd, *The Life of John Brainerd* (New York: A.D.F. Randolph, 1865), 378.

82. Hezekiah Calvin to Eleazar Wheelock, August 14, 1767, in *Letters of Eleazar Wheelock's Indians*, 57–58.

83. Hezekiah Calvin to Eleazar Wheelock, October 12, 1767, in ibid., 59. It is not clear what trade he had been put to, but he complained that the master was often away and that he was therefore learning little. Wheelock's account book records the purchase of a "leathern apron" for him. Indian Charity School Records, DA 403, Box 5399, Ledger 1763–1769, 30, Dartmouth University Special Collections.

84. Hezekiah Calvin to Eleazar Wheelock, March 1768, in *Letters of Eleazar Wheelock's Indians*, 63. See also letters of January 29 and May 5.

85. See Mary Secuter's Confessions and Letters, in ibid., 235–238.

86. Mary Secuter to Eleazar Wheelock, November 16, 1768, in ibid., 67.

87. Edward Deake to Eleazar Wheelock, June 21, 1768, in ibid., 65.

88. Hezekiah Calvin to Eleazar Wheelock, n.d. 1768, in ibid., 66–67.

89. Comment cited in ibid., 47.

90. John Brainerd to Eleazar Wheelock, February 3, 1769, in Thomas Brainerd, *The Life*, 381–382.

91. John Brainerd to Eleazar Wheelock, June 22, 1769 in ibid., 382.

92. John Brainerd to Eleazar Wheelock, December 25, 1772, in ibid., 395.

93. Eleazar Wheelock to Andrew Gifford, February 24, 1763, in *Letters of Eleazar Wheelock's Indians*, 69–71. She is mentioned in at least two other letters as well.

94. Indian Charity School Records, DA 403, Box 5399, Ledger B, 5; and Day Book 1765–1767, 29, 63, Dartmouth University Special Collections.

95. Mirriam Storrs [Stores] to Eleazar Wheelock, November 24, 1768, in *Letters of Eleazar Wheelock's Indians*, 239.

96. John Brainerd to Eleazar Wheelock, February 3, 1769, in Thomas Brainerd, *The Life*, 381–382. Brainerd reported that she had brought him EW's letter on her arrival the preceding November.

97. John Brainerd to Eleazar Wheelock, August 25, 1769, in ibid., 383.

98. Smith, *History of Nova Caesaria*, 442.

99. *The Papers of Sir William Johnson* (Albany, NY: University of the State of New York: 1957), 12:305, cited in Weslager, *Delaware Indians:* A History (New Brunswick, NJ: Rutgers University Press, 1972), 271–272, and Flemming, *Brotherton*, 63.

100. Burlington Council meetings, May 30, 1771, New Jersey Historical Society, cited in Weslager, *Delaware Indians,* 272–273. Discussions continued on June 1, 1777, at which point it was revealed that Calvin had proceeded without full consensus on the part of his people. The councilors criticized what they perceived at that time as his erratic behavior and attributed it to alcohol.

101. The Lenape name is repeated without attestation by several historians. It is given as Wilted Grass, but since in a number of indigenous languages the idea of "flattened grass" is not pathetic but rather powerful (where an animal has slept, or a wind passed through), I have chosen to amend the English translation.

102. Thomas Brainerd, *The Life,* 460.

103. Cited in Weslager, *Delaware Indians,* 304–306 (emphasis added).

104. Colonel George Morgan to Congress, May 12, 1784, Morgan Letters, Library of Congress, cited in Weslager, *Delaware Indians,* 306.

105. Journals of the Continental Congress, October 8, 1783, Library of Congress, cited in Anne Gossen, *Princeton 1783: The Nation's Capital* (Princeton, NJ: Morven Museum & Garden, 2009), 61–62. The collection also houses the letters from Thomas Killbuck to the Congress, begging to be allowed to go home.

106. John Hunt's journal, June 8, 1779, cited in Flemming, *Brotherton*, 69.

107. Thomas Brainerd, *The Life*, 417–419. They were headed to the Stockbridge mission in upstate New York; from there, they would later move west.

108. Letter to the Legislature, in John W. Barber and Henry Howe, *Historical Collections of the State of New Jersey* (New Haven, CT: John Barber, 1868), 510–511.

109. Samuel L. Mitchill, "The Life, Exploits, and Precepts of Tammany: the Famous Indian Chief: Being the Anniversary Oration, Pronounced before the Tammany Society, or Columbian Order, in the Old Presbyterian Church, in the City of New York, on Tuesday, the 12th May, 1795." Approximately forty-four of the published pamphlets survive. (New York: J. Buel) no. 153, 1795.

110. See, for example, "Constitution and By-Laws of the Leni Lenape Lodge Number 15, The Independent Order of Odd Fellows of New Jersey" (1843), surviving copy in Rutgers University Special Collections. The inside cover of the pamphlet is a card reading, "This is to certify that Brother _____ was elected a Member of this lodge on the _____ day of the year 18___."

111. Mitchill, "Life, Exploits and Precepts," 5.

112. Ibid., 10–11. It is not clear in context if Mitchill was taking sides here in the flurry of discussion of slavery that occurred in the early national period or if he was merely critiquing Federalist policy in heightened language.

113. Ibid., 26.

114. Ibid., 33.

115. John Davis, *The First Settlers of Virginia: An Historical Novel* (New York: Riley & Co, 1806), 275.

116. James Barker's introduction to his play *Marmion*, cited in John Crowley, "James Nelson Barker in Perspective," *Educational Theater Journal* 24, no. 4 (1972): 363–364.

117. James Barker, *The Indian Princess; or, La Belle Sauvage: An Operataic Melo-drama in Three Acts*, Performed at the Theatre Philadelphia, April 6, 1808.

118. Barker, *Indian Princess*, 15. Of course, in Algonkian society, only men hunted. No girl would have been out in the woods practicing with her bow.

119. Ibid., 18.

120. See Robert Tilton, *Pocahontas: The Evolution of an American Narrative* (New York: Cambridge University Press, 1994).

121. Samuel Macpherson Janney, *The Last of the Lenape and Other Poems* (Philadelphia: Henry Perkins, 1839), 35.

122. Nicholas Marcellus Hentz, *Tadeuskund, the Last King of the Lenape* (Boston: Cummings & Hilliard, 1825), 27.

123. The *Christian Intelligencer*, fall issues 1830, beginning September 4 (for mentions of Rutgers University) and all issues 1830–1832 (for the advertisements for the grammar school). The ads continue sporadically after that. A full run of the paper is held at the Gardner A. Sage Library of the New Brunswick Theological Seminary.

124. E. T. Corwin, *Manual of the Reformed Church in America* (New York: Reformed Church in America, 1879), 546. After stepping down from the paper, Westbrook served as rector of Rutgers grammar school.

125. James Van Hoeven, "Salvation and Indian Removal: The Career Biography of the Rev. John Freeman Schermerhorn, Indian Commissioner" (PhD diss., Vanderbilt University, 1972). It is fascinating to watch Schermerhorn's hope of patronage from Andrew Jackson grow, hand-in-hand with what he convinced himself were truly benevolent views concerning Removal. On the Dutch Reformed Church's relations with Indians in general, see Leroy Koopman, *Taking the Jesus Road: The Ministry of the Reformed Church in America among Native Americans* (Grand Rapids, MI: Eerdman's, 2005).

126. McCormick, *Rutgers*, 69.

127. *Christian Intelligencer*, November 27, 1830.

128. James Evan, "Death of a Christian Indian," written April 1830 and published in the *Christian Intelligencer*, October 2, 1830.

129. See, for example, *Christian Intelligencer*, December 31, 1831. In this piece Cass argues that Indians continue to worship fire because of their immovable ignorance of the "true religion."

130. *Christian Intelligencer*, April 28, 1832. The editor, Cornelius Westbrook, thus introduced another man's contribution.

131. E. T. Corwin, ed., *Digest of Constitutional and Synodical Legislation of the Reformed Church in America*, vol. 1: *1831* (New York Reformed Church, 1906), 29–30. The Minutes of the Synod include discussions of the affiliated United Foreign Missionary Society, a description of Indians "melting before the white population, and the remnant of them now lying like Lazarus at our very doors," and a statement of the need for hands "stretched out for their relief." But there is no record of expenditures for new missions, except for the fact that graduates of the Theological Seminary were to be sent to form "new congregations in destitute [white] settlements."

132. On this see McCormick, *Rutgers*, especially chap. 3.

133. Corwin et al., *Eccesliastical Records*, 3:2303–2308. (The energized disputes from which we quote took place in 1725–1726.)

134. A Theodore Frelinghuysen Jr. of Somerville is listed as a graduate in the *Christian Intelligencer* in July 1831. Since neither the senator nor his brother had a child of this name,

the young man had to have descended from one of the other branches of the family founded by the original Theodorus a century earlier. Frederick Frelinghuysen, the senator's nephew and adopted son, arrived at Rutgers in 1831 and graduated in 1836.

135. For the full speech see *Register of Debates in Congress* (Washington, DC: U.S. Government Printing Office), 6:311–316.

136. An excellent short study of the crisis is Theda Perdue and Michael D. Green, eds., *The Cherokee Removal: A Brief History with Documents* (New York: Bedford, 2005).

137. Philoclean Society Records, Minutes, February 4, 1831, Box 4, Folder 1, SC/UA.

138. *Christian Intelligencer*, July 23, 1831.

139. Theodore Frelinghuysen, *An Address Delivered before the Philoclean and Peithessophian Societies of Rutgers College, July 31, 1831* (New Brunswick: Van Doorn & McReady, 1831), 4–6.

140. Ibid., 17.

141. Ibid., 23.

142. Philoclean Society Records, Minutes, Box 4, Folder 1, September 20 and November 4, 1831, SC/UA. The students' correspondence also indicates that they were energized by Frelinghuysen's visit.

143. Peithessophian Society Records, Minutes, Box 9, Folder 1, October 27, 1831, SC/UA.

144. For example, at the end of the Philoclean Society Minutes book for the period during which he was the secretary, he wrote out his full name "Frederick Theodore Frelinghuysen" in gorgeous letters, and a friend wrote in squiggly ones, "What a long name!" Philoclean Society Records, Minutes, Box 4, Folder 1, inside back cover of volume, SC/UA.

145. The next governor of Georgia pardoned him so that he was able to return home.

146. Barber and Howe, *Historical Collections*, 510–511.

147. The General Assembly of the State of New Jersey, "An Act for the Extinguishment of Every Right, Title or Claim, which the Delaware Tribe of Indians, Formerly Residents of New Jersey, and Now Located at Green Bay, in the Territory of Michigan, Now Have, or Ever Had, to Any Part of the Territory of New Jersey or Its Franchises, in *Acts of the Fifty-Sixth General Assembly of the State of New Jersey* (Trenton: Joseph Justice, 1832), 148. See also *Votes and Proceedings of the Fifty-Sixth General Assembly of the State of New Jersey* (Newton, NJ: Grant Finch, 1832), 146, 250–251.

148. *Votes and Proceedings of the Fifty-Sixth General Assembly*, 319–320.

149. On this see McCormick, *Rutgers*, especially chap. 5.

150. The Quakers of Philadelphia distributed an 1891 pamphlet, "An Address of the Representatives of the Religious Society of Friends, from Pennsylvania, New Jersey and Delaware to their fellow citizens on behalf of the Indians." A copy survives in the Rutgers University Special Collections. Its defensive tone suggests that local opinion was decidedly hostile to the Indians. No mention of the matter was made in the pages of the *Targum* or other student records.

151. There was a real Tom Quick, of a Dutch family of settlers in Pennsylvania, whose father was killed in the Seven Years' War. In 1851, the story of the revenge he purportedly sought became a popular series in the magazine *Republican Watchman* and the author had the stories printed as a book. J. E. Quinlan, *Tom Quick, Indian Slayer* (Monticello, NY: DeVoe & Quinlan, 1851). At the very end of the Indian wars in the West, the story became popular again, inspired by William Bross, *Legend of the Delaware: An Historical Sketch of Tom Quick* (Chicago: Knight and Leonard, 1887). Judge James Allerton, of Port Jervis, New York (just above the New Jersey border, on the Delaware River), wrote a play and saw its production through to extensive local performance. Rutgers University Special Collections (Philhower Papers, Box 84) houses his original handwritten

manuscript, as well as copies that were made for the actors to learn their parts, local signage, newspaper coverage of the opening, etc. It was clearly well received in the area.

152. Philhower Papers, Box 20, Indian Subjects: Newark Normal College Course on Native Americans (1938–1940), SC/UA. Amateur New Jersey archaeologist and writer Charles Philhower taught a course in the late 1930s which was discontinued during the Second World War. The collection contains not only Philhower's lectures but also index cards filled out by each student who took the course.

153. The *Targum*, March 8, March 9, March 12, March 13, March 15, March 27, 1973.

154. Collected between 1905 and 1910 in eastern Oklahoma. Manuscript in the M. R. Harrington Papers, Box OC 161, Folder 1, Archives, Museum of the American Indian, Washington, DC. Printed in Bierhorst, *Mythology of the Lenape*, 101–102

CHAPTER 2: Old Money

1. Craig Steven Wilder, *Ebony and Ivy: Race, Slavery, and the Troubled History of America's Universities* (New York: Bloomsbury Press, 2013), 1–2.

2. James Gigantino, *The Ragged Road to Abolition: Slavery and Freedom in New Jersey, 1775–1865* (Philadelphia: University of Pennsylvania Press, 2014), 11–12.

3. Ibid., 12–14.

4. Thomas Frusciano and Benjamin Justice., "History and Politics," in *Rutgers: A 250th Anniversary Portrait*, ed. Nita Congress (London: Third Millennium Publishing, 2015), 29–30.

5. Wilder, *Ebony and Ivy*, 33.

6. Ibid., 93.

7. Ibid., 49.

8. Gigantino, *The Ragged Road to Abolition*, 12, 236–237. For more on the history of the Dutch Reformed Church in the American colonies, see Gerald Francis De Jong, *The Dutch Reformed Church in the American Colonies* (Grand Rapids, MI: Eerdmans, 1978); and John W. Coakley, *New Brunswick Theological Seminary: An Illustrated History, 1784–2014* (Grand Rapids, MI: Eerdmans, 2014).

9. Wilder, *Ebony and Ivy*, 48.

10. Ibid., 78.

11. Ibid., 76.

12. Ibid., 74.

13. Ibid. See also Graham Russell Hodges, *Root and Branch: African Americans in New York and East Jersey* (Chapel Hill: University of North Carolina Press, 1999), 1–32.

14. Wilder, *Ebony and Ivy*, 69–70.

15. The college's original 1766 and 1770 charter lists "Robert Livingston" as a trustee. However, it is difficult to determine exactly which Robert Livingston was the founding trustee, since there were four living Roberts in the Livingston family at the time of the college's founding. Robert R. Livingston, "The Chancellor" (1746–1813), is sometimes credited as holding the position, yet he was the youngest of the four—only twenty years old in 1766—and probably not the trustee. The other three Roberts were the Chancellor's father and grandfather from Claremont Manor and his uncle from Livingston Manor. His father, Robert R. Livingston, "The Judge" (1718–1775), could possibly be the trustee since he was forty-eight years old in 1766 and in the prime of his career; this Robert was the cousin of trustee Philip Livingston (1716–1778) and they were of the same generation. The oldest living Robert at the time was the Chancellor's grandfather,

Robert Livingston (1688–1775), of Claremont Manor, who was seventy-eight years old in 1766 and seemingly spending his time at his estate in upstate New York. There was one more Robert: Robert Livingston (1708–1790), the third Lord of Livingston Manor, who was the wealthiest of the four Roberts; he was fifty-eight years old at the college's founding and was the brother of trustee Philip Livingston (1716–1778). Thus, it is probable that he is actually the trustee listed on the original charter.

16. Cynthia A. Kierner, *Traders and Gentlefolk: The Livingstons of New York, 1675–1790* (Ithaca, NY: Cornell University Press, 1992), 129.

17. John W. Coakley, "John Henry Livingston (1746–1825): Interpreter of the Dutch Reformed Tradition in the Early American Republic," in *Transatlantic Pieties: Dutch Clergy in Colonial America*, ed. Leon van den Broeke, Hans Krabbendam, and Dirk Mouw (Grand Rapids, MI: Eerdmans, 2013), 296–297.

18. Roberta Singer, "The Livingstons as Slave Owners: The 'Peculiar Institution' of Livingston Manor and Clermont," in *The Livingston Legacy: Three Centuries of American History*, ed. Richard T. Wiles (Annandale-on-Hudson, NY: Bard College Office of Publications, 1987), 68–69.

19. For more on the Livingstons as slave traders see Kierner, *Traders and Gentlefolk*; Philip Misevich, "In Pursuit of Human Cargo: Philip Livingston and the Voyage of the Sloop 'Rhode Island,'" *New York History* 86, no. 3 (2005): 185–204; Singer, "The Livingstons as Slave Owners"; and Wiles, *The Livingston Legacy*.

20. Singer, "The Livingstons as Slave Owners," 70.

21. Wilder, *Ebony and Ivy*, 69–70.

22. Singer, "The Livingstons as Slave Owners," 70–71.

23. For a list of early trustees see Rutgers College and John Howard Raven, *Catalogue of the Officers and Alumni of Rutgers College, 1766 to 1916* (Trenton, NJ: State Gazette Publishing Co., 1916), 7–23.

24. Milton M. Klein, "The Other Livingston: William," in Wiles, *The Livingston Legacy*, 230.

25. Ibid., 235.

26. Ibid., 236.

27. Ibid., 242; Kierner, *Traders and Gentlefolk*, 206.

28. Gigantino, *The Ragged Road to Abolition*, 66.

29. Alexander Gunn, *Memoirs of the Rev. John H. Livingston* (New York: Rutgers Press, 1829), 251–254.

30. For instance, Susan Livingston Kean, the niece of former governor William Livingston, had a close relationship with slavery. Her deceased husband, John Kean of South Carolina, owned over one hundred slaves. After Kean's death in 1795, Susan owned and traded those slaves. Gigantino, *The Ragged Road to Abolition*, 64.

31. Ibid., 72.

32. Raven, *Catalogue of the Officers and Alumni of Rutgers College*, 27.

33. Coakley, *New Brunswick Theological Seminary*, 10.

34. Singer, "The Livingstons as Slave Owners," 83.

35. Gunn, *Memoirs of the Rev. John H. Livingston*, 43–45.

36. Ibid., 64–69.

37. For more on the Livingstons as slave traders see Kierner, *Traders and Gentlefolk*; Misevich, "In Pursuit of Human Cargo"; Singer, "The Livingstons as Slave Owners"; and Wiles, *The Livingston Legacy*.

38. Coakley, *New Brunswick Theological Seminary*, 10.

39. Release from John Henry Livingston, D.D., Thomas Jones, and Brockholst Livingston, to William Bleeker, for the 5/24th share of Sarah Livingston, in the estate of Philip

Livingston (her father) deceased May 10, 1794, Philip Livingston Papers, Box 3, New-York Historical Society.

40. Account of the Administration of Brockholst Livingston and John H. Livingston, surviving trustees and administrators of the estate of Phillip Livingston, deceased July 19, 1803, Philip Livingston Papers, Box 3, New-York Historical Society.

41. Release from John Henry Livingston, D.D., Thomas Jones, and Brockholst Livingston, to William Bleeker, for the 5/24th share of Sarah Livingston, in the estate of Philip Livingston (her father) deceased.

42. Though gradual abolition was passed in 1804, those born before were slaves for life and those born after July 4, 1804, would remain "slaves for a term" until at least 1825. Gigantino, *The Ragged Road to Abolition*, 6–7.

43. Benjamin C. Taylor, "Recollections of Old Ministers, No. III: Rev. John H. Livingston, D.D.," *Christian Intelligencer*, February 29, 1872.

44. Raven, *Catalogue of the Officers and Alumni of Rutgers College*, 15.

45. George J. Lankevich, *New York City: A Short History* (New York: New York University Press, 2002), 6–7.

46. For more on the Van Rensselaer family see Walter Whipple Spooner, "The Van Rensselaer Family," *American Historical Magazine*, January 1907, vol. 2, no. 1: 129–143; Palmer Chamberlain Ricketts, *History of Rensselaer Polytechnic Institute, 1824–1914* (New York: J. Wiley and Sons, 1914).

47. Reformed Church in America, *Acts and Proceedings of the General Synod of the Reformed Dutch Church in North America*, vol. 2, pt 1: *1813–1820 with Index*, 50.

48. Raven, *Catalogue of the Officers and Alumni of Rutgers College*, 16.

49. Adam Rothman, *Slave Country: American Expansion and the Origins of the Deep South* (Cambridge, MA: Harvard University Press, 2007), 6.

50. Seth Rockman, *Scraping By: Wage Labor, Slavery, and Survival in Early Baltimore* (Baltimore: The Johns Hopkins University Press, 2009), 2–3.

51. Gigantino, *The Ragged Road to Abolition*, 32–33.

52. Ibid., 6, 67.

53. John Patrick Wall and Harold E. Pickersgill, eds. *History of Middlesex County, New Jersey, 1664–1920* (New York: Lewis Historical Publishing Company, 1921), 286–287.

54. Ibid., 287.

55. Ibid., 288.

56. Frusciano and Justice, "History and Politics," 24.

57. Ibid.

58. James Grant Wilson and John Fiske, eds., *Appleton's Cyclopedia of American Biography*, vol. 4: *1888*, 651, http://archive.org/details/AppletonsCyclopediaOfAmericanBiographyVol.4.

59. Manumission of Slaves, 1800–1825, Middlesex County (NJ) Records, 1688–1929, Vol. XI, 192, 341, Rutgers University Special Collections and University Archives (hereafter SC/UA).

60. Jacob Dunham, Account book, 1816–1841 (Ledger), 184, MC 71, SC/UA.

61. Thelma Doyle, "History of the Neilson Family in New Brunswick" (MA thesis, Rutgers University, 1935), 7.

62. Ibid., Appendix III: "Inventory of the Personal Estate of James Neilson, Esq. deceased, Estimated by Mr. John Lyell and Peter Vredenburgh Esq. March 1783," 71–72.

63. Ibid., 12.

64. This was an unusually large sum for the time. Ibid., 12. Doyle's citation for this sale is "MS: Letter from John Van Enburgh to John Neilson, Toms River, November 30, 1778."

65. Neilson Family Papers, MC 933, Folder 15, SC/UA.

66. "Receipt from Thomas Bullman to John Neilson for the purchase of a slave," November 30, 1777, Neilson Family Papers (Ac. 589), Box 2, SC/UA, cited in David J. Fowler, "Report on John Neilson for New Brunswick Public Sculpture, Inc.," 2015, 9 (copy at SC/UA).

67. "Bill and receipt from John Henry to John Neilson for the purchase of a slave," October 1779, Neilson Family Papers (Ac. 589), Box 2, SC/UA, cited in Fowler, "Report on John Neilson," 9.

68. "Bill of sale from Anthony L. Bleecker of New York to John Neilson, January 31, 1787, Neilson Family Papers (Ac. 589), Box 4, SC/UA, cited in Fowler, "Report on John Neilson," 10.

69. Robert T. Thompson, *Colonel James Neilson: A Business Man of the Early Machine Age in New Jersey, 1784–1862* (New Brunswick, NJ: Rutgers University Press, 1940), 260–261.

70. "Bill of sale for Tony, and Tony's consent to be purchased," Neilson Family Papers (Ac. 589), Box 4, SC/UA, cited in Fowler, "Report on John Neilson," 10.

71. Neilson Family Papers (Ac. 589), Box 4, SC/UA.

72. Neilson Family Papers (Ac. 589), Box 4, Folder 27, SC/UA.

73. Neilson Family Papers (Ac. 589), Box 4, Folder 35, SC/UA.

74. Neilson Family Papers (Ac. 589), Box 4, Folder 35, SC/UA.

75. Doyle, "History," 55.

76. Thompson, *Colonel James Neilson*, 304–305.

77. Doyle, "History," 54.

78. William Henry Van Benschoten, *Concerning the Van Bunschoten or Van Benschoten Family in America: A Genealogy and Brief History* (Poughkeepsie, NY: A. V. Haight Co., 1907), 41.

79. Ibid., 35–36.

80. Ibid.

81. Ibid., 32.

82. Will of Teunis Van Bunschoten, recorded May 13, 1788 (Dutchess County), New York Wills and Probate Records, 1659–1999 (online database), Ancestry.com.

83. Ibid.

84. Van Benschoten, *Concerning the Van Bunschoten or Van Benschoten Family in America*, 38.

85. *The Historical Magazine and Notes and Queries Concerning the Antiquities, History and Biography of America*, vol. 8, Second Series (Morrisania, NY: Henry B. Dawson, 1870), 116–117.

86. Van Benschoten, *Concerning the Van Bunschoten or Van Benschoten Family in America*, 38.

87. Ibid., 51.

88. Ibid., 39.

89. Ibid.

90. David J. Fowler was exceptionally generous in sharing his research on Henry Rutgers for this report and is much appreciated.

91. David J. Fowler, "Benevolent Patriot: The Life and Times of Henry Rutgers—Introduction," *Journal of the Rutgers University Libraries* 68, no. 1 (2016): 39.

92. Ibid., 33; Wilder, *Ebony and Ivy*, 245–246.

93. This bell is currently rung on special occasions such as commencement, anniversaries, and signature accomplishments of Rutgers athletics. On Henry Rutgers's gifts and the renaming of Queen's College in his honor, see Thomas J. Frusciano, "From Queen's College to Rutgers College," *Journal of the Rutgers University Libraries* 68, no. 1 (2016): 19–28.

94. Frusciano and Justice, "History and Politics," 29–30.

95. David J. Fowler, "Benevolent Patriot: The Life and Times of Henry Rutgers—Part One: 1636–1776," *Journal of the Rutgers University Libraries* 68, no. 1 (2016): 49, 53–54, 56.

96. Fowler, "Benevolent Patriot—Introduction," 33.

97. David J. Fowler, "Benevolent Patriot: The Life and Times of Henry Rutgers—Part Three: Back Home: 1783 to 1800," *Journal of the Rutgers University Libraries*, 20, preprint draft used with permission from the author.

98. Fowler, "Benevolent Patriot—Introduction," 33; Wilder, *Ebony and Ivy*, 245–46.

99. "An Oration Delivered at Princeton," 5–12 (quotes: 7, 9, 12). Quoted in Gigantino, *The Ragged Road to Abolition*, 189–190.

100. Frusciano et al., *Rutgers*, 24–29.

CHAPTER 3: His Name Was Will

1. James Albert Ukasaw Gronniosaw, *A Narrative of the Most Remarkable Particulars in the Life of James Albert Ukawsaw Gronniosaw, an African Prince, as related by himself* (Bath, Somerset: Printed by W. Gye in Westgate-Street, and sold by T. Mills, Bookseller, in King's-Mead Square, 1772), 12.

2. Kenneth Edward Marshall, *Manhood Enslaved: Bondmen in Eighteenth- and Early Nineteenth-Century New Jersey* (Rochester, NY: University of Rochester Press, 2011), 59–60; Terry Novak, "James Albert Ukasaw Gronniosaw," in *African American Autobiographers: A Sourcebook*, ed. Emmanuel Nelson (Westport, CT: Greenwood, 2002), 171.

3. Brothers Johannes Frelinghuysen (1727–1754) and Theodorus Frelinghuysen (1724–1761) preached in Dutch and used the Dutch versions of their names; they are commonly known in Rutgers history by the Anglicized versions of their names, and here we follow secondary sources in referring to the brothers as John and Theodore. Thomas Frusciano and Benjamin Justice, "History and Politics," in *Rutgers: A 250th Anniversary Portrait*, ed. Nita Congress (London: Third Millennium Publishing, 2015), 16.

4. For the early history of the college and the Frelinghuysen family, see ibid., 16–18, 20, 31; and chap. 2 in William H. S. Demarest, *A History of Rutgers College, 1766–1924* (New Brunswick, NJ: Rutgers College, 1924), 23–46.

5. Histories of Rutgers College include Demarest, *History*; Richard P. McCormick, *Rutgers: A Bicentennial History* (New Brunswick, NJ: Rutgers University Press, 1966); and Frusciano and Justice, "History and Politics."

6. Vincent Carretta, "Gronniosaw, Ukasaw (1710x14–1775)," *Oxford Dictionary of National Biography* (Oxford University Press, 2004), online edition, May 2015, doi:10.1093/ref:odnb/71634.

7. Gronniosaw, *Narrative*, 5.

8. Ibid., 7–10.

9. The Middle Passage refers to the journey that slave ships undertook from Africa across the Atlantic Ocean to the Caribbean and the Americas. African captives experienced inhumane treatment and high mortality rates aboard these ships. For more on the Middle Passage, see Stephanie E. Smallwood, *Saltwater Slavery: A Middle Passage from Africa to American Diaspora* (Cambridge, MA: Harvard University Press, 2007).

10. Gronniosaw, *Narrative*, 10.

11. Ibid., 12.

12. Ibid.

13. Ibid., 13.

14. Ibid., 14.

15. Ibid., 15–16.

16. Ibid., 16.

17. Ibid., 17.

18. Ibid.

19. Ibid.
20. Ibid., 18.
21. Ibid.
22. Ibid., 19.
23. Ibid.
24. Ibid., 19–20. Gronniosaw's narrative does not make it clear exactly when he left the Frelinghuysen family, only that his young masters died in succession and that he left after one of the brothers died. Two of the brothers, Jacobus and Ferdinandus, studied at the University of Utrecht and died of smallpox upon their return to America in 1753. John (Johannes) lived at Raritan and passed away in 1754. Henricus lived in New York and died in 1757. The last to depart was Theodore (Theodorus), who preached at Albany, and who mysteriously perished on his return voyage from Europe around 1761. Gronniosaw does not talk of going to Europe at this time, so it is safe to assume that he did not accompany any of the brothers on their voyages to the Netherlands but rather served the family in New Jersey and New York. Demarest, *History*, 46.
25. Dina Van Bergh to Henricus Frelinghuysen, November 29, 1754, reprinted in J. David Muyskens, ed., *The Diary of Dina Van Bergh*, trans. Gerard Van Dyke (New Brunswick, NJ: Historical Society of the Reformed Church in America, 1993), 117.
26. Jacob Hardenbergh's brother Charles owned Sojourner Truth's parents. For more on the Hardenbergh family and slaveholding, see the essay "I Hereby Bequeath" by Beatrice Adams and Miya Carey in this volume (Chapter 4); also see Margaret Washington, "Part 1, Bell Hardenbergh and Slavery Times in the Hudson River Valley," in Sojourner Truth's America (Chicago: University of Illinois Press, 2009), esp. 16, 19–20.
27. Demarest, *History*, 34–37.
28. Gronniosaw, *Narrative*, 20.
29. Ibid., 21.
30. Ibid., 27.
31. Carretta, "Gronniosaw, Ukasaw (1710x14–1775)"; "On Thursday died . . . James Albert Ukasaw Gronniosaw," *Chester Chronicle, or, Commercial Intelligencer*, October 2, 1775, reprinted in "Personal Accounts," *Understanding Slavery Initiative*, http://www.understandingslavery.com/index.php?option=com_content&view=article&id=375&Itemid=230.
32. "Run Away on the 23rd of August Past from Philip French," *American Weekly Mercury* (Philadelphia), August 27, 1741, reprinted in Graham Russell Hodges and Alan Edward Brown, eds., *"Pretends to Be Free": Runaway Slave Advertisements from Colonial and Revolutionary New York and New Jersey* (New York: Garland, 1994), 17.
33. For example, on November 22, 1767, the Christ Church in New Brunswick recorded the baptism of "Toney, a negro belonging to Philip French, Esq," by Reverend Abraham Beach; see Robert McKean and Abraham Beach, "Some Early Records for Christ Church, New Brunswick, and Saint James Episcopal Church, Piscataway: Marriages, Baptisms and Burials, 1758–1759 and 1767–1784," *Genealogical Magazine of New Jersey* 91 (January 2016): 8.
34. The 1916 version of the Rutgers Catalogue includes names of nearly all early affiliates and their dates of affiliation with the school. John Howard Raven, *Catalogue of the Officers and Alumni of Rutgers College (Originally Queen's College) in New Brunswick, NJ, 1766 to 1916* (Trenton, NJ: State Gazette Publishing Co., 1916), especially 8 (for Philip French) and see 7–10 (for the complete list of founding trustees).
35. Land deed from Philip French to Queen's College, New Brunswick, NJ, 1771, Philip French Papers, Folder A, 1732–1786 (MC 1249), Rutgers University Special Collections

and University Archives (hereafter SC/UA); Demarest notes that the purchase was technically structured as a fifty-year lease for two lots at a price of five pounds, two shillings, sixpence per year (Philip French sold most of his property by way of a lease, possibly due to legal issues with his land title). Twenty years later, the college sold the lease and moved to another location. Demarest, *History*, 86–87.

36. "June 12, 1769 Run-Away on Saturday," *New-York Journal; or, The General Advertiser*, June 15, 1769, reprinted in Hodges and Brown, *Pretends to Be Free*, 152.

37. Raven, *Catalogue*, 8. See information about Reverend Van Harlingen and his family throughout chap. 4 of Demarest, *History*, 84–99.

38. Andrew Hansen, "The Van Harlingen Homestead—Seat of Queen's College in 1780," *Somerset County Historical Quarterly* 6, no. 3 (July 1917): 173–176; Demarest, *History*, 125.

39. Raven, *Catalogue*, 10.

40. In 1808, Ernestus Van Harlingen reported that an enslaved woman in his household gave birth to a child; see "Additional Slaveholders' List in Somerset [Part 1]," *Somerset County Historical Quarterly* 6, no. 2 (April 1917): 98.

41. Raven, *Catalogue*, 68, 70, 72.

42. Ibid., 7.

43. "Calendar of the Sir William Johnson Manuscripts," *New York State Library Annual Report* 91, pt. 2 (Albany: University of the State of New York, 1910), 437.

44. Ibid.

45. Lucas Von Beverhoudt also owned a plantation in Hanover, Morris County, New Jersey. The estate had a wealth of "buildings, houses, horses, cows, oxen, sheep, . . . negroes with their wives and offspring and . . . plantation tools and chattels." New Jersey Historical Society, *Proceedings of the New Jersey Historical Society: A Magazine of History, Biography, and Genealogy* 4: 128–129. For more on slavery in St. Thomas and St. Croix see N.A.T. Hall and B. W. Higman, *Slave Society in the Danish West Indies: St. Thomas, St. John, and St. Croix* (Mona, Cave Hill, and St. Augustine: University of the West Indies Press, 1992).

46. Alexander Clarence Flick, *Loyalism in New York during the American Revolution* (New York: Columbia University, 1901), 32.

47. Captain Adam Hyler used whaleboats to make his raids on New York Harbor, which was occupied by the British Navy. He was stationed in New Brunswick and would take his prisoners and plunder up the Raritan River because the large British vessels could not pursue him up the shallow river. John P. Wall, *Commanders of New Brunswick's Navy in the War of the Revolution* (New Brunswick, NJ: Times Publishing Co., 1905), 5–6; Lorenzo Sabine, *Biographical Sketches of Loyalists of the American Revolution* (Bedford, MA: Applewood Books, 1864), 2:28.

48. James Gigantino, *The Ragged Road to Abolition: Slavery and Freedom in New Jersey, 1775–1865* (Philadelphia: University of Pennsylvania Press, 2014), 58.

49. "Eight Dollars Reward. RAN Away . . . a Negro Boy Named Sam," *Brunswick Gazette*, May 1, 1792.

50. Raven, *Catalogue*, 35, 69; Demarest, *History*, 163.

51. "Eight Dollars Reward. RAN Away . . . a Negro Boy Named Sam." For a discussion of the significance of scars on enslaved runaways, see Marisa J. Fuentes, *Dispossessed Lives: Enslaved Women, Violence, and the Archive* (Philadelphia: University of Pennsylvania Press, 2016).

52. Because the father and son share the same name, it is difficult to tell who the teacher was at the grammar school in 1809–1811; Raven and Demarest provide conflicting information on this point. It seems most likely that the junior James Stevenson served as the grammar school teacher while he attended classes at Queen's College, but it is also

possible that his father (whom the trustees earlier attempted to call to the grammar school) agreed to come teach grammar school classes while his son was a college student. Raven, *Catalogue*, 35, 72; Demarest, *History*, 191, 218.

53. Hiram Edmund Deats, *The Jerseyman* (H. E. Deats, editor and publisher, 1900), 13–14.

54. See digitized copy of birth certificate for Daniel dated December 5, 1809, "Hunterdon County Birth Certificates of Children of Slaves 1804–1835," New Jersey Department of State, http://www.nj.gov/state/archives/chnc1004.html.

55. "Freeholders Past to Present 1739–2015," Hunterdon County, New Jersey, http://www.co.hunterdon.nj.us/frholder/pastpresent.htm; "Hunterdon County Birth Certificates."

56. "Twenty Dollars Reward," *Guardian; or, New-Brunswick Advertiser*, November 12, 1807, typewritten copy of newspaper item found in folder "Freeman, Alpheus 1788," Box 2, Rutgers University Biographical Files: Alumni (Classes of 1774–1922), SC/UA.

57. Raven, *Catalogue*, 69.

58. "To Rent, THAT Elegant and Established Stand for Business," *Guardian; or, New-Brunswick Advertiser*, April 13, 1815, SC/UA.

59. For more on how enslaved individuals experienced slave sales, see Walter Johnson, *Soul by Soul: Life inside the Antebellum Slave Market* (Cambridge, MA: Harvard University Press, 2001).

60. Raven, *Catalogue*, 69.

61. Ibid., 12, 23.

62. Craig Steven Wilder, *Ebony and Ivy: Race, Slavery, and the Troubled History of America's Universities* (New York: Bloomsbury Press, 2013), 123. For Hardenbergh's acquisitions in 1793 and 1795, Wilder cites County Tax Ratables, Somerset County, Eastern Precinct, 1793–1795, Reel 18, New Jersey State Archives, Trenton.

63. "FOR SALE BY the Subscriber, a Negro Wench, of about Thirty Five Years of Age," *Guardian; or, New-Brunswick Advertiser*, March 27, 1801, SC/UA.

64. Raven, *Catalogue*, 10.

65. John Neilson to Robert Finley, February 25, 1794, Folder 45—Papers Relating to the Purchase of Slaves, Box 4, Neilson Family Papers, 1768–1908 (MC 933), SC/UA.

66. Robert Finley to John Neilson, February 27, 1794, Folder 45—Papers Relating to the Purchase of Slaves, Box 4, Neilson Family Papers, 1768–1908 (MC 933), SC/UA.

67. The Blauvelt family continued to send their sons to Queen's College for generations, and by the time of the Civil War, nine of them had graduated from the school, including Abraham Blauvelt's three sons. Raven, *Catalogue*, 68, 69, 72, 73, 76, 83, 99, 124; Demarest, *History*, 208.

68. Raven, *Catalogue*, 13, 23.

69. The construction of Old Queens is commonly recognized as taking place between 1809 and 1811, because the cornerstone of the building was ceremoniously laid on April 27, 1809. However, construction work at the site, including foundation work and carting materials, began in the fall of 1808. Demarest, *History*, 211.

70. Middlesex County Birth of Slaves, 1804–1844 [Register of black children], 51, Vol. X, Middlesex County (NJ) Records, 1688–1929 (MC 784.1), SC/UA (hereafter cited as Middlesex County Birth of Slaves).

71. For more on "slaves for a term," see Gigantino, *Ragged Road to Abolition*, 7.

72. W. Woodford Clayton, ed., *History of Union and Middlesex Counties, New Jersey: With Biographical Sketches of Many of Their Pioneers and Prominent Men* (Philadelphia: Everts & Peck, 1882), 528.

73. "TO BE SOLD. A HEALTHY, Likely Negro Girl," *Guardian; or, New-Brunswick Advertiser*, November 11, 1794, SC/UA.

74. "FOR SALE, the Time of BLACK WOMAN," *Guardian; or, New-Brunswick Advertiser*, July 13, 1809, SC/UA.

75. "A BLACK BOY Nine Years Old," *Guardian; or, New-Brunswick Advertiser*, July 20, 1809, SC/UA.

76. Abraham Blauvelt published slave sale advertisements inviting readers to "enquire of the printer" long before and long after the summer of 1809. See for example, "FOR SALE, THE Time of an Indented NEGRO GIRL," *Guardian; or, New-Brunswick Advertiser*, May 28, 1799; "FOR SALE, A NEGRO MAN, Slave for Life," *Guardian; or, New-Brunswick Advertiser*, October 27, 1814; and "For Sale. AT Her Own Request, a Strong, Healthy NEGRO WOMAN," *Guardian; or, New-Brunswick Advertiser*, March 16, 1815, SC/UA.

77. John Patrick Wall and Harold E. Pickersgill, *History of Middlesex County, New Jersey, 1664–1920* (New York: Lewis Historical Publishing Co., 1921), 1:259; Clayton, *History of Union and Middlesex Counties*, 514.

78. Azariah Dunham served as trustee from 1783 until his death in 1790. Jacob Dunham's older brother Lewis Ford Dunham was also active in the college's affairs, having been elected to the board of trustees upon his father's death in 1790. In 1807 Lewis Ford Dunham (who also inherited substantial landholdings and wealth from Azariah Dunham) offered to give land to Queen's College for the new campus, though the college trustees ultimately chose James Parker's land for this purpose. Raven, *Catalogue*, 11, 12; Demarest, *History*, 208, 233; Isaac Watson Dunham, *Dunham Genealogy: English and American Branches of the Dunham Family* (Norwich, CT: Bulletin Print, 1907), 255–256; Azariah Dunham's will and estate inventory, 7527–7558L.B.30, 481. W and Cod. 1790. Inv. 1790, Middlesex-Monmouth County Wills, Wills and Inventories, ca. 1670–1900, New Jersey State Archives, Trenton.

79. See entry 15 in Abraham Blauvelt, Account book, 1794–1809 (Ledger), MC 720, SC/UA.

80. See entry 130 in ibid.

81. Jacob Dunham, Account book, 1816–1841 (Ledger), MC 71, SC/UA.

82. Ibid., 8.

83. See manuscript manumission records from slaveholder Thomas Hill recorded in Middlesex County Manumission of Slaves, 1800–1825, Vol. XI, Middlesex County (NJ) Records, 1688–1929 (MC 784.1), SC/UA (hereafter cited as Middlesex County Manumission of Slaves). See in particular the manumission of a twenty-four-year-old woman named Sarah recorded on December 1, 1820 (329), the manumission of a twenty-one-year-old woman named Jane recorded on August 7, 1824 (384), and the manumission of a twenty-one-year-old woman named Hannah recorded on February 17, 1825 (426).

84. Dunham, Account book, 35.

85. Ibid.

86. Ibid., 47.

87. Demarest, *History*, 211. Blauvelt's account book for the building does not list James Chapman as one of the contractors paid out in the early stages of the construction project. However, Blauvelt's account book ends in March 1810, and work on the building continued, so it is possible Chapman may have worked on the building at a later stage.

88. Dunham, Account book, 82.

89. Raven, *Catalogue*, 13.

90. See manumission record for twenty-eight-year-old Benjamin recorded on July 27, 1822, Middlesex County Manumission of Slaves, 362.

91. Dunham, Account book, 352, 212, 220.

92. Ibid., 120.

93. Ibid., 326.

94. 1830 U.S. Census record for Jacob Dunham (North Brunswick Township, Middlesex County, NJ), imaged from NARA microfilm publication series M19, Roll 83, Ancestry. com (online database).

95. Variously spelled John P. Sandford or John P. Sanford, this contractor received payments totaling $3,633.83 between May 20, 1809 and February 14, 1810. See Blauvelt, Account book. Efforts to locate information about Sandford's construction business are ongoing.

96. For a discussion of John Smalley, see the essay "I Hereby Bequeath" by Adams and Carey in this volume (Chapter 4); John Smalley and his son John Smalley Jr. also appear in Middlesex County records: Middlesex County Birth of Slaves, 78, 80; Middlesex County Manumission of Slaves, 178; James Dehart reported that an enslaved woman in his household gave birth to a baby boy named Nicholas in 1809, Middlesex County Birth of Slaves, 35; Michael Garrish reported numerous births of enslaved children in his household including Martha (1806), Catherine (1817), James (1819), Lucy (1822), Sophia (1824), and Sarah (1829), ibid., 16, 80; Jacob Van Deventer reported that an enslaved woman in his household gave birth to a child named Denyaun in 1807, Ibid., 22.

97. Middlesex County records provide evidence of extensive slaveholding in the Voorhees family; see Middlesex County Birth of Slaves, 13, 31, 64, 72; Middlesex County Manumission of Slaves, 164, 202, 305; see also local newspaper items: "Ten Dollars Reward. Runaway . . . A NEGRO GIRL, Named Jane," *Fredonian* (New Brunswick, NJ), April 20, 1815; "A Negro Boy for Sale," *Fredonian* (New Brunswick, NJ), September 7, 1815; "Ten Cents Reward. RUNAWAY . . . a Negro Woman by the Name of Dinah," *Guardian; or, New-Brunswick Advertiser,* February 22, 1816; "PUBLIC SALE, OF REAL ESTATE," *Fredonian* (New Brunswick, NJ), December 20, 1821, SC/UA.

98. Raven, *Catalogue,* 11, 23, 66.

99. Bill of Sale from John Voorhees of Hunterdon County to James Schureman of New Brunswick (sale of Luck, February 26, 1813), James Schureman Papers, 1689–1902 (MC 1379), SC/UA.

100. Raven, *Catalogue,* 24.

101. "VENDUE. At the Farm Late of James Bennet, Esq. WILL BE SOLD AT AUCTION," *Fredonian* (New Brunswick, NJ), March 8, 1821.

102. "For Sale or Rent, THAT Capital Stand for Business in Burnet Street," *Fredonian* (New Brunswick, NJ), February 28, 1822.

103. "VENDUE. Will Be Sold at Public Auction, At the Late Residence of Capt. George Farmer," *Fredonian* (New Brunswick, NJ), November 5, 1818.

104. In 1823, William Deare reported that an enslaved woman in his household gave birth to a baby boy named Elias, Middlesex County Birth of Slaves, 71, SC/UA.

105. Raven, *Catalogue,* 13, 23, 71.

106. See George Farmer's will dated May 19, 1817, Middlesex County (Wills, Vol. A–B, 1804–1824), and George Farmer estate papers, Case 7734, Middlesex County (Unrecorded Estate Papers, 7683–7912); both items in New Jersey Wills and Probate Records, 1739–1991, Ancestry.com (online database).

107. Gigantino, *Ragged Road to Abolition,* 149–152.

108. Ibid., 149, 155–161.

109. William P. Deare's connection to the slave-trading ring requires further review. Some evidence suggests that Deare provided legal counsel to Van Wickle's co-conspirators; see Jarrett Drake, "Off the Record: The Production of Evidence in 19th Century New Jersey," New Jersey Studies: An Interdisciplinary Journal 1, no. 1 (2015): 111. Whether Deare profited from the slave-trading business is not clear, but it is clear that Deare was well

acquainted with Van Wickle's operation. Deare was in a prime position to stop the flow of human traffic, but he willfully turned a blind eye to the situation and enabled Van Wickle to remove black children, women, and men out of Middlesex County, and he possibly provided further assistance to Van Wickle's associates.

110. Adam Rothman, *Slave Country: American Expansion and the Origins of the Deep South* (Cambridge, MA: Harvard University Press, 2007), 192; James Gigantino, "Trading in Jersey Souls: New Jersey and the Interstate Slave Trade," *Pennsylvania History: A Journal of Mid-Atlantic Studies 77*, no. 3 (2010): 290.

111. Middlesex County Manumission of Slaves, 208–209, SC/UA.

112. William Van Deursen, the father, served as trustee during 1785–1793 while his oldest sons, Staats Van Deursen (class of 1791) and Henry Van Deursen (class of 1794), were enrolled in the school; Staats Van Deursen served as trustee during 1807–1823, and his much younger brother William Van Deursen (class of 1809) served as trustee during 1823–1873; Staats Van Deursen's son John Schureman Van Deursen graduated in 1814 and died five years later before he had a chance to serve as an officer of his alma mater; see Raven, *Catalogue*, 11, 13, 14, 24, 70, 72, 74; Albert Harrison Van Deusen, *Van Deursen Family* (New York: Frank Allaben Genealogical Co. [ca. 1912]), 109–110, 213–214; Clayton, *History of Union and Middlesex Counties*, 521.

113. As treasurer, Staats Van Deursen handled the accounts while the college struggled financially from 1813 to 1823. Van Deursen's account book shows that during this time the college held bonds in amounts of $500 or $1,000 and collected 7 percent interest on the bonds. A preliminary review of Van Deursen's records reveals that Queen's College issued bonds to many local slaveholders, and more research is needed to fully understand the college's investment in the local economy. See Staats Van Deursen, Treasurer's Ledger of Queen's College, 1813–1824, Location 120–121, SC/UA.

114. U.S. Senate, *Report from the Register and Receiver of the Land Office at Monroe, Louisiana, Under Act of 1851, for the Settlement of Certain Classes of Private Land Claims within the Bastrop Grant*, 32d Cong., 2d Sess., 1852, S. Doc. 4, 558; Merritt M. Robinson, *Reports of Cases Argued and Determined in the Supreme Court of Louisiana* (New Orleans, LA: E. Johns & Co., 1842), 25.

115. By 1820, Jacob Klady was selling a group of enslaved individuals in Louisiana. He sold a twenty-two-year-old woman named Felicity for $1,400 and a thirty-five-year-old man named Dick for the same price, while prices of enslaved workers in New Jersey rarely exceeded $300. See these items in Gwendolyn Hall's online database "Afro-Louisiana History and Genealogy, 1719–1820": Sale of Felicity from Jacob Klady to Michel LeVillian (Ouachita, LA, April 22, 1820), http://www.ibiblio.org/laslave/individ.php?sid=88042; Sale of Dick from Jacob Klady to Michel LeVillian (Ouachita, LA, April 22, 1820), http://www.ibiblio.org/laslave/individ.php?sid=88041.

116. Middlesex County Manumission of Slaves, 229, SC/UA.

117. Ibid., 243.

118. Staats Van Deursen's friend and fellow Queen's College officer James Schureman also sat on this committee. Clayton, *History of Union and Middlesex Counties*, 745–746; John Patrick Wall and Harold E. Pickersgill, *History of Middlesex County, New Jersey, 1664–1920* (New York: Lewis Historical Publishing Co., 1921), 424.

119. See minutes from November 7, 1823, in New Brunswick (NJ) Common Council, *Minutes of the New Brunswick N.J. Common Council, 1796–1819* (New Brunswick, NJ: New Brunswick Historical Society, 1910), 18, http://archive.org/details/minutesofnewbrun00newb.

120. See minutes from March 5, 1824, in ibid., 16.

121. Gigantino, *Ragged Road to Abolition*, 117.

122. Ibid., 125–126.

123. Between 1800 and 1825, a total of 279 manumissions were recorded in Middlesex County. See Middlesex County Manumission of Slaves, SC/UA.
124. Ibid., 35.
125. Raven, *Catalogue*, 12; Frusciano and Justice, "History and Politics," 24.
126. Raven, *Catalogue*, 328; Demarest, *History*, 140–141, 189, 198.
127. Middlesex County Manumission of Slaves, 83, SC/UA.
128. Ibid., 274.
129. James Parker served as trustee during 1812–1868. Raven, *Catalogue*, 13; Frusciano and Justice, "History and Politics," 24; Demarest, *History*, 209.
130. Middlesex County Manumission of Slaves, 364, SC/UA.
131. Ibid., 351.
132. Bill of Sale from Anthony Bleecker of New York City to John Neilson (sale of Flora, Phillis, and Ann, January 31, 1787), Folder 45—Papers Relating to the Purchase of Slaves, Box 4, Neilson Family Papers, 1768–1908 (MC 933), SC/UA. In the 1780s, John Neilson on multiple occasions served as the president of the board of trustees; Demarest, *History*, 144.
133. Middlesex County Manumission of Slaves, 362, 373, 432, SC/UA.
134. Middlesex County Birth of Slaves, 79, SC/UA.
135. Gigantino, *Ragged Road to Abolition*, 130.
136. Middlesex County Manumission of Slaves, 328, SC/UA.
137. Raven, *Catalogue*, 13; Demarest, *History*, 189–195.
138. Raven, *Catalogue*, 35. After studying medicine with Dr. Moses Scott of New Brunswick, Charles Smith became one of the few men to receive a medical degree from Queen's College in 1792 during the school's short-lived early attempt to establish a medical college. Clayton, *History of Union and Middlesex Counties*, 517.
139. Raven, *Catalogue*, 13.
140. Middlesex County Manumission of Slaves, 382, SC/UA.
141. For more on Henry Rutgers, see the essay "Old Money" by Kendra Boyd, Miya Carey, and Christopher Blakley in this volume (Chapter 2); see also David J. Fowler, "Benevolent Patriot: The Life and Times of Henry Rutgers—Introduction," *Journal of the Rutgers University Libraries* 68, no. 1 (January 2016): 29–41.

CHAPTER 4: "I Hereby Bequeath . . ."

1. Craig Steven Wilder, *Ebony and Ivy: Race, Slavery, and the Troubled History of America's Universities* (New York: Bloomsbury Press, 2013), 1–2.
2. Van Artsdalen's surname may also appear as "Van Arsdalen." Henry P. Thompson, *History of the Reformed Church at Readington, New Jersey, 1719–1881* (New York: Board of Publication of the Reformed Church, 1883), 73, https://archive.org/stream/historyofreforme00thom/historyofreforme00thom_djvu.txt.
3. *Somerset County Historical Quarterly* 8 (1919): 102; E. T. Corwin, *Manual of the Reformed Church in America* (New York: Board of Publication, R.C.A., 1902), 807.
4. "Reverend Simeon Van Artsdalen," Wills and Inventories, ca. 1670–1900, Hunterdon-Mercer County Wills, 1363J.B. 28:210, W. 1786, Inv. (2), 1786.Ren.1786, New Jersey State Archives, Trenton (hereafter NJSA).
5. Ibid.
6. James Gigantino, *The Ragged Road to Abolition: Slavery and Freedom in New Jersey, 1775–1865* (Philadelphia: University of Pennsylvania Press, 2014), 12.
7. John Nelson Abeel, undated 1780s sermon, John Nelson Abeel Papers, New Jersey Historical Society. Quoted in Gigantino, *The Ragged Road to Abolition*, 70, 268. See also

John Howard Raven, *Catalogue of the Officers and Alumni of Rutgers College, 1766 to 1916* (Trenton, NJ: State Gazette Publishing Co., 1916); Edward Tanjore Corwin, *Manual of the RCA* (New York: Board of Publications, 1903), 163. John Nelson Abeel graduated from Princeton in 1787 and then briefly studied theology under the tutelage of John Henry Livingston in New York. He continued his theological studies with President John Witherspoon at Princeton. Other members of Abeel's family with ties to Rutgers include his brother David, who was a contractor for the Queen's College building, and his son Gustavus Abeel, who received an A.M. degree from Rutgers College in 1829 and served as a trustee from 1845 to 1887.

8. Raven, *Catalogue of the Officers and Alumni of Rutgers College*, 8.

9. Russell L. Gasero, *Historical Directory of the Reformed Church in America, 1628–2000* (Grand Rapids, MI: Eerdmans, 2001), 207.

10. Will of John Schuneman, in Albany County (New York) Surrogate's Office, *Wills, Letters Testamentary, Letters of Administration, Etc., 1787–1902* (Salt Lake City, UT: Genealogical Society of Utah, 1968).

11. Ibid.

12. Ibid.

13. Joanne Melish Pope, *Disowning Slavery: Gradual Emancipation and "Race" in New England, 1780–1860* (Ithaca, NY: Cornell University Press, 1998), 60.

14. Dylan C. Penningroth, *The Claims of Kinfolk: African American Property and Community in the Nineteenth-Century South* (Chapel Hill: University of North Carolina Press, 2003), 78.

15. Nell Irvin Painter, *Sojourner Truth: A Life, a Symbol*, (New York: W. W. Norton, 1996), 171.

16. Raven, *Catalogue*, 7; Painter, *Sojourner Truth*, 11.

17. Raven, *Catalogue*, 7.

18. Olive Gilbert and Sojourner Truth, *Narrative of Sojourner Truth* (Battle Creek, MI: For the Author, 1878), 13; Painter, *Sojourner Truth*, 3.

19. Gilbert and Truth, *Narrative of Sojourner Truth,* 13.

20. William H. S. Demarest, *A History of Rutgers College, 1766–1924* (New Brunswick, NJ: Rutgers College, 1924), 47, 79, 81; *Cyclopedia of New Jersey Biography* (Newark, NJ: Memorial History Company, 1916), 333; Painter, *Sojourner Truth*, 12.

21. Gilbert and Truth, *Narrative of Sojourner Truth*, 33; Morgan, *Slave Counterpoint*, 665.

22. Gilbert and Truth, *Narrative of Sojourner Truth*, 14.

23. Ibid., 13.

24. Ibid., 25.

25. Will of John Smalley, in New Jersey, Surrogate's Court (Middlesex County), *Probate Records (1780–1930) and Indexes (1803–1971)* (Salt Lake City, UT: Genealogical Society of Utah, 1972).

26. Ibid.

27. Ibid.

28. Gigantino, *The Ragged Road to Abolition*, 73.

29. Ibid., 116–117, 125.

30. Ibid., 92–96.

31. Historians of gender, sexuality, and slavery have examined this extensively. See Joshua D. Rothman, *Notorious in the Neighborhood: Sex and Families across the Color Line in Virginia, 1787–1861* (Chapel Hill: University of North Carolina Press, 2003), 50–51; Deborah Gray White, *Ar'n't I a Woman?: Female Slaves in the Plantation South* (New York: W. W. Norton, 1985); Ira Berlin, *Slaves without Masters: The Free Negro in the Antebellum South* (New York: New Press, 2007); and Daina Berry Ramey, *"Swing the Sickle for the Harvest Is Ripe": Gender and Slavery in Antebellum Georgia* (Urbana: University of Illinois Press, 2007).

32. La Rue Vrendenburgh, "The Vrendenburgh Family of Somerset, New Jersey," vreden-burgh.org/vrendenburgh/pages/somerset.htm.

33. Middlesex County Records, vol. XI, Manumission of Slaves 1800–1825, Control # CMICL009, 390 and 392, NJ State Archives, Trenton, NJ.

34. "Peter Vrendenburgh," Wills and Inventories, ca. 1670–1900, Middlesex-Monmouth County Wills, 10962L. W. 1823. Inv. 1823, NJSA.

35. Gigantino, *The Ragged Road to Abolition*, 136–137.

36. James Schureman Papers, 1698–1902, Rutgers Special Collections and University Archives; Raven, *Catalogue*, 7, 13, 23, 40.

37. "James Schureman," Wills and Inventories, ca. 1670–1900, Middlesex-Monmouth County Wills, 11022L. W. 1824. Inv. 1824, NJSA.

38. Gigantino, *The Ragged Road to Abolition*, 92–96.

39. "James Schureman," Wills and Inventories.

40. Wilder, *Ebony and Ivy*, 1–2.

CHAPTER 5: "And I Poor Slave Yet"

1. David Listokin, Dorothea Berkhout, and James W. Hughes, *New Brunswick, New Jersey: The Decline and Revitalization of Urban America* (New Brunswick, NJ: Rutgers University Press, 2016), 5.

2. "To the PUBLIC," *New Brunswick Political Intelligencer and New-Jersey Advertiser*, March 16, 1784; "For want of employ, will be Sold Cheap at Private Sale," *Guardian; or, New Brunswick Advertiser*, October 23, 1793; "FOR SALE Nine years service of a Black Girl," *Fredonian*, January 18, 1818; "For sale, a BLACK WOMAN," *Guardian; or New Brunswick Advertiser*, April 13, 1815, SC/UA.

3. Lucia McMahon and Deborah Schriver, eds., *To Read My Heart: The Journal of Rachel Van Dyke, 1810–1811* (Philadelphia: University of Pennsylvania Press, 2000), 10.

4. J. M. Robert, Illus., *Plan of the City of New-Brunswick: From Actual Survey* (New Brunswick, NJ: A. A. Marcelus and Terhune & Letson, 1829), Library of Congress, https://www.loc.gov/item/2011587019/.

5. For a discussion of making history from fragmentary primary sources of enslaved people, see Marisa J. Fuentes, *Dispossessed Lives: Enslaved Women, Violence, and the Archive* (Philadelphia: University of Pennsylvania Press, 2016).

6. James Gigantino, "Trading in Jersey Souls: New Jersey and the Interstate Slave Trade," *Pennsylvania History: A Journal of Mid-Atlantic Studies 77*, no. 3 (2010): 281–302.

7. New Brunswick Common Council, *Minutes of the New Brunswick N.J. Common Council, 1796–1819* (New Brunswick, NJ: New Brunswick Historical Society, 1910), 591.

8. M. W. St. Clair Clarke, "Abstract of the Returns of the Fifth Census Showing the Number of Free People, the Number of Slaves, the Federal or Representative Number, and the Aggregate of Each County of Each State in the United States" (Washington, DC: Duff Green, 1832), http://www.census.gov/prod/www/decennial.html. The gender breakdown for the 1828 local census and the 1830 national census are as follows: New Brunswick (1828): 2,191 white men (49%) and 2,244 white women (51%); 159 free black men (42.5%) and 215 free black women (57.5%); 20 male slaves for life (35%) and 37 female slaves for life (65%); 47 male slaves for a term (37%) and 80 female slaves for a term (63%). New Jersey (1830): 152,529 white males (50.8%) and 147,737 white females (49.2%); 9,501 free black men (51.9%) and 8,802 free black women (48.1%); 1,059 male slaves for life (46.9%) and 1,195 female slaves for life (53.1%). Across all racial categories, New Brunswick exaggerates the gender imbalance.

9. Wilbur H. Siebert, *The Underground Railroad: From Slavery to Freedom* (New York: Russell & Russell, 1967 [1898]), 120–125.

10. Larry Greene, "Civil War and Reconstruction: State and Nation Divided," in *New Jersey: A History of the Garden State*, ed. Maxine N. Lurie and Richard Veit (New Brunswick, NJ: Rutgers University Press, 2012), 153.

11. Siebert, *The Underground Railroad*, 120–125.

12. *Fredonian*, April 12, 1826, SC/UA.

13. C. W. Larison, *Silvia Dubois, A Biografy of the Slav Who Whipt Her Mistres and Gand Her Fredom*, ed. and trans. Jared C. Lobdell (New York: Oxford University Press, 1988), 69–70 (spelling and punctuation as in original text).

14. In New York and East Jersey, some counties and municipalities issued "freedom papers" to manumitted slaves to use as proof of their free status. For more information, see Graham Russell Hodges, *Root and Branch: African Americans in New York and East Jersey, 1613–1863* (Chapel Hill: University of North Carolina Press, 1999), 160–167.

15. Fuentes, *Dispossessed Lives*, 8.

16. "AFRICAN SCHOOL," *Fredonian*, January 1, 1823.

17. For a discussion of architectures of control in an urban slave environment see Fuentes, *Dispossessed Lives*, esp. chap. 1.

18. *Plan of the City of New-Brunswick*. Today, the site of the gaol in nineteenth-century New Brunswick is occupied by a chain of stores.

19. Susan O'Donovan, "Universities of Social and Political Change: Slaves in Jail in Antebellum America," in *Buried Lives: Incarcerated in Early America*, ed. Michele Lise Tarter and Richard Bell (Athens: University of Georgia Press, 2012), 124–148.

20. *"Pretends to Be Free": Runaway Slave Advertisements from Colonial and Revolutionary New York and New Jersey*, ed. Graham Russell Hodges and Alan Edward Brown (New York: Taylor and Francis, 1994), xxvi. Trenton and Somerset were also common locations for local authorities to imprison suspected runaways.

21. *New Jersey Gazette*, November 7, 1781. Reprinted in Austin Scott, ed., *Documents Relating to the Revolutionary History of the State of New Jersey*, vol. 4: *Extracts from American Newspapers Relating to New Jersey, October, 1780–July, 1782* (Trenton, NJ: State Gazette Publishing Co., 1917), 319.

22. *Fredonian*, April 2, 1812, SC/UA.

23. *New York Gazette*, August 28, 1768 (spelling and punctuation as in original), SC/UA.

24. New Brunswick Common Council, *Minutes*, 65, 555, 567 (Emphasis added), SC/UA.

25. Ibid., 569 (spelling and punctuation as in original).

26. Ibid., 555.

27. *New York Packet, and the American Advertiser*, July 1, 1779. Reprinted in William Nelson, ed., *Documents Relating to the Revolutionary History of the State of New Jersey*, vol. 3: *Extracts from American Newspapers Relating to New Jersey, 1779* (Trenton, NJ: John L. Murphy Publishing Company, 1914), 460.

28. New Brunswick Common Council, *Minutes*, 555–569.

29. James Gigantino, *The Ragged Road to Abolition: Slavery and Freedom in New Jersey, 1775–1865* (Philadelphia: University of Pennsylvania Press, 2014), 123–124.

30. Fuentes, *Dispossessed Lives*, 38.

31. Ibid.

32. Benjamin H. Manning, "Map of Land late of Mr. Phillip French late of New Brunswick deceased . . . ," 1790, Manuscript Map #20,015, Rutgers Special Collections and University Archives (hereafter SC/UA). As printed in Richard L. Porter, "History and Land Use Change: The New Brunswick Copper Mining and Processing Complex, Rutgers

University, and Johnson & Johnson," *New Jersey Studies: An Interdisciplinary Journal* (Winter 2016): 103–104.

33. Porter, "History and Land Use Change," 103–104. King Street no longer exists in New Brunswick but it formerly extended northward from where Neilson Street dead-ends into Albany Street.

34. Lucia McMahon and Deborah Schriver, eds., *To Read My Heart: The Journal of Rachel Van Dyke, 1810–1811* (Philadelphia: University of Pennsylvania Press, 2000), 44.

35. New Brunswick Common Council, *Minutes*, 555; McMahon and Schriver, *To Read My Heart*, 10 (spelling and capitalization as in original).

36. Gigantino, *Ragged Road to Abolition*, 123–124.

37. Jacob Dunham, Account book, 1816–1841 (Ledger), MC 71, SC/UA.

38. Fuentes, *Dispossessed Lives*, 15. While Fuentes's book deals specifically with eighteenth-century Barbados, her findings are applicable to Anglo slaveholding practices at large. More to the point, the slave codes developed by Barbadian planters were largely transplanted into East Jersey by Dutch and English immigrants. In the merging of East and West Jersey, the much more brutal East Jersey slave codes took precedence. See Gigantino, *The Ragged Road to Abolition*, 13.

39. "VENDUE STORE," *New Brunswick Political Intelligencer and New Jersey Advertiser*, March 9, 1784 (spelling and punctuation as in original), SC/UA.

40. "TO THE PUBLIC," *New Brunswick Political Intelligencer and New Jersey Advertiser*, March 16, 1784, SC/UA.

41. "NOTICE: THE SUBSCRIBER," *Fredonian*, March 25, 1823, SC/UA.

42. Fuentes, *Dispossessed Lives*, 37.

43. "NOTICE," *Fredonian*, April 18, 1822, SC/UA.

44. Michael Gomez, *Exchanging Our Country Marks: The Transformation of African Identities in the Colonial and Antebellum South* (Chapel Hill: University of North Carolina Press, 1998), 257.

45. Hodges and Brown, *Pretends to Be Free*, xv.

46. While the data set for the entire essay stretches from 1766 (the date of the earliest surviving printed runaway slave advertisement relevant to New Brunswick) to 1835 (the date when blacks in New Brunswick were no longer regarded as prima facie slaves), the breadth of slave sale advertisements in New Brunswick newspapers is narrowed to 1780–1835. The reason for this is simply that the earliest surviving printed advertisement for the sale of a slave in New Brunswick dates to 1780. In any case, it is unlikely that slave sales between 1766 and 1780 bucked the trends established by the narrower data set.

47. "TO BE SOLD," *Brunswic Gazette*, April 28, 1792; "TO BE SOLD, A HEALTHY LIKELY NEGRO GIRL," *Guardian; or, New-Brunswick Advertiser*, November 11, 1794; "TO BE SOLD, A YOUNG BLACK GIRL," *Arnett's New Jersey Federalist*, January 15, 1795; "FOR SALE, A LIKELY HEALTHY NEGRO WENCH," *Genius of Liberty and New Jersey Advertiser*, October 26, 1795; "FOR SALE," *Fredonian*, July 10, 1811, SC/UA.

48. Gigantino, "Trading in Jersey Souls," 283.

49. Gigantino, *Ragged Road to Abolition*, 100–101.

50. Ibid., 8.

51. This figure is calculated from fifty-five advertisements for the sale of slaves taken from seven newspapers printed in New Brunswick between 1785 and 1835: *New Brunswick Political Intelligencer and New Jersey Advertiser* (April 20, 1785–May 3, 1786; October 14, 1783–April 5, 1785; April 20, 1785–May 3, 1786); *New Jersey Journal and Political Intelligencer* (May 10, 1786–December 31, 1788); *Brunswic Gazette* (June 7, 1791–May 1, 1792);

Guardian; or, New Brunswick Advertiser (October 23, 1793–February 12, 1816); *Arnett's New Jersey Federalist* (July 3, 1794–January 15, 1795); *Genius of Liberty and New Jersey Advertiser* (October 26, 1795); and *Fredonian* (June 26, 1811–December 24, 1834). Most of the newspapers used in calculating these figures were not continuous and were missing several installments. These figures also exclude advertisements for the sale of slaves in which gender is not specified. However, these cases are the exception rather than the rule and are typically for slave children added on to the sale of a gender-specified adult.

52. Gigantino, *Ragged Road to Abolition*, 134.

53. Ibid., 133.

54. For a discussion of enslaved women and reproduction see Jennifer L. Morgan, *Laboring Women: Reproduction and Gender in New World Slavery* (Philadelphia: University of Pennsylvania Press, 2004).

55. Austin Scott, ed., *Documents Relating to the Colonial History of New Jersey: New Jersey Archives, Newspaper Extracts, Second Series*, vol. 5: *1780–1782* (Paterson, NJ: State of New Jersey, 1917), 147.

56. See note 59.

57. "Dry Goods, to be sold," *Guardian; or, New-Brunswick Advertiser*, October 23, 1793; "WANTED TO PURCHASE, two active negro boys," *Genius of Liberty, and New-Jersey Advertiser*, October 26, 1795.

58. "FOR SALE, OR TO BE EXCHANGED FOR A BLACK GIRL," *Fredonian*, December 30, 1813, SC/UA.

59. Steven Deyle, *Carry Me Back: The Domestic Slave Trade in America* (Oxford: Oxford University Press, 2005), 27.

60. "FOR SALE, A YOUNG BLACK GIRL," *Arnett's New-Jersey Federalist*, January 15, 1795, SC/UA.

61. Thavolia Glymph, *Out of the House of Bondage: The Transformation of the Plantation Household* (Cambridge: Cambridge University Press, 2008), 58–59.

62. Daina Ramey Berry, "'In Pressing Need of Cash': Gender, Skill, and Family Persistence in the Domestic Slave Trade," *Journal of African American History* 92, no. 1 (2007): 30.

63. Graham Russell Hodges, *Root and Branch: African Americans in New York and East Jersey, 1613–1863* (Chapel Hill: University of North Carolina Press, 1999), 75.

64. Deborah Gray White, *Ar'n't I a Woman?: Female Slaves in the Plantation South*, 2nd ed. (New York: W. W. Norton, 1999), 122.

65. McMahon and Schriver, *To Read My Heart*, 18.

66. "To the PUBLIC," *New Brunswick Political Intelligencer and New Jersey Advertiser*, March 16, 1784, SC/UA.

67. "TO BE SOLD, A Young healthy likely NEGRO WOMAN," *Brunswic Gazette*, May 1, 1792 (spelling and punctuation as in original), SC/UA.

68. "FOR SALE, the time of an indented NEGRO GIRL," *Guardian; or, New-Brunswick Advertiser*, May 28, 1799, SC/UA.

69. "For Sale, AT her own request," *Guardian; or, New-Brunswick Advertiser*, March 16, 1815, SC/UA.

70. "FOR SALE, THE TERM OF 7 OR 8 YEARS, A BLACK MAN," *Fredonian*, May 1, 1823, SC/UA.

71. "FOR SALE," *Fredonian*, December 23, 1813, SC/UA.

72. Gigantino, "Trading in Jersey Souls," 282.

73. Berry, "In Pressing Need of Cash," 25.

74. McMahon and Schriver, *To Read My Heart*, 181.

75. Ibid., 275.

76. Ibid., 44.

77. Ibid., 18.

78. M.W. St. Clair Clarke, Clerk of the House of Representatives of the United States, "Abstract of the Returns of the Fifth Census Showing the Number of Free People, the Number of Slaves, the Federal or Representative Number, and the Aggregate of Each County of Each State in the United States," (Washington, DC: Duff Green, 1832).

79. "FOR SALE," *Fredonian*, April 27, 1820, SC/UA.

80. See for example, Keith C. Barton, "'Good Cooks and Washers': Slave Hiring, Domestic Labor, and the Market in Bourbon County, Kentucky," *Journal of American History* 84, no. 2 (1997): 455.

81. Glymph, *Out of the House of Bondage*, 6.

82. Ibid., 108.

83. Margaret Nevius Van Dyke, "Van Dyke Memoir Recalls Dutch Traditions, Household Slaves," in *The Princeton Recollector* 4, no. 4 (January 1979), 6, SC/UA.

84. Deyle, *Carry Me Back*, 165.

85. "BLACK WOMAN FOR SALE," *Fredonian*, October 7, 1813, SC/UA.

86. "To be SOLD at private sale," *Guardian; or, New Brunswick Advertiser*, October 23, 1793, SC/UA.

87. Glymph, *Out of the House of Bondage*, 66–68.

88. For a preliminary conversation on the slaveholding practices of Dutch mistresses in New York, see Hodges, *Root and Branch*, 114.

89. Ibid., 54–55.

90. "VENDUE at the farm late of James Bennet, Esq.," *Fredonian*, March 8, 1821, SC/UA.

91. "FOR SALE, A black girl," *Fredonian*, December 16, 1819; "FOR SALE, a smart active black boy," *Fredonian*, November 15, 1821, SC/UA.

92. "FOR SALE by the subscriber . . . ," *Guardian; or New Brunswick Advertiser*, March 27, 1801, SC/UA.

93. "For sale, At her own request," *Guardian; or, New-Brunswick Advertiser*, March 16, 1815, SC/UA.

94. Gigantino, *Ragged Road to Abolition*, 117.

95. Deyle, *Carry Me Back*, 82.

96. New Brunswick, N.J., First Presbyterian Church, Records 1784–1909, Microfilm copy D-2, SC/UA. John and Ann Bartley's daughter was baptized on May 3, 1827. In the church register, "colored" in many instances is abbreviated simply as "col'd."

97. "AFRICAN SCHOOL," *Fredonian*, January 1, 1823; African Association of New Brunswick Minute Book, 35, 37, SC/UA. Peter Upshur served as moderator of the association for a number of years (not always concurrently) until his death in July of 1823. Even after his death, meetings were held at the home of "Mrs. Nancy Upshur," Peter's widow. Birth dates found from their gravestones in the North Brunswick First Presbyterian Cemetery.

98. "Marriages Performed by Rev. Joseph Clark, 1797–1839," *Genealogical Magazine of New Jersey*, 66 (1991): 91–96; McMahon and Schriver, *To Read My Heart*, 19.

99. Gigantino, *Ragged Road to Abolition*, 128.

100. Eddie S. Glaude, *Exodus!: Religion, Race, and Nation in Early Nineteenth-Century Black America* (Chicago: University of Chicago Press, 2000), 22.

101. Because of the association's relationship with influential white "advisors," we refrain from using the term "black autonomous space," favoring the phrase "exclusively black space" instead. Without dismissing the value inherent in an exclusively black space, "autonomy" would imply that the African Association was free from external influence and manipulation and that was simply not the case. Due to the power that white trustees maintained over the association's finances, autonomy is in this case an inaccurate descriptor.

102. African Association of New Brunswick Minute Book, 35, SC/UA.

103. "AFRICAN SCHOOL," *Fredonian*, January 1, 1823. Records are conflicting as to when the school actually opened (either 1823 or 1824).

104. Ibid.

105. L. A. Greene, "A History of Afro-Americans in New Jersey," *Journal of Rutgers University Libraries* 56, no. 1 (1994): 16.

106. Ibid., 17, 26.

107. Gigantino, *Ragged Road to Abolition*, 214; Greene, "History of Afro-Americans in New Jersey," 1, 29.

108. African Association of New Brunswick Minute Book, 1, SC/UA. The African School of New Brunswick may not have been the very first school for blacks in New Brunswick. According to William H. S. Demarest, "In 1816 a free evening school for the education of people of color was opened; it was held on Monday and Wednesday evenings under the superintendence of gentlemen belonging to the theological school whose services were gratuitously rendered to this object; about eighty adults and children were giving attendance; and the public were urged to appreciate the movement and even to enforce regular attendance of their slaves." *The History of Rutgers College, 1766–1924* (New Brunswick, NJ: Rutgers College, 1924), 251.

109. Gigantino, *Ragged Road to Abolition*, 183.

110. Ibid.

111. African Association of New Brunswick Minute Book, 1–3, SC/UA. Slavery attendance is more difficult to quantify because reduced membership fees could have meant the individual was enslaved or it could have been a subsidized fee based in ability to pay. Additionally, only five permission slips survived the archive, making permission slips an ineffective way to measure general slave attendance.

112. Ibid., (spelling and punctuation as in original).

113. Gigantino, *Ragged Road to Abolition*, 127–128.

114. African Association of New Brunswick Minute Book, 4, SC/UA; "Obituary.—Rev. Leverett I. F. Huntington," *Christian Spectator* 2, no. 1 (January 1820): 46.

115. Annual Report of the American Colonization Society, Vol. 28, Pts. 1845–1853, 15; Gigantino, *Ragged Road to Abolition*, 220; African Association of New Brunswick Minute Book, 28, 32, 34, SC/UA.

116. John Howard Raven, *Catalogue of the Officers and Alumni of Rutgers College, 1766 to 1909* (Trenton, NJ: State Gazette Publishing Co., 1916), 9; Gigantino, *Ragged Road to Abolition*, 238–239; African Association of New Brunswick Minute Book, 28, 29, 31, SC/UA.

117. Gigantino, *Ragged Road to Abolition*, 5.

118. Ibid., 184.

119. Ibid.

120. Permission slips from Mr. Brash, March 1, 1817, and Rev. Norre, January 1, 1819, African Association of New Brunswick Minute Book, SC/UA.

121. African Association of New Brunswick Minute Book, 31, SC/UA (spelling and punctuation as in original).

122. Glaude, *Exodus*, 162.

123. Ibid., 163.

124. African Association of New Brunswick Minute Book, 3, SC/UA.

125. Ibid., 23.

126. Ibid., 23–25 (spelling and punctuation as in original).

127. Ibid., 2.

128. Ibid., 20.

129. Ibid., 18 (spelling and punctuation as in original).
130. Gigantino, *Ragged Road to Abolition*, 185.
131. African Association of New Brunswick Minute Book 2, 3, SC/UA.
132. Ibid., 4.
133. African Association of New Brunswick Minute Book, 1–2, SC/UA (spelling and punctuation as in original).
134. The minutes books also reveal that due to the strict policy males-only leadership meetings were often canceled due to "not meeting a quorum." African Association of New Brunswick Minute Book, 16–17, SC/UA, lists a few examples.
135. Greene, "History of Afro-Americans in New Jersey," 20.
136. Female attendance percentage as recorded from African Association of New Brunswick Minute Book, SC/UA: 1817—28% (31M/12F); 1818—20% (26M/7F); 1819—29% (22M/9F); 1820—37% (20M/12F, January), 37% (17M/10F, July); 1821—42% (15M/11F, January). In another book "members for 1821"—31% (22M/10F, January), 25% (11M/7F, July); 1822—35% (17M/9F, January), 42% (12M/9F, July); 1823—17% (20M/4F, January); 1824—28% (13M/5F, January), 22% (14M/4F, July).
137. African Association of New Brunswick Minute Book, 3, SC/UA.
138. "Phillis Nelson" appears four times in the association minutes books: January 1, 1820; June 3, 1820; January 1, 1821; January 1, 1820, SC/UA.
139. Historians of the nineteenth century have explored many general questions regarding the autonomy of women in black institutions, highlighting the centrality of the black church as a public sphere in both religious and political arenas. Evelyn Brooks Higginbotham, *Righteous Discontent: The Women's Movement in the Black Baptist Church, 1880–1920* (Cambridge, MA: Harvard University Press, 1993), 1. Higginbotham argues that black church women were "crucial to broadening the public arm of the church and making it a powerful institution of racial self-help in the African American community" in the late nineteenth century. Elsa Barkley Brown, "Negotiating and Transforming the Public Sphere: African American Political Life in the Transition from Slavery to Freedom," *Public Culture 7*, no. 1 (Fall 1994): 107–109, 146. Barkley Brown investigates Richmond's First African Church in the immediate emancipation era and contends that African Americans enforced "their understandings of a democratic political discourse through mass meetings attended and participated in . . . by men, women, and children." According to Barkley Brown, women's participation in mass meetings in the postwar period "[contradicted] gender-based assumptions with larger society about politics, political engagement and appropriate forms of political behavior" (108). Brown rejects the gendered public-private dichotomy of Reconstruction literature, suggesting the "problematic of applying such generalizations to African American life in the late-nineteenth century South" (109). She specifically critiques the belief forwarded by Jacqueline Jones that "Black men predominated in this arena, because like other groups in nineteenth-century America, they believed that males alone were responsible for and capable of serious business of politicking. This notion was reinforced by laws that barred female suffrage," Jacqueline Jones, *Labor of Love, Labor of Sorrow: Black Women, Work, and the from Slavery to the Present* (New York: Basic Books, 2009 [1985]), 66. Martha S. Jones, *All Bound Up Together: The Woman Question in African American Public Culture, 1830–1900* (Chapel Hill: University of North Carolina Press, 2007), 4, 8. Jones investigates how the "woman question" influenced black public culture, especially free black communities in the North. Beginning in the 1830s through the nadir (the period from 1877 to the early twentieth century when African Americans faced extreme racism and racial violence), Jones frames much of the discussion around formal institutions

like the Negro convention movement, early antislavery societies, and women's suffrage organizations, tracing the shifting contours of black women's participation in each.

140. Gigantino, *Ragged Road to Abolition*, 184.

141. Ibid., 184–185.

142 African Association of New Brunswick Minute Book, 38, 40, SC/UA.

143. To be clear, this is not a comment on the interior, romantic, or intimate nature of their relationship. While many women might have pursued similar relationships with respected or established men, these intimate ties were negotiated within a complicated, patriarchal society. Moreover, some relationships were coerced and even violent. For more information about how free black and enslaved women negotiated autonomy, agency, and freedom through their relationships, intimate and otherwise, see Amrita Myers, *Forging Freedom: Black Women in the Pursuit of Liberty in the Antebellum South* (Chapel Hill: University of North Carolina Press, 2011); Emily Clark, *The Strange History of the American Quadroon: Free Women of Color in the Revolutionary Atlantic World* (Chapel Hill: University of North Carolina Press, 2013); Marisa Fuentes, "Power and Historical Figuring: Rachael Pringle Polgreen's Troubled Archive," in *Gender & History* (Special Issue: "Historicising Gender and Sexuality" ed. Kevin P. Murphy and Jennifer M. Spear) 22:3 (November 2010): 564-584; White, *Ar'n't I a Woman?*, 29-44.

144. African Association of New Brunswick Minute Book, SC/UA. The Utt women were either sisters or a mother/daughter team; they were often listed together in the records books.

145. Ibid., 23.

146. Ibid., 18 (spelling and punctuation as in original).

147. Ibid., 24.

148. Ibid., 1, 37.

CHAPTER 6: From the Classroom to the American Colonization Society

1. Theodore Frelinghuysen, *An Oration: Delivered at Princeton, New Jersey, Nov. 16, 1824, Before the New Jersey Colonization Society by the Honourable Theodore Frelinghuysen* (Princeton, NJ: Princeton Press, 1824), 12 (spelling and punctuation as in original).

2. Ibid., 6.

3. Ibid.

4. James D. Bratt, *Dutch Calvinism in Modern America: A History of a Conservative Subculture* (Grand Rapids, MI: Eerdmans, 1984), 4; Sydney E. Ahlstrom, *A Religious History of the American People* (New Haven, CT: Yale University Press, 1972), 203; John W. Coakley, *New Brunswick Theological Seminary: An Illustrated History, 1784–2014* (Grand Rapids, MI: Eerdmans, 2014), 15.

5. Historian Thomas Frusciano argues, "There were however, abolitionist voices in the denomination—including presumably from persons no less Calvinist than the others—which come out in the General Synod debate in 1855 that included How's presentation, and in the pamphlet exchanges that followed" (editorial comment). See also Edward Tanjore Corwin, *A Digest of Constitutional and Synodical Legislation of the Reformed Church in America* (New York: Board of Publications of the Reformed Church in America, 1906), 467–468.

6. Douglas Greenberg, "The Middle Colonies in Recent American Historiography," *William and Mary Quarterly* 36 (1979): 396–398, 408–409, 412–413, 422–425; James Gigantino, *The Ragged Road to Abolition: Slavery and Freedom in New Jersey, 1775–1865* (Philadelphia: University of Pennsylvania Press, 2014), 9–10, 85–86; Emily Blanck, "Slavery in New Jersey: A Roundtable," *New Jersey History* 127, no. 1 (2012): 2, 4, 14. For a more recent interpretation of the Middle Colonies as pluralistic and distinct, see Maxine N.

Lurie, "Colonial Period: The Complex and Contradictory Beginnings of a Mid-Atlantic Province," in *New Jersey: A History of the Garden State*, ed. Maxine N. Lurie and Richard Veit (New Brunswick, NJ: Rutgers University Press, 2012), 33. For an overview of the Mid-Atlantic's long history of political "accommodations," see Kenneth J. Heineman, "The Only Thing You Will Find in the Middle of the Road Are Double Yellow Lines, Dead Frogs, and Electoral Leverage: Mid-Atlantic Political Culture and Influence across the Centuries," *Pennsylvania History: A Journal of Mid-Atlantic Studies* 82, no. 3 (Summer 2015): 311.

7. Ahlstrom, *A Religious History*, 201; Kim Todt, "'Women Are as Knowing Therein as the Men': Dutch Women in Early America," in *Women in Early America*, ed. Thomas A. Foster (New York: New York University Press, 2015), 45–46; Robert Juet, "The Third Voyage of Master Henry Hudson," in *Narratives of New Netherland, 1609–1664*, ed. J. Franklin Jameson (New York: Scribner's, 1909), 19.

8. Susanah Shaw Romney, "'With & Alongside His Housewife': Claiming Ground in New Netherland and the Early Modern Dutch Empire," *William and Mary Quarterly* 73, no. 2 (April 2016): 190; Ahlstom, *A Religious History*, 201–202.

9. Patricia U. Bonomi, "'Swarms of Negroes Comeing about My Door': Black Christianity in Early Dutch and English North America," *Journal of American History* 103, no. 1 (June 2016): 38, 40, 43–44; Joyce D. Goodfriend, "Burghers and Blacks: The Evolution of a Slave Society at New Amsterdam," *New York History* 59 (April 1978): 126–127, 134–136, 139; Gerlad Francis De Jong, "The Dutch Reformed Church and Negro Slavery in Colonial America," *Church History* 40, no. 4 (December 1971): 423, 426; Ira Berlin, *Many Thousands Gone: The First Two Centuries of Slavery in North America* (Cambridge, MA: Harvard University Press, 1998), 50–51; Graham Russell Hodges, *Root and Branch: African Americans in New York and East Jersey* (Chapel Hill: University of North Carolina Press, 1999), 20–23; George L. Smith, *Religion and Trade in New Netherland: Dutch Origins and American Development* (Ithaca, NY: Cornell University Press, 1973), 126–128.

10. "Letter of Reverend Jonas Michaëlius," in *Narratives of New Netherland, 1609–1664*, ed. J. Franklin Jameson (New York: Scribner's, 1909), 129–130; De Jong, "Dutch Reformed Church," 427.

11. Susanah Shaw Romney, *New Netherland Connections: Intimate Networks and Atlantic Ties in Seventeenth-Century America* (Chapel Hill: University of North Carolina Press, 2014), 211–214, 233–235, 243; Romney, "Claiming Ground," 192.

12. "Rev. Henricus Selyns to the Classis of Amsterdam," in *Narratives of New Netherland, 1609–1664*, ed. J. Franklin Jameson (New York: Scribner's, 1909), 408–409; Bonomi, "Swarms of Negroes," 39, 43. See also Hodges, *Root and Branch*, 18–25 for further discussion.

13. For a nuanced account of the Dutch, religion, and slavery, see Gerald Francis De Jong, *Dutch Reformed Church in the American Colonies* (Grand Rapids, MI: Eerdmans Publishing Company, 1978), 161–169.

14. "Constitution of 1792," in Corwin, *A Digest of Constitutional and Synodical Legislation*, lxvi. Theological scholar and professor John Coakley explains the technicality of this language: "The term 'complaint' is a technical one, and implies the invoking of a procedure that's elsewhere described in the Constitution, which applies to all disciplinary matters. That is, refusal of baptism is not seen here as a matter of personal complaint by the refused person, as though it were a lawsuit brought by a plaintiff—but as a matter of violation of the discipline of the church" (editorial comment by John Coakley).

15. Richard P. McCormick, *Rutgers: A Bicentennial History* (New Brunswick, NJ: Rutgers University Press, 1966), 1–5; William H. S. Demarest, *A History of Rutgers College, 1766–1924* (New Brunswick, NJ: Rutgers College, 1924), 25, 33–36, 57; Coakley, *New Brunswick*

Theological Seminary, 1–2; Ahlstrom, *A Religious History*, 376–377; "Proceedings of the Twelfth Reverend Coetus of New York," in *The Acts and Proceedings of the General Synod of the Reformed Protestant Dutch Church in North America* (New York: Board of Publications of the Reformed Protestant Dutch Church, 1859), xci–xcii. At this point in time New Jersey was a colony of England with an appointed royal governor. As an interesting historical note, William Franklin was the illegitimate son of Benjamin Franklin.

16. McCormick, *Rutgers*, 25–26; Thomas J. Frusciano, "From Queen's College to Rutgers College," *Journal of the Rutgers University Libraries* 68, no. 1 (2016): 20–21; Coakley, *New Brunswick Theological Seminary*, 6, 10.

17. McCormick, *Rutgers*, 7; Wallace N. Jamison, *Religion in New Jersey: A Brief History* (Princeton, NJ: D. Van Nordstrand, 1964), 86, 90, 92.

18. Jamison, *Religion in New Jersey*, 104–105; Paul F. Conkin, *The Uneasy Center: Reformed Christianity in Antebellum America* (Chapel Hill: University of North Carolina Press, 1995), 177; Clifford Stephen Griffin, *Their Brothers' Keepers: Moral Stewardship in the United States, 1800–1865* (New Brunswick, NJ: Rutgers University Press, 1960), 186–188; Louis Filler, *The Crusade against Slavery, 1830–1860* (New York: Harper, 1960), 124–125.

19. Geography informed the Reformed Church's internal debates and response to the impulses of the Second Great Awakening. Since the 1619 Synod of Dordrecht, Dutch Reformed Calvinism had upheld predestination. Salvation was solely in God's hands, and his election to salvation was unconditional—it was not shaped by a person's actions or character. In the early nineteenth century, congregations in the northern reaches of the American Reformed Church, clustered around Albany, offered increasingly liberal interpretations of Calvinist principles and notions of election. Ministers embraced revivals and considered the place of human choice and action in their own salvation. The Second Great Awakening's emphasis on conversion, repentance, and personal action would lead to the founding of a number of reform organizations. By stressing the belief that through his or her own efforts every individual could achieve salvation, Protestantism laid the groundwork for amelioration or improvement on a much larger scale. From teetotalers in favor of temperance to proponents of women's suffrage to welfare advocates, the spirit of reform suffused antebellum culture and society. The larger religious transformations and movements toward liberal reform in upstate New York likely informed these shifting interpretations. Yet more southern congregations, concentrated in New Jersey and New York City, rejected these liberal tendencies. They remained strict in their beliefs about divinely dictated salvation, and they made the New Brunswick Theological Seminary an intellectual bastion of old-school Calvinism. The influence of a conservative Calvinism dictated how the Second Great Awakening played out in the Mid-Atlantic region, and in New Jersey specifically. This conservatism would ultimately manifest itself in an antislavery activism committed above all to upholding social and racial hierarchies. See James D. Bratt, ed., *Antirevivalism in Antebellum America: A Collection of Religious Voices* (New Brunswick, NJ: Rutgers University Press, 2006), 54; Conkin, *Uneasy Center*, 178; Coakley, *New Brunswick Theological Seminary*, 15; and James Tanis, *Dutch Calvinistic Pietism in the Middle Colonies: A Study in the Life and Theology of Theodorus Jacobus Frelinghuysen* (The Hague: Martinus Nijhoff, 1967), 119.

20. For works considering the ACS a conservative antislavery organization, see Early Lee Fox, *The American Colonization Society, 1817–1840* (Baltimore: Johns Hopkins University Press, 1919); Frederic Bancroft, "The Colonization of American Negroes, 1801–1865," in *Frederic Bancroft: Historian*, ed. Jacob E. Cooke (Norman: University of Oklahoma Press, 1957); and Philip J. Staudenraus, *The African Colonization Movement, 1816–1865* (New York: Columbia University Press, 1961). For works critical of or altogether unwilling

to consider the ACS an antislavery organization, see Eric Foner's *Free Soil, Free Labor, Free Men: The Ideology of the Republican Party before the Civil War* (Oxford: Oxford University Press, 1995 [1970]); George M. Frederickson, *The Black Image in the White Mind: The Debate on Afro-American Character and Destiny, 1817–1914* (New York: Harper & Row, 1971); Leonard P. Curry, *The Free Black in Urban America, 1800–1850* (Chicago: University of Chicago Press, 1981); and Amos J. Beyan, *The American Colonization Society and the Creation of the Liberian State* (Lanham, MD: University Press of America, 1991). See also Douglas R. Egerton, *Rebels, Reformers, and Revolutionaries: Collected Essays and Second Thoughts* (New York: Routledge, 2002); Bruce Dorsey, *Reforming Men and Women: Gender in the Antebellum City* (Ithaca, NY: Cornell University Press, 2002); and Eric Burin, *Slavery and the Peculiar Solution: A History of the American Colonization Society* (Gainesville: University Press of Florida, 2005).

21. Karen Halttunen, *Confidence Men and Painted Women: A Study of Middle-Class Culture in America, 1830–1870* (New Haven, CT: Yale University Press, 1986), xvi.

22. Gigantino, *The Ragged Road to Abolition*, 81.

23. James Gigantino, "Trading in Jersey Souls: New Jersey and the Interstate Slave Trade," *Pennsylvania History: A Journal of Mid-Atlantic Studies 77*, no. 3 (2010): 282.

24. United States Bureau of the Census, *A Century of Population Growth: From the First Census of the United States to the Twelfth, 1790–1900* (Washington, DC: Government Printing Office, 1909), 133.

25. Gigantino, *The Ragged Road to Abolition*, 9.

26. L. A. Greene, "A History of Afro-Americans in New Jersey," *Journal of the Rutgers University Libraries 56*, no. 1 (1994): 29–30.

27. Rachel Van Dyke, "Book 3. June 10–23, 1810," in *To Read My Heart: The Journal of Rachel Van Dyke, 1810–1811*, ed. Lucia McMahon and Deborah Schriver (Philadelphia: University of Pennsylvania Press, 2000 First Edition), 44.

28. Ibid.

29. Larry Greene, "Civil War and Reconstruction: State and Nation Divided," in *New Jersey: A History of the Garden State*, ed. Maxine N. Lurie and Richard Veit (New Brunswick, NJ: Rutgers University Press, 2012), 149.

30. See the *Fredonian*, October 11, 1830, SC/UA.

31. "Memorial to the Legislature of Virginia,". *Annual Report of the American Colonization Society, Vol. 28, Parts 1845-1853* (Washington, DC: C. Alexander, Printer, 1845), 41.

32. Ibid.

33. Ibid.

34. Ibid., 45.

35. Ibid.

36. In an article interrogating the origins of the ACS, however, historian Douglas R. Egerton argues that there is some evidence to prove that Charles Fenton Mercer, a wealthy congressman from Virginia, was the true progenitor of the colonizationist movement. Egerton claims that the Virginian had revived the colonization scheme much earlier in 1816, believing that Africa could act as a safety valve, relieving the United States of the dual burdens of slavery and the pauperism that would most certainly befall free blacks. During a trip to New York State that summer, Mercer shared his plan to introduce the idea to the state legislature with friends, among them Elias B. Caldwell, who subsequently shared them with his brother-in-law Robert Finley. The latter, who saw in colonizationism a way to derive meaning from his life, would spearhead the national organization, which neutralized Mercer's own state-level plans. Egerton goes on to suggest that from the beginning, Northerners wanted to deny the ACS its Southern roots

in order to appeal to a broader audience. Finley, a Northern minister who embodied political moderation and the spirit of antebellum reform, made a much more acceptable founding father. Ultimately, Northern colonizationists were more likely to challenge the paternity of the ACS than its racial politics. See Douglas R. Egerton, "'Its Origins Is Not a Little Curious': A New Look at the American Colonization Society," *Journal of the Early Republic* 5, no. 4 (Winter 1995): 163–180.

37. Corwin, *Digest of Constitutional and Synodical Legislation*, 20–21; Daniel Walker Howe, *What Hath God Wrought: The Transformation of America, 1815–1848* (New York: Oxford University Press, 2007), 262.

38. Richard Allen, trans., *Leaves from a Century Plant: Report of the Centennial Celebration of Old Pine St. Church* (Philadelphia: Henry B. Ashmead, 1870), 170–171.

39. David D. Demarest, *Centennial of the Theological Seminary of the Reformed Church in America (Formerly Ref. Prot. Dutch Church) 1784–1884* (New York: Board of Publication of the Reformed Church in America, 1885), 440.

40. Philip Milledoler, *Address, Delivered to the Graduates of Rutgers College: At Commencement Held in the Reformed Dutch Church, New Brunswick, N.J., July 20, 1831* (New York: Rutgers Press, 1831), 8.

41. Ibid., 13.

42. See Burin, *Slavery and the Peculiar Solution*.

43. Milledoler, *Address*, 14.

44. "Reports of Agents," *African Repository and Colonial Journal* 7 (1831–1832): 375.

45. Frelinghuysen, *An Oration*, 8.

46. Ibid., 9.

47. Ibid.

48. Robert J. Eells, "Theodore Frelinghuysen, Voluntaryism and the Pursuit of the Public Good," *American Presbyterians* 69, no. 4 (Winter 1991): 258.

49. Ibid., 259.

50. Harvey Strum, "Frelinghuysen, Theodore," in *Encyclopedia of New Jersey*, ed. Maxine N. Lurie and Marc Mappen (New Brunswick, NJ: Rutgers University Press, 2004), 293.

51. "Amos Kendall," *Whig Standard*, June 15, 1844, 2. As a figure, both literary and material, the meticulously dressed black dandy troubled the conventions of race, gender, class, and sexuality. "As a social practice that mounts a critique against the hierarchies that order society," argues literary scholar Monica L. Miller, "dandyism appears to be a phenomenon particularly suited to blacks, who experienced an attempted erasure or reordering of their identities in the slave trade." Indeed, as black dandies began to "dress the part from slavery to freedom" during the antebellum period, conveying not only self-respect but increased social status and fitness for citizenship, they emerged as a threat to elite, middle-class, working-class, and immigrant whites. See Monica L. Miller, *Slaves to Fashion: Black Dandyism and the Styling of Black Diasporic Identity* (Durham, NC: Duke University Press, 2009), 10, 103.

52. It is likely Frelinghuysen owned slaves as his father inherited the slaves of his mother, Dinah Frelinghuysen Hardenbergh (wife of Jacob Sr.) (editorial comment by Professor Thomas Frusciano).

53. Frelinghuysen, *An Oration*, 6.

54. *The Thirteenth Annual Report of the American Colonization Society for Colonizing the Free People of Colour of the United States, with an Appendix Second Edition* (Georgetown, DC: James C. Dunn, 1830), xiii.

55. Frelinghuysen, *An Oration*, 7.

56. Ibid., 9.

57. Theodore Frelinghuysen, "Review of Anti-Slavery Publications, and Defence of the Colonization Society," *African Repository and Colonial Journal* 10, no. 1 (March 1834): 3.

58. Robert Finley, "Thoughts on the Colonization of Free Blacks," *African Repository and Colonial Journal* 9 (1834 [1816]): 334.

59. For more on the relationship between environmentalism and racial difference see Mia Bay, *The White Image in the Black Mind: African-American Ideas about White People, 1830–1925* (Oxford: Oxford University Press, 2000); and Bruce Dain, *The Hideous Monster of the Mind: American Race Theory in the Early Republic* (Cambridge, MA: Harvard University Press, 2002).

60. Finley, "Thoughts on the Colonization of Free Blacks," 334 (emphasis as in original document).

61. John S. Rock, "Right of Suffrege [sic]," *The North Star*, February 8, 1850, http://find.gale-group.com.proxy.libraries.rutgers.edu/ncnp/start.do?prodId=NCNP&userGroupName=new67449.

62. Ibid.

63. William Lloyd Garrison, *Thoughts on African Colonization: Or an Impartial Exhibition of the Doctrines, Principles and Purposes of the American Colonization Society, Together with the Resolutions, Addresses and Remonstrances of the Free People of Color*, pt. 2 (Boston: Garrison and Knapp, 1832), 46.

64. See Howard Holman Bell, ed., *Minutes of the Proceedings of the National Negro Conventions, 1830–1864* (New York: Arno Press, 1969). It is the case that by the 1850s, free blacks were beginning to differ about the exact meanings of home and emigration. The majority of abolitionists such as Frederick Douglass, James McCune Smith, and William J. Watkins rejected freedom upon condition of exile and fought to make life better for African Americans within the United States. Contrastingly, a small group of antislavery activists including Martin R. Delany and Henry Highland Garnet, frustrated with the slow and uneven meting out of justice for African Americans, embraced emigration as the only way to achieve true liberation. It is important to note that though a small number of African Americans believed that emigration to West Africa, Canada, or the Caribbean offered the best avenue for freedom, their views were not interchangeable with those of the ACS. Black nationalism and antiblack racism should not be conflated.

65. Greene, "A History of Afro-Americans in New Jersey," 24.

66. "The American Colonization Society," *The North Star*, February 8, 1850,http://find.gale-group.com.proxy.libraries.rutgers.edu/ncnp/start.do?prodId=NCNP&userGroupName=new67449.

67. Benjamin F. Butler, future major general in the Union Army, would become famous during the Civil War for circumventing the Fugitive Slave Law by classifying runaway slaves as "contraband" in order to recruit them as laborers.

68. Samuel E. Cornish and Theodore S. Wright, *The Colonization Scheme Considered, In Its Rejection by the Colored People—In Its Tendency to Uphold Caste—In Its Unfitness for Christianizing and Civilizing the Aborigines of Africa, and For Putting a Stop to the African Slave Trade: In a Letter to the Hon. Theodore Frelinghuysen and the Hon. Benjamin F. Butler* (Newark: Printed by Aaron Guest, 1840), 7 (emphasis as in original document).

69. Ibid., 8 (emphasis as in original document).

70. Ibid., 26.

71. Samuel B. How, *Slaveholding Not Sinful: Slavery, the Punishment of Man's Sin: It's Remedy, the Gospel of Christ* (New York: John Terhume, 1856), 9, 12–13, 29–30, 33.

72. Ibid., 18–19, 49.

73. Craig Steven Wilder, *Ebony and Ivy: Race, Slavery, and the Troubled History of America's Universities* (New York: Bloomsbury Press, 2013), 10.

74. Ibid.

75. Joseph Story and Thomas M. Cooley, *Commentaries on the Constitution of the United States, with a Preliminary Review of the Constitutional History of the Colonies and States before the Adoption of the Constitution* (Clark, NJ: Lawbook Exchange, 2008), 204.

76. Francis Wayland, *The Elements of Moral Science* (Boston: Gould, Kendall, & Lincoln, 1835), 216, 207.

77. Claude Clegg Andrew, *The Price of Liberty: African Americans and the Making of Liberia* (Chapel Hill: University of North Carolina Press, 2004), 3.

78. Wilder, *Ebony and Ivy*, 182.

79. Ibid., 207.

80. Ibid., 228.

81. Ibid., 212.

82. Ibid., 213, 217, 225. Hosack received his education from the College of New Jersey (Princeton), and earned his medical degree from the University of Pennsylvania in 1791. He completed his medical training at the University of Edinburgh. For more on Hosack see David Hosack, *Inaugural Discourse, Delivered at the Opening of the Rutgers Medical College*; Hosack, *An Introductory Lecture on Medical Education; Delivered at the Commencement of the Annual Course of Lectures on Botany and the Materia Medica* (New York: T. and J. Swords, 1801). On the history of Queen's and Rutgers College and early medical instruction, see David L. Cowen, *Medical Education: The Queen's-Rutgers Experience, 1792–1830* (New Brunswick, NJ: The State Bicentennial Commission and the Rutgers Medical School, 1966).

83. Ibid., 216, 225.

84. Wilder, *Ebony and Ivy*, 216, 223, 225. Mitchill was raised in a large Quaker family on Long Island. He manumitted his slaves Jenny Jiggins months after the trial, Ned in 1811, and Betsy in June 1816.

85. Ibid., 214 and 217.

86. Wilder, *Ebony and Ivy*, 264.

87. Bay, *White Image in the Black Mind*, 20.

88. See, for example, ibid.; Ann Fabian, *The Skull Collectors: Race, Science, and America's Unburied Dead* (Chicago: University of Chicago Press, 2010); and Melissa N. Stein, *Measuring Manhood: Race and the Science of Masculinity, 1830–1934* (Minneapolis: University of Minnesota Press, 2015).

CHAPTER 7: Rutgers

1. See Camilla Townsend et al., "'I Am Old and Weak . . . and You Are Young and Strong . . .': The Intersecting Histories of Rutgers University and the Lenni Lenape," in this volume (Chapter 1).

2. For example, in 1863 the New Jersey Assembly passed a bill entitled An Act to Prevent the Immigration of Negroes and Mulattoes by a vote of thirty-three to twenty. See L. A. Greene, "A History of Afro-Americans in New Jersey," *Journal of the Rutgers University Libraries* 56, no. 1 (1994): 4–71, 29–31.

3. The Native Archives system was established by Congress in 1934.

4. *100 Milestone Documents*, National Archives (Washington, DC: National Archives and Records Administration, 1995), 57, https://ourdocuments.gov/doc.php?doc=33.

5. In 1887, the act was amended by the Hatch Act, and later the Smith-Lever Act in 1914. For more information see "Our History: How George H. Cook Shaped Rutgers," Executive Dean of Agriculture and Natural Resources, Rutgers University, https://execdean-agriculture.rutgers.edu/george-h-cook.html.

6. Samuel Dumont Halliday, *History of the Agricultural College Land Grant Act of July 2, 1862: Devoted Largely to the History of the "Land Scrip" Which under That Grant Was Allotted to the State of New York and Afterwards Given to Cornell University* (Ithaca, NY: Ithaca Democrat Press, 1906), 5. The Morrill bill presented in 1862 was nearly identical to the original bill. An amendment was included that provided for military training as a requirement for each student.

7. Ibid., 5.

8. Ibid.

9. Ibid. See also https://www.archives.gov/publications/prologue/2012/winter/homestead.pdf.

10. United States, General Land Office, *Annual Report of the Commissioner of the General Land Office to the Secretary of the Interior* (Washington, DC: The Office, 1868), 24, http://www.archive.org/stream/annualreportcom370ffigoog/#page/n23/mode/2up.

11. Ibid. The total amount was 7,041,114.50 acres. Other public lands were disposed through military bounty-land warrants and homesteads. http://www.archive.org/stream/annualreportcom370ffigoog/#page/n23/mode/2up.

12. As slaves and noncitizens, African Americans were not seen as part of this project of nation-building.

13. Justin Smith Morrill, *Speech of Hon. Justin S. Morrill, of Vermont, on the Bill Granting Lands for Agricultural Colleges* (Washington, DC: Congressional Globe Office, 1858), 9, https://archive.org/stream/speechofhonjusti01morr#page/8/mode/2up.

14. Ibid.

15. James Buchanan, "Veto Message," February 24, 1859. Online at Gerhard Peters and John T. Woolley, *The American Presidency Project*, http://www.presidency.ucsb.edu/ws/?pid=68368 (emphasis added).

16. Ibid.

17. Ibid.

18. Jean Wilson Sidar, *George Hammell Cook: A Life in Agriculture and Geology* (New Brunswick, NJ: Rutgers University Press, 1976), 85.

19. Thomas LeDuc, "State Disposal of the Agricultural College Land Scrip," *Agricultural History* 28, no. 3 (July 1954): 99–107.

20. Thomas Frusciano explains that "this is the James Bishop who built Bishop House that is on the College Avenue campus. He had major interests in the shipping and rubber industries. As a result of the Panic of 1873, he sold the mansion to Mahlon Martin in 1874 and Rutgers acquired the mansion and surrounding property from Martin in 1925" (editorial comment).

21. LeDuc, "State Disposal," 101.

22. Benjamin F. Andrews, *The Land Grant of 1862 and the Land-Grant Colleges* (Washington, DC: Government Printing Office, 1918), 34, https://archive.org/details/landgrantof1862100andrrich.

23. Sidar, *George Hammell Cook*, 85.

24. Ibid.

25. See chap. 6 in Sidar, *George Hammell Cook* for more information on the bidding war between Rutgers and Princeton, especially 86–92.

26. Ibid., 85.

27. Ibid., 84–85. It would be naïve to suggest that the Morrill Act was enacted because of a pure commitment to a white democratic educational vision. As stated earlier, the act itself served as a branch in a growing war effort.

28. For an example of the way the Morrill Act is often remembered and discussed today, see Christopher P. Loss, "Why the Morrill Land-Grant Colleges Act Still Matters, *The Chronicle for Higher Education,* July 16, 2012. http://www.chronicle.com/article/Why-the-Morrill-act-Still/132877/?cid=at.

29. Cynthia L. Jackson and Eleanor F. Nunn, *Historically Black Colleges and Universities: A Reference Handbook* (Santa Barbara, CA: ABC-CLIO, 2003), 13–14.

30. "Historically Black Colleges and Universities and Higher Education Desegregation," U.S. Department of Education, U.S. Department of Education, Office for Civil Rights, Regional Civil Rights Offices, Washington D.C., March 1, 1991. http://www2.ed.gov/about/offices/list/ocr/docs/hq9511.html.

31. Jackson and Nunn, *Historically Black Colleges and Universities,* 30.

32. Ibid., 15. The tenuous position of black land-grant colleges is evidenced in the case of the private Hampton Agricultural and Normal Institute in Virginia. When the institute was founded in 1872 by the American Missionary Association, it received one-half of the funds from the 1862 act that the state of Virginia had received. By 1920, the state had transferred the funding from Hampton to Virginia Normal and Industrial College (now Virginia State University).

33. Helen W. Ludlow, "Hampton Indian Students at Home," in *Hampton Institute 1868–1885: Its Work for Two Races,* ed. Mary Frances Armstrong (Hampton, VA: Normal School Press Print, 1885), 10.

34. Donal F. Lindsey, *Indians at Hampton Institute, 1877–1923* (Urbana: University of Illinois Press, 1995), 9–11. As Lindsey continues, "Behind this policy was a commitment to 'education' as the vehicle for the complete cultural transformation of the Indian" (12).

35. Ibid., 96.

36. Ibid., 98.

EPILOGUE

1. Robin D. G. Kelley, "Black Study, Black Struggle," *Boston Review,* March 27, 2016, http://bostonreview.net/forum/robin-d-g-kelley-black-study-black-struggle.

2. "Campus Demands," *The Demands,* http://www.thedemands.org/.

3. Craig Steven Wilder, *Ebony and Ivy: Race, Slavery, and the Troubled History of America's Universities* (New York: Bloomsbury Press, 2013), 33.

4. *The Report of the Working Group on Slavery, Memory, and Reconciliation to the President of Georgetown University* (Washington, DC: Georgetown University, 2016), http://slavery.georgetown.edu/report/#_ga=1.62721580.1064456366.1473560107.

5. *Slavery and Justice: Report of the Brown University Steering Committee* (Providence, RI: Brown University, 2006), http://brown.edu/Research/Slavery_Justice/documents/SlaveryAndJustice.pdf.

6. *Report of the Trustee Committee on Woodrow Wilson's Legacy at Princeton* (Princeton, NJ: Princeton University, 2016), https://www.princeton.edu/vpsec/trustees/Wilson-Committee-Report-Final.pdf.

7. Ibid.

LIST OF CONTRIBUTORS

Beatrice Adams is a third-year doctoral student in African American and African diaspora history at Rutgers University. She received an MA in social sciences from the University of Chicago and a BA in history from Fisk University. Her doctoral research examines African Americans' relationship to the American South, focusing on issues of identity, belonging, and migration.

Shaun Armstead received her BA in history from Auburn University. She is currently a second-year doctoral student in the history program at Rutgers University, where she focuses on women's transnational activism after World War II.

Jesse Bayker is a PhD candidate in history. He received a BA in history and LGBTQ studies from CUNY Brooklyn College in 2010. He studies women's and gender history, with a particular focus on transgender history in the nineteenth century. He is currently completing his dissertation, entitled "Before Transsexuality: Crossing the Borders of Gender in the United States, 1850–1960."

Christopher Blakley is a PhD candidate in the Department of History at Rutgers University. His expertise is in early American environmental history, the history of science, and Atlantic world slavery. His dissertation questions how interactions between enslaved Africans and nonhuman animals throughout the diaspora shaped imperialism and colonization in the eighteenth-century British Atlantic world.

Kendra Boyd is a PhD candidate in African American history at Rutgers University. She holds a BS in business administration from Wayne State University and studies black business and racial capitalism. She is completing her dissertation,

"Freedom Enterprise: The Great Migration and Black Entrepreneurship in Detroit."

Miya Carey is a PhD candidate and is in her sixth year in the Department of History at Rutgers University, New Brunswick. She specializes in twentieth-century African American and women's and gender history. Her dissertation, "'That Charm of All Girlhood': African American Girlhood and Girls in Washington, D.C., 1930–1965," explores shifting definitions of girlhood through an examination of black girls' social organizations and youth culture in the nation's capital.

Kaisha Esty is a PhD candidate in African American and women's and gender history at Rutgers. She holds a BA and MRes in American studies from the University of Nottingham, UK. Currently in her fifth year, she is working on her dissertation, "'A Crusade against the Despoiler of Virtue': Black Women, Social Purity, and the Gendered Politics of the Negro Problem."

Marisa J. Fuentes is an associate professor at Rutgers University, New Brunswick, in the Departments of Women's and Gender Studies and History. Her first book, *Dispossessed Lives: Enslaved Women, Violence and the Archive* (2016), explores the spatial, historical, and symbolic confinement enslaved women experienced in eighteenth-century Bridgetown, Barbados. Her research interests include gender and early modern slavery, critical historical methodologies, Black Atlantic history, and the links between the slave trade and capitalism. Her work has been supported by the Fulbright Program, the Ford Foundation, Harvard's Charles Warren Center for Studies in American History, and the Schomburg Center for Research in Black Culture—with support from the National Endowment for the Humanities.

Tracey Johnson graduated with her BA in history from The College of William and Mary in 2014. She is currently a second-year doctoral student in the History Department at Rutgers. She is interested in the Black Arts movement, particularly the ways in which New York City museums served as a space of activism during the civil rights and Black Power movements.

Daniel Manuel is a third-year doctoral candidate in the women's and gender history program. His research explores AIDS activism and policy in the U.S. South in the 1980s and 1990s. Prior to attending Rutgers, he earned his BA and MA in history from the University of Louisiana at Lafayette.

Jomaira Salas Pujols is a second-year doctoral candidate in the Sociology Department at Rutgers University whose research is focused on higher education, race, and academic achievement for students of color. She studies various forms of resistance to structural racism on college campuses by analyzing campus protests and the everyday academic strategies of blacks and Latinas in colleges and universities in the United States. Pujols uses mixed-methods and participatory action research to develop new epistemologies of underrepresented communities.

Brenann Sutter earned her BA in history and sociology from the University of California, San Diego, in 2010. In 2012, she completed her MA in history at New York University. Sutter is currently in the third year of her doctoral program at Rutgers University, pursuing twentieth-century American history with a concentration in women and gender. Her research explores the social and political negotiations between sexuality, citizenship, and consumerism.

Camilla Townsend is a professor of Native American history at Rutgers, New Brunswick. She is the author of several books, among them *Pocahontas and the Powhatan Dilemma* and *American Indian History: A Documentary Reader*. For her work on the history of indigenous peoples she has received grants from the American Philosophical Society, the National Endowment for the Humanities, and the John Simon Guggenheim Memorial Foundation. Ugonna Amaechi, Jacob Arnay, Shelby Berner, Lynn Biernacki, Vanessa Bodossian, Megan Brink, Joseph Cuzzolino, Melissa Deutsch, Emily Edelman, Esther Esquenazi, Brian Hagerty, Blaise Hode, Dana Jordan, Andrew Kim, Eric Knittel, Brianna Leider, Jessica MacDonald, Kathleen Margeotes, Anjelica Matcho, William Nisley, Elisheva Rosen, Ryan Von Sauers, Ethan Smith, Amanda Stein, and Chad Stewart are undergraduate students at Rutgers who conducted extensive research for Chapter 1 as part of her course "Native American History."

Pamela Walker is a second-year doctoral student specializing in African American and women's and gender history. She received her BA in history from the University of Tennessee at Knoxville in 2011 and an MA in history from the University of New Orleans in 2015. She studies the intersections of motherhood, activism, and survival during the twentieth-century black freedom struggle. Walker's current research explores cross-racial antipoverty activism and civil rights participation during the 1960s in the American South and Northeast United States.

Deborah Gray White is Board of Governors Distinguished Professor of History at Rutgers University, New Brunswick, New Jersey. She is author of *Ar'n't I A Woman? Female Slaves in the Plantation South*, *Too Heavy a Load: Black Women in Defense of Themselves, 1894–1994*, several K–12 textbooks on U.S. history, and *Let My People Go: African Americans 1804–1860*. Her edited works include *Telling Histories: Black Women in the Ivory Tower*, a collection of personal narratives written by African American women historians that chronicle the entry of black women into the historical profession and the development of the field of black women's history. *Freedom on My Mind: A History of African Americans*, a coauthored text, is her most recent publication. As a fellow at the Woodrow Wilson International Center for Scholars in Washington, DC, and as a John Simon Guggenheim Fellow, White conducted research on her newest book, *Lost in the USA: Marching for Identity from the Promise Keepers to the Million Mom March*.

Meagan Wierda is a second-year doctoral student jointly interested in the history of slavery and the history of medicine in the United States during the nineteenth century. Her interests center on questions of race, embodiment, and knowledge production. She examines how African American abolitionists mounted a specifically scientific challenge to slavery in the decades leading up to the Civil War. Before coming to Rutgers, Meagan earned an MA in history from Concordia University (Montréal) and a BA in history and lettres françaises from the University of Ottawa.

Caitlin Wiesner is a second-year doctoral student in the Department of History at Rutgers University. She earned her BA with highest honors in history and women's and gender studies at the College of New Jersey in 2015. She specializes in twentieth-century U.S. women's history, in particular the history of sexual violence and antirape activism. Her current research focuses on the ways African American women responded to professionalization, institutionalization, and black nationalism within antirape organizations.

ABOUT THE EDITORS

Marisa J. Fuentes is an associate professor in women's and gender studies and history at Rutgers University, New Brunswick, New Jersey. She is the author of *Dispossessed Lives: Enslaved Women, Violence, and the Archive.*

Deborah Gray White is a Board of Governors Distinguished Professor of History at Rutgers University, New Brunswick. She is the author or editor of numerous books including, *Ar'n't I a Woman? Female Slaves in the Plantation South.*